CW00540640

LIFE, DEATH AND MONEY

Staple Inn Hall, the home of the Institute of Actuaries.

LIFE, DEATH AND MONEY

ACTUARIES AND THE CREATION OF FINANCIAL SECURITY

Edited by Derek Renn

MAKING FINANCIAL SENSE OF THE FUTURE

BLACKWELL
Publishers

Copyright © Institute of Actuaries 1998

First published 1998

2 4 6 8 10 9 7 5 3 1

Blackwell Publishers Ltd
108 Cowley Road
Oxford OX4 1JF
UK

Blackwell Publishers Inc.
Commerce Place
350 Main Street
Malden, Massachusetts 02148
USA

British Library Cataloguing in Publication Data

A CIP catalogue record for this book is available from the British Library.

Library of Congress Cataloging-in-Publication Data

Life, death and money : actuaries and the creation of financial
    security / edited by Derek Renn.
        p. cm.
    Includes bibliographical references and index.
    ISBN 0-631-20906-9 (alk. paper)
    1. Actuaries. 2. Insurance—Mathematics. 3. Risk management.
4. Investment analysis. I. Renn, D. F. (Derek Frank)
    HG8781.L53 1998
    368'.01—dc21
                                                                    97–38759
                                                                         CIP

ISBN 0-631-20906-9

Typeset in 10 on 12pt Sabon by York House Typographic Ltd, London
Printed in Great Britain by MPG Books Bodmin, Cornwall

This book is printed on acid-free paper

Contents

List of figures

List of tables

List of contributors

W. M. Abbott, M.A., F.I.A. Educated at King Edward VII School, Sheffield and Corpus Christi College, Oxford, Bill Abbott qualified as an actuary in 1970. After working with Equity & Law and the Port of London Authority Pension Fund, he joined Legal & General and became Group Actuary in 1987. He has been a Council member and treasurer of the Institute of Actuaries, and its national representative on the Council of the International Actuarial Association, where he was secretary of its investment section (AFIR) from 1989 to 1997.

C. D. Daykin, C.B., Hon. D.Sc., M.A., F.I.A., Hon. F.F.A., F.S.S., A.S.A. Chris Daykin has been the UK Government Actuary since 1989. He joined the department with a first-class honours degree in mathematics from Cambridge and qualified as an actuary in 1973. He has been a member of the council of the Institute of Actuaries, and was its President from 1994 to 1996. He played a major role in the development of joint actuarial examinations of the Institute and Faculty, and in the development of actuarial education in central and eastern Europe. He is a prolific author of actuarial papers and the joint author (with Teivo Pentikanen and Marti Pesonen) of *Practical Risk Theory for Actuaries*. Chris is the chairman of the Permanent Committee for Statistical, Actuarial and Financial Studies of the International Social Security Association, chairman of the education committee of the Groupe Consultatif des Associations d'Actuaires Européennes, a council member of the International Actuarial Association and chairman of the International Forum of Actuarial Associations.

L. M. Eagles, B.A., B.Sc. (Econ.), F.I.A. Lawrence Eagles has spent the whole of his career with Bacon & Woodrow, the actuaries and consultants. He qualified as an actuary in 1965 and became a partner in 1974. He has written several papers on general (non-life) insurance, but for the past ten years has specialized in aspects of life, sickness and medical expenses insurance and new developments, most recently long-term care. Much of his work has been with friendly societies of all kinds.

J. V. Evans, B.A., F.I.A. Jillian Evans started her working life in the

Government Actuary's Department, qualifying in 1964. It was there that she first became involved in population studies and an abiding interest in the subject was engendered. She moved to Rodney Barnett & Company (later Barnett Waddingham) and became a partner in 1970. For many years, she has been involved in the work of the Continuous Mortality Investigation Bureau, which carries out mortality and morbidity research under the aegis of the Faculty and Institute of Actuaries.

D. G. R. Ferguson, M.A., Dip.Ag.Sci., F.I.A., A.S.A. Duncan Ferguson joined Bacon & Woodrow from Cambridge. He went to Cape Town as the Actuary and Assistant General Manager of Metropolitan Life, where he qualified as an actuary in 1970. On his return to the UK, he became a director of the international division of Eagle Star. He rejoined Bacon & Woodrow in 1988 and became senior partner in 1994. After serving on Council, he became President of the Institute of Actuaries in 1996.

P. H. Grace, B.Sc., F.F.A. Educated at Bedford Modern School and St Andrews' University, Paul Grace joined Scottish Equitable and qualified as an actuary in 1964. He left to join Zurich Insurance, becoming Actuary and Life Manager, but later rejoined Scottish Equitable as Actuary. He became an executive director in 1987 and is Managing Director and Actuary of the Scottish Equitable Policyholders' Trust and chairman of the Association of British Insurers' Life Taxation and Regulation Committee. He has served of the Council of the Faculty of Actuaries and became its President in 1996. He is the author of *Introduction to Life Office Practice*, published in 1988.

D. J. Le Grys, F.I.A. Desmond Le Grys qualified as an actuary in 1962 and has mainly worked in life and disability insurance. He has written and lectured extensively on a range of topics, including financial management, underwriting, AIDS and risk management. He joined the Munich Reinsurance Company in 1974 and founded their London life operation. He was the Managing Director and Actuary until 1996 and continues as a director. He is a Fellow of the Assurance Medical Society and was chairman of the Continuing Care Conference in 1997.

C. G. Lewin, F.I.A., F.S.S., F.P.M.I. Chris Lewin qualified as an actuary in 1964, and has pioneered the profession's corporate finance initiative since 1992. He is Head of Group Pensions at Guinness plc, and a council member of the Occupational Pensions Advisory Service. Chris is also a Fellow of the Pensions Management Institute and honorary treasurer of the National Association of Pension Funds.

G. H. Lockwood, F.I.A. Graham Lockwood joined Eagle Star in 1962 to take the position of Resident Actuary in Australia, where his interest in general insurance began. After returning to the UK, he became a senior manager concerned with general insurance operations overseas and other corporate activities. In 1984 he was appointed executive director for all life and general insurance activity outside the UK, and for the London-based marine and reinsurance business. In 1991 he became Deputy Chairman and Group Actuary, and concentrated on improving risk management practice and the London market business.

C. S. S. Lyon, M.A., F.I.A., F.S.A. Stewart Lyon qualified as an actuary in 1954, and from then until his retirement held a succession of posts at Legal & General, the last being that of General Manager (Financial) and Group Chief Actuary. He was President of the Institute of Actuaries from 1982 to 1984 and was awarded the Institute's Gold Medal in 1991. He was a member of the Occupational Pensions Board and subsequently of the Fowler Enquiry into Provision for Retirement, and was a trustee and treasurer of the Independent Living Fund. Currently he is a vice-president of the Disablement Income Group. In addition, he is a past president and gold medallist of the British Numismatic Society.

D. F. Renn, C.B.E., Ph.D., F.I.A., F.S.S., F.S.A. Educated at Queen Elizabeth's Grammar School, Barnet, Derek Renn entered the Civil Service through an open executive competition, which posted him to the Government Actuary's Department where he served for 44 years, ending up as Senior Actuary and Establishment Officer. He was an Institute tutor in demography, friendly societies, life interests and reversions, and editor of the *Journal of the Institute of Actuaries* (now the *British Actuarial Journal*). He has written extensively on medieval castles, the subject of his doctoral thesis.

R. S. Skerman, C.B.E., B.A., F.I.A. Ronald Skerman entered the actuarial profession straight from school, as did most entrants before the Second World War, and qualified in 1940. He joined the Prudential Assurance Company, becoming Chief Actuary in 1968, a director of the Prudential Corporation in 1980 and Deputy Chairman until his retirement in 1987. He has been a tutor and examiner, has served on Council and was President of the Institute of Actuaries from 1970 to 1972. He was awarded the Institute's Gold Medal in 1980. He has been chairman of the Life Offices Association, of the British Insurers European Committee and of the Common Market Working Group of the Comité Européen des Assurances. Ronald was a member of the Royal Commission on Civil Liability and Compensation for Personal Injury. His papers include the seminal one (to the German Actuarial Society) proposing principles that should underlie a statutory solvency basis for life assurance businesses.

C. M. Stewart, C.B., F.I.A. Born and educated in Glasgow, Colin Stewart saw wartime service in the Fleet Air Arm before joining the Government Actuary's Department and qualifying in 1953. He advised on the financing of the UK and other social security schemes, including research into demography and population projections. He was also for some years involved in the supervision of insurance companies, advising on new legislation to provide greater policyholder protection. After retiring from government service, he was engaged in research into the funding of occupational pension schemes. Colin has published many papers on these subjects. He served the Institute of Actuaries as an examiner, as editor of its *Journal* and as Council member and Treasurer, and was also a council member of the International Actuarial Association.

The City of London has been a global financial centre for centuries. Lombard Street and the Royal Exchange had the original responsibility of securing goods, cargoes and later, lives, against risk of damage or loss.

In 1575 the Lord Mayor introduced the rules of insurance practice and appointed the first 'regulatory body', "The Commissioners of Assurances". In 1662, a Birchin Lane haberdasher (John Graunt) created the first life table, based on local death records. Exactly a century later another City mathematician (James Dodson) published the principles of scientific life assurance. After his death a new company was devised, which was set up in order to put Dodson's principles into practice by initiating contracts of insurance. That company is now known as 'The Equitable'.

Since then, actuaries around the world have continued to use their judgement, as well as their scientific training, to assess future financial impacts and risks in the many areas of commercial activity. This book of essays demonstrates how the UK actuarial profession has made contributions to many social and financial developments for a century and a half, and how its ideas will 'make financial sense of the future' in an increasing variety of fields for many years to come.

The headquarters of the profession in England and Wales - the oldest corporate body of actuaries in the world - since 1887, has been a Tudor building fronting on High Holborn and now within the City of London . Staple Inn Hall was formerly an Inn of Court, and as a lawyer myself I am extremely familiar with and supportive of institutions such as the Institute of Actuaries and its counterpart, the Faculty of Actuaries in Edinburgh, and the contribution which their old and valuable traditions continue to make in safeguarding the Public Interest. I am therefore delighted to wish the actuarial profession every success for the next 150 years.

Richard Nichols.

Preface

A publication describing the development of actuarial theory and practice has been contemplated for many years. In 1991, Douglas McKinnon and Stewart Lyon, past Presidents of the Faculty and Institute of Actuaries respectively, put forward an outline for this book, designed to be part of the 150th anniversary of the profession. However, its focus has been altered, since a comprehensive textual study entitled *The History of Actuarial Science* was published in 1995. Therefore, this new book describes the work of actuaries past, present and even future. It aims to improve public awareness and understanding of the actuarial profession (primarily within the United Kingdom) by explaining how actuarial concepts contribute to social and financial developments.

Even if you are not a mathematician, you should read this book if you are interested in how the scientific basis of the insurance and pension industry has grown up and how it works. The contributors are all eminent actuaries who have spent all their working lives (and much of their leisure time) in the industry, and who are among the leading experts in their particular field. These are their own views; this book is not necessarily the official opinion of the profession, nor does it pretend to be the last word on any of the subjects discussed.

Editors often feel that it is incumbent upon them to write part of the book as well. I was not the originator and I cannot claim any special expertise, so I have limited my role to suggesting changes to improve clarity. I must thank Sally Grover and Mark Symons of the Institute of Actuaries staff and the editorial team at Blackwells for their strenuous efforts in organizing the work of so many authors into a coherent whole; and, not least, the authors themselves, who have responded positively to much red ink and many changes of plan.

Every effort has been made to trace the owners of the copyright of the illustrations, and apologies are offered to anyone whose rights may have been inadvertently infringed. Thanks are due to the Equitable Life Assurance Company for the portrait of William Morgan; and to the Government Actuary for the portrait of Sir Alfred Watson, and also to the latter for material used in table 7.2 and in figure 5 members and beneficiaries.

The Office of National Statistics allowed us to use Crown Copyright material in figure 2. Figure 8 was reproduced by kind permission of the PA News Photo Library.

Derek Renn

Further reading

Davidson, A. R. 1956: *The History of the Faculty of Actuaries in Scotland 1856–1956*. Edinburgh.

Haberman, S. and Sibbett, T. A. (eds) 1995: *History of Actuarial Science*. London.

Menzler, F. A. A. 1960: *Institute of Actuaries Students' Society. The First Fifty Years 1910–1960. An Appreciation*. London.

Moorhead, E. J. 1989: *Our Yesterdays: the history of the actuarial profession in North America 1808–1979*. Schaumburg, Illinois.

Simmonds, R. C. 1948: *The Institute of Actuaries 1848–1948*. Cambridge.

Stewart, C. M. 1985: *The Students' Society Log 1960–1985. Twenty-five Years of Enterprise*. London.

Actuaries make financial sense of the future   1

Duncan Ferguson and Paul Grace

The title of this introductory chapter sums up what the members of one of Britain's smaller professions do. It is the slogan chosen by actuaries to mark the 150th birthday of the profession in the UK, where it began.

Actuaries are proud of being guardians of the financial interests of millions of people and strive to protect those interests ethically, using skills acquired through a fiendishly difficult mathematically based qualification.

Actuaries are generally not well-known. Few of them deal directly with the public. Most advise or manage insurance companies, pension funds and other financial institutions. One aim of this book is that more should become known about the profession.

When you insure your car, your house or your life, an actuary is involved. He or she probably assessed the basis for the premium that you have been charged, and will be monitoring the funds of your insurer to make sure that your claim will be met. The actuary is also concerned in another major aspect of your future. Your biggest financial asset is probably the value of your pension rights. The value of your State Basic Pension alone can amount to more than £50 000 (in today's money) by the time you retire, and ten million people in the UK have an additional pension provided by their employer. Again, an actuary will have assessed the contributions required to provide the pension and will be monitoring the funds set aside to do so.

Actuaries are constantly engaged in calculating the value of the liabilities and assets of insurance companies and pension schemes, to make sure that the managers of those organizations should have enough money and other resources at the right time to provide the benefits promised to each and every policyholder or scheme member. This calculation work goes on continuously, because the value of assets, as well as the likelihood of and amount of claims, are changing all the time.

This is the traditional field of actuarial work, but today actuarial techniques are used in many other fields, under many different names.

Before we look at the wide variety of actuarial work, let us look at the profession as a whole. What do actuaries do, where do they do it, who do they do it for, what is their professional credo, and how did it all start? This is what this chapter is all about.

What exactly do actuaries do?

Every profession aims to improve the quality of life for others in some way; the Church, nursing and teaching are examples. Actuaries analyse the many risks to financial security, so that suitable safeguards and protection can be arranged at a fair price. They are responsible for the financial management of the savings of millions of people (especially through insurance and pensions) in a continually changing world. Actuaries have been doing this for centuries, but their role is little-known, since their numbers are small and actuaries have been reluctant self-publicists.

An actuary is a practical person, skilled in financial modelling and risk analysis in many different areas of business. These skills combine with those of a statistician, an economist and a financier, together with generous helpings of law, marketing and the art of management. But the actuary is the very opposite of a 'Jack of all trades and master of none' – he or she selects and uses the skills appropriate to each task. An actuary has the ability to identify and solve a wide range of business problems. He or she can apply a mathematical approach to the solution of long-term financial problems, particularly (but not exclusively) problems of insurance, investment and pensions. Long-term is just that: pensions may go on being paid for 70 years or more after the individual first joined the pension scheme.

History seldom repeats itself exactly, but the past can be some guide to the future, and actuaries are experts at using available data intelligently. All statistical data is subject to random fluctuations, and data are expensive to collect and process. There must therefore be a 'trade-off' of investigation costs against an acceptable level of uncertainty. Risks may be reduced but not removed, and the funnel of uncertainty widens the further ahead we try to look. However, repeated monitoring of results over time allows 'homing in' on a moving target.

Actuaries are not simply technicians; they seek continually to develop and improve their mathematical theories and the collection of data on matters of life, health and finance. Up-to-date information and research can be vital, especially at a time of rapid change. Actuaries also extend unchanging proven principles into new areas, such as the appraisal of capital investment projects.

Consider the building of a new hospital for an NHS Trust. The project manager must first examine the risks involved – identifying, analysing and managing them. These risks would extend beyond design and construction into environmental concerns, human resources and relationships, and the likely demand for services many years into the future. A suitable and consistent set of assumptions about each subset of risks (and their cost) would be integrated with the possible alternative financial arrangements to pay for the project and to secure the desired profit on the money employed. It would be important that everyone was comfortable with *all* the assumptions being used before the final decision was taken for the project to go ahead. As part of the project team, an actuary 'adds value' to the decision-making process by taking charge of the financial modelling, the risk analysis and the sensitivity of the project to changes in the assumptions.

Where do actuaries work?

Many actuaries are employed by *life assurance companies*. Some provide expert advice on investments, while others specialize in information technology, in planning, in the marketing of the company's products, or in strategic risk measurement. Others work in general administration and in top management, directing the strategy for the future business of the company. More traditional fields for actuaries within an insurance company include designing and pricing contracts, monitoring the adequacy of the funds to provide the promised benefits, and recommending the fair rate of bonuses to be added to with-profit policies.

Actuaries are also active in the *'non-life'* side of the insurance industry, covering property (from homes and cars to satellites), as well as other insurable risks, such as legal liability and loss of profits. Here the actuaries define the risk factors, advise on the premiums to be charged and the reinsurance to be purchased, calculate the reserves for outstanding claims and carry out financial modelling.

Many actuaries work as consultants, either as individual practitioners or in partnership with other actuaries. Some now work in multidisciplinary practices that offer wider business advice (for instance, on information technology, taxation, employee benefits, risk management, general as well as life insurance, and investment). Others work in the *public service* (the Government Actuary's Department), either as consultants to government and its agencies or as advisors to the regulators of the insurance, investment and pensions industry.

Most *consulting actuaries* are involved in advising employers on the package of financial rewards to be given to their staff. This involvement commenced with work on retirement benefits, where actuaries have statutory responsibilities concerning the funding for pension liabilities. It moved on to other aspects of remuneration – sickness insurance, bonus schemes and the like. Consultants may also advise insurance companies either on special problems or, more generally, where the company is too small to have its own actuary.

Actuaries can be found in *stockbroking* and other investment firms, assisting with analysis, management and control of securities, including derivatives. The profession is probably best-known to the investment world at large for the *Financial Times* – Actuaries Indices, which are published daily, showing the prices and yields of various groups of companies, such as that of the top 100 UK companies.

A growing area of actuarial work is *health insurance*, including the provision of long-term care for the elderly and permanent health insurance for the disabled. As governments seek to transfer costs from the welfare state to individuals who can afford to look after themselves, this area of work is set to grow. Professions often co-operate with each other at a national level. Permanent health insurance or sickness insurance has long been familiar territory to actuaries, but a new area is the study of methods for financing long-term care in old age, where the actuarial profession has joined the UK Continuing Care Conference. In 1996 the UK profession, together with the Royal Society of London, organized a conference to consider: 'Human Genetics – Uncertainties and the Financial Implications Ahead'. This demonstrated the ability of the actuarial profession to work with scientists from other fields in the advancements for social benefit.

Actuaries also work for individuals with problems such as the valuation of insurance policies, the calculation of the value of interests in trusts or estates, splitting pension arrangements on divorce, the loss of pension rights arising from injury or damages for unlawful discrimination, and claims for injury or death.

Research and education is the life-blood of every profession, and several actuaries are employed in universities or in providing distance learning/training to students. Many actuaries devote their spare time to developing their science, for the benefit of everyone. Important work has been published recently on the behaviour of capital markets, on the systems of performance measurement of fund managers, and on a variety of reserving techniques.

Actuaries abroad

There is an insatiable call for actuarial services throughout the world, particularly from developing countries and those of the former Eastern bloc. International standards of professional education are leading to mutual recognition of qualifications.

As the world's first professional actuarial body was established in the UK, it is not surprising that the UK has been a net exporter of actuaries and actuarial services. A third of the members of the Faculty and Institute live and work overseas. Members from the UK established the actuarial profession in many of the Commonwealth countries and students of many of these associations still take the examinations set in the UK. A number of actuaries trained in the UK still move overseas to work; some permanently, while some who are employed in UK-based consultancies, work on assignments in overseas territories.

The actuarial bodies in the European Union established the Groupe Consultatif des Associations d'Actuaires des Pays des Communautés Européennes, the Secretariat of which is based in Oxford, to act as a focal point for discussing actuarial issues with Brussels. The Groupe Consultatif has encouraged the individual associations to develop a professional image, by establishing Codes of Practice and Disciplinary Schemes.

Professional behaviour

Ethical business practice is good business. Recent scandals in the financial sector, as well as in other professions, have often been due to neglect of this maxim. Professional people should always try to do good and avoid harm, both by being fair and honest in their dealings with others and by keeping promises. They should be concerned with the consequences of their personal views and test them against others. An actuary should say to himself: 'Can I share my decision in good conscience with my family, my colleagues and public representatives?'

The actuarial profession is charged with certain statutory duties by the regulators of pensions and life assurance business. Part of the profession's code of conduct is a set of guidance notes, many of which are mandatory, and these are continually revisited. It is a mark of public confidence that actuaries have resolved the apparent conflict for a self-regulating professional body between its 'watchdog' role and that of promoting the status of actuaries. Recently, we have provided Lloyd's of London with opinions on the solvency reserves of syndicates, the Building Societies

Commission with our views on mortgage indemnity insurance and (more publicly) on the proper valuation of derivative instruments.

Actuaries guard their independence jealously. All of them have to comply with high standards of behaviour or they will be expelled from the profession by their peers. Those standards cover honesty, integrity, competence (knowledge and experience) and professional judgement. Actuaries serve both the public interest and the individual interest; they have a duty of care to others who might rely on their advice or information, and are responsible for both the quality of their work and for the way in which it is carried out.

Advising the client

There must be a close relationship between any professional and any client, based on mutual trust and openness. The actuary must be clear whom he or she is advising, and the client must understand in what capacity that advice is being offered.

Thus, the actuary must check:

- What are the terms of reference?
- Have I the necessary experience and knowledge?
- Is my advice being given to an individual (employer or employee) or to a group or committee (directors or trustees)?
- Am I advising as an individual or as a representative of my employer?
- Will the advice be passed on to others through the client?
- Will the advice that I give be timely, positive, clear and unambiguous?

The actuary must ensure that the client is equally aware and understands fully what he or she is getting in response to his or her needs. Any advice offered should be unbiased. An actuary must scrupulously check on his or her freedom – both actual and perceived – from influences that might affect the advice that is given or might limit its scope. The client must be informed of any possible conflict of interest that might affect that independence. Advice should be not simply defensive; that is, offering alternatives without recommendations. The actuary must ensure that he or she is identifiable as the source of the advice given, especially if it is to be passed on. Care must be taken to make sure that any expectation aroused does not automatically become a guarantee to be met.

What makes a good actuary?

Numeracy and the ability to communicate are among the attributes of every actuary. He or she must be ready to listen, interpret, guide and explain, either to individuals or to groups. Interpretation and guidance requires an understanding of technicalities, as well as of practical and commercial issues. Explanation may need to be at one or more levels, ranging from a concise description to step-by-step tuition.

A brief history

Simple valuation techniques have been in use since Roman times, but they were refined at the time of the Renaissance, that great age of discovery and world trade. Mathematical practitioners – the forerunners of today's actuaries – offered solutions to the arithmetical problems of charging of interest, because it was realised that the value of money varies with time. The latter part of the seventeenth century saw the greatest development to date of probability theory and the invention of the life table, one of the actuary's oldest tools. A hundred years later, in 1762, the first scientific life assurance company was founded in England – and the Equitable is still with us today. In around 1900 there was a resurgence of interest in actuarial principles among leading mathematicians. Pioneering works, which became worldwide standard texts on demography and social security, were written by actuaries.

The principles of operational research (used during the Second World War), of discounted cash flow and of spreadsheets were familiar to actuaries a century earlier. Techniques such as risk analysis, the control cycle and option pricing, which have been used by actuaries for many years, are now used widely outside insurance. Today there is a greater appreciation of the need for policyholders' protection, combined with the need for a sound yield on the capital employed, through profit testing of various possible scenarios of business development and experience.

Under UK insurance legislation, the authorities have powers to wind up an insurance company if they believe that policyholders' reasonable expectations ('PRE') are endangered. PRE is not defined and has not yet been tested in the Courts, although it is generally considered that an insurance company should be prudently managed, and that whenever the directors exercise discretion they will do so in the interests of all policy-holders.

The actuary at play

Actuaries are seldom dull or boring people; many find further outlets for their energies. There is a City livery company of actuaries, which supports an ever-changing spread of charities. We can count in our ranks actors, aircraft pilots, authors, barristers, historians, ministers of religion, musicians, racing drivers and tour guides. Many of our members have represented their country on the sporting field.

Just as many actuaries enjoy some form of recreational activity, many also enjoy the fellowship and conviviality of a dining club. At the last count, 18 actuarial dining clubs were identified, but it is believed that a number of other groups dine together regularly. Some of the dining clubs have obvious affinities – for example, those working in the Lloyd's market – whereas others draw their membership from a broader base.

Now read on

It remains to explain 'how they do it' in more detail in the rest of this book. Each of the authors has many years of experience of the subject about which they have written. Necessarily, they have had to pick and choose and a few subjects are not covered. Nevertheless, we hope that this book will increase your awareness and understanding of the actuarial profession.

As we said at the beginning, this is a small profession but it has great influence and is proud of its value to society.

'Mathematics possesses not only truth but supreme beauty – a beauty cold and austere, like that of sculpture.'

Bertrand Russell

Earliest days

2

Chris Lewin

'Doth not the wise merchant, in every adventure of danger, give part to have the rest assured?'

Sir Nicholas Bacon, 1559

Before actuaries were even thought of, mankind was trying to make sense of the patterns of life and death. Rudimentary forms of insurance developed to meet business risks, with crudely estimated probabilities of survival being used to calculate the sums of money to be paid. Towards the end of the seventeenth century, mathematics, statistical analysis and compound interest were combined to produce the foundations of actuarial science as we know it today.

None of us knows when we will die. The range of uncertainty is very wide. Gender, age, hereditary influences, present state of health, lifestyle, accidents, disease, medical advances and wars all play a part.

However, given a large group of people, predictions can be made with considerable confidence about how many of them will normally die this year, how many next year and so on. If an insurance scheme were set up for the group, to provide future payments on each person's death for the benefit of his or her family, we could work out nowadays how much money each person in the group would have to contribute in advance to a common fund to pay for the scheme, assuming that the rate of interest that would be obtainable on the fund were known.

How the insurance principle developed from primitive beginnings, and how we discovered ways of predicting how long a group of people would live, based on experience, is a fascinating story. Methods were developed of combining these mortality predictions with compound interest techniques, in order to work out the sums of money that needed to be contributed for insurance and pension schemes.

The insurance principle

Although, if valid predictions are to be made, we have to look at the mortality experience of a group of people, rather than an individual, the basic need for insurance and pension arrangements stems from individual risk and uncertainty. If you go on a journey or voyage, there is a risk of losing any goods entrusted to you, or your possessions, or even your life. Your house may catch fire, and you and your family may be left without a roof over your heads. If you are a breadwinner, you face the risk of dying too soon and leaving your dependants destitute or, conversely, you may live for too long after retirement and fall into poverty after your savings are exhausted. These risks have existed from the earliest times, and the traditional method of dealing with the poverty that resulted was to relieve it by charitable donations from those who were more fortunate. This was never very satisfactory, however, both because of the inadequacy of the protection often provided and because of the stigma attached to the receipt of charity. It was natural, therefore, to look for some means whereby the necessary relief could be provided as of right at an adequate level, out of funds earmarked for the purpose, and hence the insurance principle was born.

Perhaps our first glimpses of the insurance principle appear in early Hebrew writings. An extract from the law code of Hammurabi, who reigned over Babylon in the first half of the eighteenth century BC, reads as follows:

If a merchant lent money to a trader for benefit, and he saw a loss where he went, he shall pay back the principal of the money to the merchant. If, when he went on the road, an enemy made him give up what he was carrying, the trader shall so affirm by God and then shall go free.

The *Baba Kama* describes life among the Jews in the first two centuries AD:

It shall be lawful for ass drivers to come to an understanding whereby they may agree, whenever one of the members of the company shall lose an ass by robbers or wild beasts, to furnish another in place of the one lost; provided, however, that in case a driver shall have lost his ass through his own negligence, it shall not be necessary to supply him with another. Whenever an ass is lost without any fault on the part of the driver, another ass shall be furnished him. In case the owner says, give me the value of my ass, and I will purchase a new ass for myself, the offer need not be accepted; let an ass be bought for him and placed at his disposal.

It shall be lawful for ship-owners to enter into an agreement to this effect: Whenever a ship belonging to one of us is lost, we agree to furnish the loser another ship. In case, however, the ship is lost through his own negligence, we shall not be bound to furnish him with another. If the loss occurs without fault on his part, we are bound to make it good to him. If he ventured into waters that were not navigable, we are not bound to make good the loss.

These passages demonstrate the existence of rudimentary forms of social insurance in those far-off days. However, the origins of modern insurance can be traced more directly to the protection sought by medieval merchants when consigning cargoes of goods.

Originally, the finance for a sea voyage was commonly put up by one or more wealthy individuals, who agreed not to seek repayment if the cargo was lost. If the ship arrived safely, the money was repaid with a heavy rate of interest, which covered both the risk premium for the possible loss and the true interest on the loan.

The separation of the protection element from the financing came during the period 1300–1350, because of a need to widen the sources of finance, as trade expanded, combined with a reluctance on the part of some of the new lenders to assume the risk of loss. The latter thus had to be covered separately, and insurance was born.

The first genuine insurance policy known is dated 13 March 1350, and covers a cargo of wheat from Sicily to Tunis. The insurer, one Leonardo Cattaneo, undertook to assume all risks from act of God or of man and from perils of the sea.

One of the earliest records which survives from a firm of underwriters is a small book covering the year 1384, entitled 'This is the book of Francisco of Prato and Company, partners abiding in Pisa, and we shall write in it all the insurances we make on behalf of others. May God grant a profit and protect us from dangers'. The cargoes included wool, silk, cloth, fustian and malmsey, at rates from 3 to 8 per cent.

Insurance in London

It seems likely that English merchants at first arranged any insurance that they required through their Italian counterparts in England, whom they usually met in Lombard Street, and the risks may well have been borne in Italy. Eventually, however, it was probably found more convenient, as well as more profitable, to insure the risks at home. By about the year 1500, brokers acted as intermediaries to put the merchants who required insurance in touch with people willing to provide it.

An early attempt at an insurance fraud occurred in 1548, when one Matthew Hull complained that he had not received the cost of carrying certain goods which were consigned to his ship by their owner, who 'by fraud assured to four times the value' and then attempted to have the ship and goods cast away. In his judgement, the Protector Somerset confirmed that the goods were indeed 'upon a very false and crafty colour to deceive the assurers carried up and down'.

The extent of international competition in the insurance market, even at this early date, is demonstrated by the fact that the merchant house of Johnson and Company commissioned a voyage from England to Spain in 1552, and that the two ships that they hired were assured in England 'car il est ici toujours meilleur marché 2 ou 3 pour-cent qu'en Espaigne qu'en Anvers'. Unfortunately, both ships were attacked by French warships and completely plundered.

Some of the early insurance policies have survived, and from them we can see how the underwriting proceeded. In 1580, a cargo of hides, lead and sugar was shipped from Weymouth to Rouen. It was valued at £529 and insured at a premium of 3 per cent, the risks covered being:

> Of the seas, men of war, fire, enemies, pirates, rovers, thieves, jettisons, letters of mark and countermark, arrests, restraints and detainments of kings and princes and of all other persons, barratry of the master and mariners, and of all other perils, losses and misfortunes whatsoever they be or howsoever the same shall chance, happen or come, to the hurt, detriment or damage of the said hides, lead and sugars, or of any part or parcel hereof.

There were 17 underwriters in all, who took varying sums on risk. Once fully underwritten, the policy was copied into the Register of the Office of Assurances.

What was the Office of Assurances? It appears that the real motivation behind its establishment in 1575 was a desire by the Privy Council to regulate the insurance market, which had become a troublesome source of dispute, since numerous cases in which the assurers had refused to pay up had needed to be referred to the Privy Council for decision. The other important step which was taken by the Privy Council at the same time was to require the Lord Mayor of London to put down in writing the practices governing assurance policies, specifying in great detail the circumstances in which payment should be made. This the Lord Mayor eventually did, but only after numerous reminders from the Privy Council. It is probable that the resulting document formed the basis of the very detailed practice book of the Office of Assurances, which survives in the British Library.

The role of the Commissioners of Assurances was set out in a resolution of the Court of Aldermen in January 1577. Seven merchants had to attend the Office of Assurances at the west end of the Royal Exchange twice a week, on Mondays and Thursdays, to resolve disputes, with Richard Candeler acting as their clerk. It is pleasing to note that a box for the poor was provided at the Office and, every time judgement was passed by the Commissioners, the assured person had to put twelvepence in the box! In effect, the Commissioners acted as arbitrators, and the result was that litigation in the Admiralty Court about assurance matters ceased for about 20 years.

Gerard Malynes, a merchant writing in 1620, described the system of assurance at the Royal Exchange in great detail. He explained that he had attended on numerous occasions the Parliamentary committees which, in 1601, had been responsible for new legislation governing the insurance market. The main issue at that time had been that the Commissioners for Assurances did not have the power to ensure compliance with their decisions. The effect of the legislation was to vest final authority in the Lord Mayor of London, who had power to commit the underwriters to prison if they failed to pay.

Malynes pointed out that the premium for marine insurance differed according to the situation of the place, whether it was a time of war or peace, and what dangers there were thought to be from pirates, men of war, rocks and inaccessible places, seasons of the year, and so on. He quoted current premium rates that varied between 3 per cent and 15 per cent for one-way voyages. It was important when determining the premium for a particular voyage to know the full details, including the age and goodness of the ship, whether she was sailing on her own or in company with other ships, the extent to which the ship was armed, the nature of the goods to be insured and whereabouts in the vessel they were to be carried.

Early life insurance

It seems likely that life policies were issued from the commencement of the Office of Assurances in 1575, and they may even have been arranged by brokers prior to that date. However, most such policies would have been contracts for periods of one year or less, and this limitation was prescribed in the practice book of the Office of Assurances, referred to above. If insurance was required for more than a year, then it had to be arranged by a succession of separate contracts. The disadvantage of this arrangement was that premiums would rise with age, and there was always the possibility that the life would be deemed uninsurable at the time of renewal if the proposer was in poor health.

The earliest life policy known was issued in June 1583. Richard Martin, a citizen and Alderman of London, took out an assurance on the life of William Gibbons, a citizen and salter of London, for £382 6s. 8d., for a term of 12 months at a premium of 8 per cent. Gibbons died on 8 May 1584, but the underwriters refused to pay, on the ground that Gibbons 'lived the full twelve months, accounting 28 days to every month'. The case went to court and the judges ruled that the underwriters had to pay up, because 'according to the custom and usages of Lombard Street and the Royal Exchange, the month is to be accounted according to the course of the calendar'.

Malynes also cited a couple of cases in which people's lives were insured at the Office of Assurances. Someone insured the life of Sir Richard Martin, Master of the Mint (possibly the same person as the Richard Martin referred to above), who was about 90 years of age, for one year at a premium of 25 per cent. He died within the year and the insurers paid up. The second case was that of Master Kiddermaster, who bought a public office by means of a loan and took out an assurance at a premium of 4 or 5 per cent until he had repaid the loan. When underwriting life policies, it was thought best to have acquaintance of the persons whose lives were to be assured, so as to judge 'whether aged or young, of good qualities and diet, of disposition gentle or quarrelsome, a traveller or a dweller'.

Money lending

The mathematical combination of the lending of money at compound interest and the statistical measurement of the probabilities of death at each age eventually enabled life assurance and pensions to be soundly established on a long-term basis.

There is some evidence that interest may have been charged on loans in ancient Babylon and Rome. However, it was definitely practised by money lenders in the Middle Ages. These money lenders were often Jews, and they became very unpopular with their clients when debts rapidly mounted up. Many theological debates took place on whether the charging of interest should be permitted and whether a maximum rate should be fixed.

The Bible was seen to give some guidance, for example in the following passages:

> If thou lend money to any of my people that is poor by thee, thou shalt not be to him as an usurer, neither shalt thou lay upon him usury. (Exodus 22: 25).

Thou shalt not lend upon usury to thy brother; usury of money, usury of victuals, usury of any thing that is lent upon usury; Unto a stranger thou mayest lend upon usury; but unto thy brother thou shalt not lend upon usury. (Deuteronomy 23: 19–20).

A papal law passed in 1179 stated:

Since in almost every place the crime of usury has become so prevalent that many persons give up all other business and become usurers, as if it were permitted, regarding not its prohibition in both testaments, we ordain that manifest usurers shall not be admitted to communion, nor, if they die in their sin, receive Christian burial, and that no priest shall accept their alms.

Details have come down to us of a loan made in November 1183 by Avigai of London to William of Tottenham. The loan was £53 6s. 8d., of which one half had to be repaid by the following Christmas, with £2 5s. 0d. interest. The rest would continue outstanding, with interest at £1 13s. 4d. per quarter until the capital had been repaid. If the interest payments were not maintained, any balance due was to be converted into capital bearing interest at the rate of 2d. in the pound per week – a significantly higher rate.

Despite the papal views on usury, even Church authorities borrowed money at interest. In London in 1235, a prior and his convent received a loan of 100 marks from some merchants, which they undertook to repay 3 months later; but if the loan was not repaid, then they promised 'thereafter ... to pay them ... every two months one mark for every ten marks as a recompense for losses ... '. Thus interest was to be paid at the exorbitant rate of 60 per cent per annum.

Later, the City of London authorities issued various laws prohibiting usury. However, various devices were used to get round these laws, one of the favourites being a fictitious sale and repurchase of goods.

In June 1421 John Lawney, a grocer, brought a case against Walter Chartesey, a draper, complaining that the latter lent him in 1419 the sum of £22, on condition that, for the next nine years, Chartesey would have the lease of a house in Southwark which was owned by Lawney and let out to a tenant for a rental of £5 6s. 8d. per annum. An additional feature of the case was that the contract falsely showed the rent as only £3 6s. 8d. per annum, presumably in order to conceal the usurious nature of the transaction from anyone who merely examined the contract.

The line between permitted genuine commercial transactions, in which the investor accepted part of the risks of the enterprise, and forbidden usurious transactions was often a fine one. What particularly distinguished the latter was a specific interest charge and the taking of security so that risk was virtually eliminated. It was not until 1545 that it again became legal to lend money at interest, and then only at a rate (10 per cent per annum) which was much lower than that commonly insisted upon by usurers.

The borrowing of money was very common in the sixteenth century among the nobility and gentry, as well as among tradesmen and the poorer classes. Calvin was a key influence in diluting the religious opposition to usury, thus enabling a legal code to be developed which permitted money-lending within certain constraints and hence met practical needs. Calvin's doctrine was summarized by Blaxton in 1634 as implying the following cautions to be observed by usurers:

1. It must not be taken of the needy, or such as urged to borrow upon necessity.
2. The usurer must not be so addicted to gain, but that he must be still ready furnished and willing to furnish his poor neighbour in his need, freely.
3. The rule of Christ must ever be his touchstone, to deal no otherwise than he would be dealt with in the like case.
4. The borrower's gain must be so much more at the least as the usurer's interest comes unto.
5. That not only a respect be had to the borrower but to the good of the Common-wealth also, that that receive no prejudice.
6. That the usurer never exceed the stint set down in the Country or Common-wealth where he lives.

Compound interest

Now that it was becoming more respectable to charge interest, though not at exorbitant rates, the subject started to be treated by writers of mathematical textbooks. In 1558, Trenchant's book included a chapter on simple and compound interest. This included a table showing the amount to which a single payment of one would accumulate after various numbers of years, based on a rate of compound interest of 4 per cent per annum. A similar table showed the accumulation of a series of payments of one every year for various numbers of years. An example was given of a merchant who bought goods for £1548 on the basis of a payment of £100 per annum until the debt was discharged. If he wished to pay ready money instead, how much should he give (discounting at 17 per cent per annum)? The solution was obtained by finding the present value of each of the 16 payments separately and adding them together.

These were not, however, the first tables of compound interest: a fourteenth-century Italian manuscript survives, which gives tables showing the accumulation of a single payment at compound interest over a number of years.

In 1585, an arithmetic textbook published by Simon Stevin of Bruges included a number of worked examples for problems of both simple and compound interest. It also contained tables showing the present value of single payments in a number of years' time, discounting at various rates of interest from 1 to 16 per cent per annum. Similar tables were given to show the present values of a series of payments in future years.

Of particular interest are the problems in which Stevin finds the yield involved in transactions. For example, someone owes £1500 per annum to be paid over the next 22 years, and he pays his creditor £15 300 in lieu. What rate of interest does this represent? The solution is obtained by inspection of the tables and is found to be a little greater than 8 per cent per annum.

In 1613, a book on compound interest was published which reached an astonishingly high standard, and which can be regarded as one of the landmarks of actuarial science. It was written by Richard Witt, a 44-year-old mathematical practitioner of London. As well as containing a number of tables of compound interest for both accumulations and present values, the book has 124 interesting worked examples. One of these will illustrate the type of question covered:

> A man hath a Lease of certaine grounds for 8 yeares yet to come; for which he payeth £130 per Ann. Rent, viz. £65 per halfe yeare: which grounds are worth £300 per Ann., viz. £150 per halfe yeare. If this man shall surrender-in his Lease; what ready money shall he pay with it to his Land-lord for a new Lease of 21 years, not altering the Rent of £130 per Ann., reckoning such int. as men have when they buy Land for 20 years purchase, and receive the Rent halfe yearly?

Other books published later in the seventeenth century showed how logarithms could be used to ease the work of calculation. 'Napier's bones' was another contemporary calculating device which could have been used to ease the workload.

Measuring mortality

John Graunt, a London merchant, made a crucial breakthrough when, in 1662, he published a book entitled *Natural and Political Observations made upon the Bills of Mortality*. It is no exaggeration to say that this is one of the most significant books ever published, as it pointed the way to a whole new field of knowledge, of vital importance to civilization.

The Bills of Mortality were printed statements of the numbers of people who died each week in the big cities, classified according to the apparent cause of death. The original purpose was to give warning of the rise of epidemic diseases, particularly the plague, in time to enable some people at least to retreat from the city into the countryside, where the chances of infection might be less.

Graunt described how the data published in the London Bills were obtained:

> When any one dies, either by tolling, or ringing of a bell, or by bespeaking of a grave of the Sexton, the same is known to the Searchers, corresponding with the said Sexton. The Searchers here-upon (who are ancient matrons, sworn to their office) repair to the place, where the dead corpse lies, and by view of the same, and by other enquiries, they examine by what Disease or Casualty the corpse died. Hereupon they make their report to the Parish-Clerk and he, every Tuesday night, carries in an accompt of all the Burials and Christenings happening that week, to the Clerk of the Hall. On Wednesday the general accompt is made up, and printed, and on Thursdays published, and dispersed to the several families who will pay four shillings per annum for them.

Graunt produced an extensive table in which he analysed the deaths over a 20-year period according to the recorded cause of death. The number of deaths averaged about 11 500 per annum. Since the age at death was not recorded, Graunt tried to associate cause with likely age.

He observed that about one-third of all deaths occurred from 'Thrush, Convulsion, Rickets, Teeth, Worms, Abortives, Chrysomes, Infants, Liv-ergrown and Overlaid', which he guessed all related to children under four or five years old. He guessed also that perhaps half of the deaths from 'Smallpox, Swinepox, Measles and Worms without Convulsions' might be children under six years old. Taking all these categories together, plus a proportion of the deaths from 'Plague', he estimated that about 36 per cent of the deaths related to children who died before they were six years old.

Table 2.1 Graunt's life table.

Age	Number alive at given age	Deaths before next listed age
0	100	36
6	64	24
16	40	15
26	25	9
36	16	6
46	10	4
56	6	3
66	3	2
76	1	1
80	0	-

Looking at the other end of the span of life, he noted that about 7 per cent of the total deaths were described as 'aged', which he guessed as meaning over age 70.

He then derived his famous 'life table'. Taking as his starting point the conclusion, referred to above, that of one hundred conceptions, 36 die before attaining the age of six, and asserting that perhaps one survives to age 76, he then sought 'six mean proportional numbers between 64, the remainder living at 6 years, and the one which survives 76', and found that 'the numbers following are practically near enough to the truth...'.

Using modernized column headings, his numbers take the form shown in table 2.1.

The starting point of 100 apparently related to conceptions rather than live births, and the 36 per cent of deaths before age six included children who were aborted or still-born. It is apparent from Graunt's description of his method that, although the death rate for the first six years of life was based on the data from the Bills of Mortality, the other figures in the table were purely speculative and were designed so as to secure a smooth progression.

Graunt also drew a number of other conclusions from the statistics that he had analysed. In particular, he estimated that the population of London was about 384 000 people, rather than the millions which were often asserted in common talk. Modern research suggests that his figure was not far wide of the truth. He inferred that the population of London had increased considerably over the previous 70 years, and that much of the increase had been concentrated in the parishes outside the City walls (mainly to the west), where numerous large old houses had been turned into tenements.

Sir Richard Corbet, shortly before his death in 1683, devised the first

British mortality table to be subdivided by individual years of age, rather than the groups of ages used by Graunt. Like Graunt's table, Corbet's was largely a mathematical conception rather than being based on real-life data. Unfortunately, Corbet's work remained unpublished at the time, and his early death, at the age of 42, probably deprived the world of much that might have been of great value in actuarial science. One of his suggestions was that a national census should be carried out by a form of stratified sampling. In this, he was well ahead of his time; a national census was not carried out for another 120 years.

Actuarial mathematics

Actuarial science began through the combination of compound interest with life tables based on observed mortality data.

Long-term financial transactions that depended on the duration of someone's life were already commonplace by the late seventeenth century. For example, property leases were often granted for a period as long as two or three named persons survived. Governments sold life annuities in order to raise capital. The terms underlying such transactions were based on rules of thumb rather than on mathematical calculation.

The first person to make actuarial calculations combining compound interest and mortality rates was the Dutch Prime Minister, John de Witt. On 30 July 1671, he presented a report to the States-General, showing the prices at which he recommended the government to sell life annuities, payable half-yearly, in order to raise money for the State. For a life aged three years, he calculated that the purchase price should be 16 times the annual amount of the annuity, based on a rate of interest of 4 per cent per annum. This was higher than the previous going rate of 14 years' purchase, regardless of age. However, the assembly decided to stick to the previous figure, because they feared that an increase in the price would reduce sales.

De Witt's method was equivalent to taking a hypothetical group of 768 lives aged three, each of whom was entitled to an annuity of one per annum, payable half-yearly. He assumed that six of them would die in each half-year for the next 50 years. For the next ten years deaths were assumed to be at the rate of four each half-year, for the following ten years at the rate of three each half-year, and for the last seven years at the rate of two each half-year. Clearly, these rates were mathematical assumptions rather than figures derived from observed experience, although the numbers chosen may have been influenced by investigations into actual experience which have not come down to us. Looking separately at the lives assumed to die in each particular half-yearly period, he calculated (using ordinary compound interest tables) the present value at the outset of the series of payments that they would receive. The sum of these present values, divided by 768, gave the average value required for one purchaser.

John Hudde, a mathematician and a mayor of Amsterdam, made an investigation into the actual mortality experience of persons who had purchased annuities from the United Provinces in the years 1586–90. All 1495 persons were now dead and their ages at entry and death were recorded. He used his results to calculate the value of life annuities at 4 per cent per annum interest: for example, 17.2 years' purchase for a life aged six. In 1672, at around the time when Hudde became mayor, the City of Amsterdam decided to offer annuities at a price that depended on the age of the annuitant. These prices were very low, compared to Hudde's theoretical results, and one wonders whether this may have been due to some increase in the rate of interest or just a desperate need by the city for money.

The first widely circulated work on the calculation of the value of life annuities was a paper published in 1693 in the *Philosophical Transactions of the Royal Society* by Edmond Halley.

Halley's famous life table was constructed solely from the Bills of Mortality for Breslaw, which had been sent to the Royal Society by Caspar Neumann, a pastor of that city who was interested in scientific matters. The Bills showed the numbers of deaths at each age, for the two sexes separately. In total, these deaths averaged 1174 per annum for each of the five years for which the data were available. Halley did not have a census of the living population, so he was forced to make the assumption that there was a stationary population (that is, that the city's population had remained constant in size for many years). This may have introduced some inaccuracy into his work: in particular, the population structure may have been distorted by a plague epidemic in 1633, when about 30 per cent of the town's population died. If, as is likely, these people were mainly replaced by an influx of young adults from the surrounding countryside, this would have resulted in the town having a 'population bulge' of people born around 1605–15. In the period 1687–91, the years for which Neumann had extracted his figures from the Bills of Mortality, this bulge would have caused more deaths than normal in the age range 72–86. As a result, Halley's life table may have overstated the number of people normally surviving into old age.

The life table commences as shown in table 2.2, and continues up to age 84, at which there are stated to be 20 persons.

Halley used his life table in the same way as an actuary would today.

Table 2.2 Halley's life table.

Age	Persons
1	1000
2	855
3	798
4	760
5	732
6	710
7	692
8	680

Suppose that one were looking to value a life annuity payable to someone aged three years. The first payment would fall due at the age of four, and the chance of being alive to receive it would be 760/798. Its present value, assuming that it were to be received, could be evaluated from compound interest tables – let us call this value V. The present value of the payment at age four, allowing for the chance of surviving to receive it, would therefore be obtained by multiplying V by 760/798. Similarly, the present value of the payment at age five, assuming that it were to be received, could also be evaluated from compound interest tables – let us call this value W. Then the present value of this payment, allowing for the chance of surviving to receive it, would be obtained by multiplying W by 732/798.

By proceeding similarly for each future age, and summing the resulting values, we could arrive at the present value of all future payments of the annuity.

Not content with evaluating an annuity payable during the life of one person, Halley then went on to consider the value of annuities dependent on the continuation of two lives.

Halley thus pointed the way, but one significant problem remained: the amount of labour required to make such calculations was very considerable. In 1725, Abraham de Moivre published a method for reducing the work. He assumed that the numbers of those living, according to the life table, decreased in arithmetical progression, which produced results that were sufficiently close to those produced from Halley's table to be useful for practical purposes.

Practical applications

Numerous books soon appeared, giving new approximate methods or calculated values of life annuities. The theory of actuarial science was now advancing by leaps and bounds. What was happening, however, in the development of institutions providing life assurance and pensions?

The answer is that it took a number of years before the theoretical science reached a stage at which it could be applied fully in practice, and it was only as 1750 approached that the first viable institutional applications came to fruition.

Apart from the government and the City of London, the first financial institution to offer the public long-term contracts depending on human survivorship appears to have been the Mercers' Company of London. In 1690, they adopted a scheme whereby male members of the public contributed a single premium of £100, in return for which their widow received a life annuity of £30 per annum. The rate of interest at that time was 6 per cent, and the terms offered were prudent on that basis, supposing that the wives were of the same age as their husbands. Unfortunately, the scheme soon ran into difficulty, because the rate of interest obtainable on the invested fund fell. On top of this, the scheme had admitted some men at advanced ages, and in a number of cases the wives were much younger than their husbands. The annuity gradually had to be reduced until it was only half the promised £30 per annum and, eventually, more than 50 years from the outset, it had to be stopped altogether. The scheme had to be rescued by a government grant.

As late as the 1720s, life assurance was still being offered on a one-year basis by the Royal Exchange corporation and the London Assurance corporation, at a premium of £5 or £5 5s. per £100 assured irrespective of age. However, the first important breakthrough had been made some years earlier, when longer-term policies were offered for the first time. In 1706, John Hartley, a bookseller, formed a life assurance company known as the Amicable. The number of contributors was limited to 2000 and they each paid £6 4s. per annum, of which 4s. went towards maintaining the office. Hence the maximum income, after providing for the office, was £12 000 per annum. Of this sum, £2000 was to be divided amongst the nominees of those members who died in the first year, £4000 in the second year, £6000 in the third, £8000 in the fourth year and 'never less than £10,000 afterwards'. These sums were to be reduced pro rata if the membership was less than 2000.

Thus the Society would have an accumulated fund of £30 000 plus interest in five years' time and this would grow by £2000 per annum thereafter. It was hoped that the accumulation of these funds would enable future contributions to be reduced, and even to be extinguished altogether after 30 years. No thought appears to have been given, however, to the important point that the annual number of deaths would increase as the years went on and the membership aged, thus rendering these calculations invalid. In the event, the capital did not build up to the extent envisaged and some rather desperate measures to attract new members were found necessary in 1770, to stave off financial disaster; but the Society had a long and honourable life, being finally absorbed into the Norwich Union in 1866. Nevertheless, the original intention was clearly that greater funds should be built up. Had this occurred, the financial basis of the Society would have been much sounder, and claims on death could have been paid at a continuing high level without the need for an influx of new members. Nevertheless, long-term life assurance was on offer for the first time, and hence the year 1706 marks a turning point.

One of the first public-service pensions was granted in 1684 to Martin Horseham, a landwaiter in the Port of London, who was 'so much indisposed by a great melancholy that he is at present unfit for business'. The pension had to be paid by Horseham's successor. This was less of a burden for the successor than might appear at first sight, since although the pension of £40 per annum was half the post's basic salary of £80 per annum, a landwaiter could also earn about £150–250 per annum in fees. Horseham had rendered only about 18 months' public service, so the payments made to him were clearly in the nature of an ill-health retirement pension.

It was found increasingly unsatisfactory to burden the successor in this way. Clearly, there would be likely to be difficulties when one successor found himself soon relieved of his burden due to the early death of his predecessor, while his colleague could have a continuing drain on his salary for many years. In 1712, the whole system was regularized and a superannuation fund established in the Customs. The pension was now fixed at one-third of basic salary. Members had to pay $2\frac{1}{2}$ per cent of their salaries and specific regulations were brought into force to determine eligibility for a pension. The essential qualification was incapacity to work rather than the attainment of a fixed age. The idea seems to have been to fund pensions on a 'pay-as-you-go' basis rather than accumulating funds in advance for this purpose. The old principle of the successors paying for their predecessors' pensions was thus maintained, but the risks were pooled.

The inevitable soon happened, and the number of pensioners increased to such an extent that the contributions became insufficient. The pensions fell into arrears and it was thought impracticable to increase the members' contributions, so the Treasury had to make payments into the fund to meet the balance of the outgo. Eventually, this scheme led to the establishment of the Civil Service Superannuation Scheme as we know it today.

It was not until 1743, however, than an occupational pension fund was established that was soundly financed on the principle of building up monies to meet future liabilities. This was the Scottish Ministers' Widows' Fund. It was set up in Edinburgh by a private Act of Parliament and survived until 1993, a splendid record of 250 years' service and a tribute to prudent Scottish financial management.

The original subscribers (whether single or married) paid five guineas per annum and, in addition, there was a tax on members' weddings. The Fund provided every widow with an annuity of £20 per annum. If a member died without leaving a widow, his family received a lump sum of £200. The subscriber could elect at the outset to pay a higher or lower contribution than five guineas per annum, in which case his benefits were adjusted pro rata. Membership was optional for existing incumbents but compulsory for new entrants to the ministry.

The calculations on which the scheme was based were probably largely the work of Dr Robert Wallace, a clergyman who also wrote on population matters, and Colin Maclaurin, the mathematician.

Wallace stated that men could be expected to enter the Fund at about age 30 and that 'persons at 30 by the bills of mortality may be supposed to live about 28 years'. Hence he argued that age 58 was the common time at which a woman became a widow, assuming that she was about the same age as her husband. He then stated that 'persons at 58 years of age by the bills of mortality have an equal chance to live only 13 years, which is not half the time that married persons live together'. Hence the Fund would have only half as many widows to provide for as members, and this half for only half the time for which their husbands contributed. Each widow could therefore receive an annuity equal to four times their husband's annual contribution. In fact, the ratio of annuity to contribution finally adopted was just under four.

Here we see the first tangible instance of the theoretical actuarial work referred to above being applied to the setting up of a long-term financial institution.

In 1748, some projections were made of the growth of the Fund in future years, and these proved to be extremely accurate. By 1765, for example, the accumulated Fund amounted to £58 347, compared with a forecast of £58 348! Do actuaries achieve such accuracy today?

The stage is set

By the middle of the eighteenth century, therefore, insurance companies offering the public long-term life assurance and pensions contracts, financed on a sound actuarial basis, could be established. It is therefore appropriate to conclude this chapter with a notable contribution to the theory of insurance which appeared in 1747.

In that year, Corbyn Morris published *An Essay towards illustrating the Science of Insurance*. Although his arguments were illustrated by reference to marine insurance, they were clearly of wider application. The main purpose of the work was to demonstrate that an insurer's 'probability of ruin' decreases as he spreads his available wealth between more and more policies at any one time. This conclusion was arrived at by simple probability theory, using the binomial theorem.

Morris postulated a situation in which there are a number of independent voyages of different ships, each voyage having a one-third chance of failure, and hence the insurance premium (ignoring profit and expenses) is $33\frac{1}{3}$ per cent. Insurer A insures the whole risk on one voyage, so he has a one-third chance of having to meet the claim, which would mean that he would lose all his money and be ruined. Insurer B is equally wealthy, but spreads his resources out over 12 voyages, so that he takes a one-twelfth share in the underwriting of each voyage. The chance that insurer B loses all his money (that is, if all the 12 voyages fail) is only 1 in 531 441. The chance that B is a net loser (because at least five of the voyages fail) is 195 825/531 441; in other words, just over one chance in three.

Morris points out that, as the number of voyages increases, insurer B becomes less of a winner if he wins and less of a loser if he loses.

Although Morris's work may appear elementary and obvious to modern readers, it needs to be seen in context as a pioneering effort. Marine insurance was by then well established, and the results actually achieved by underwriters doubtless proved empirically the benefit of spreading out one's risks over a number of voyages rather than just over one or two at a time. However, this does not seem to have been proved mathematically before.

Further reading

General

There are numerous articles and notes by C. G. Lewin (often under the heading '1848 and all that') in *Fiasco* (the magazine of the Staple Inn Actuarial Society) and in *The Actuary* (the magazine of the Institute and Faculty of Actuaries) from 1987 onwards.

Early Jewish writing

Rabinovitch, N. L. 1973: *Probability and Statistical Inference in Ancient and Medieval Jewish Literature.* Toronto.

Marine and early life assurance

Blackstock, W. W. 1910: *The Historical Literature of Sea and Fire Insurance in Great Britain, 1547–1810.* Manchester.

Malynes, G. 1622: *Consuetudo, vel Lex Mercatoria or the Antient Law-Merchant.*

Raynes, H. E. 1964: *A History of British Insurance*, second edition. London.

Usury

Blaxton, J. 1634: *The English Usurer.*

Jones, N. 1989: *God and the Moneylenders – Usury and Law in Early Modern England.* Oxford.

Wilson, T. 1572: *A discourse upon Usury* (edited by R. H. Tawney, London, 1925).

Compound interest

Lewin, C. G. 1970: An early book on compound interest – Richard Witt's 'Arithmeticall Questions'. *Journal of the Institute of Actuaries*, 96, 121–32.

Lewin, C. G. 1981: Compound interest in the seventeenth century. *Journal of the Institute of Actuaries*, 108, 423–42.

Phillippes, H. 1654: *The Purchasers Pattern.*

Stevin, S. 1584: *La Pratique d'Arithmétique.* Leyden.

Trenchant, J. 1558: *L'Arithmétique.*

Probability, mortality and life tables

Alter, G. 1983: Plague and the Amsterdam Annuitant. *Population Studies*, 23, 37–41.

Bernstein, P. L. 1996: *Against the Odds – The Remarkable Story of Risk.* New York.

Daston, L. 1988: *Classical Probability in the Enlightenment.* Princeton, NJ.

David, F. N. 1962: *Games, Gods and Gambling – the origins and history of probability and statistical ideas from the earliest times to the Newtonian era.* London.

Glass, D. V. 1963: John Graunt and his 'Natural and political observations'. *Proceedings of the Royal Society, Series B*, 159, no. 974.

Graetzer, J. 1883: *Edmund Halley und Casper Neumann.* Breslaw.

Graunt, J. 1662: *Natural and Political Observations made upon the Bills of Mortality.* London.

Haberman, S. and Sibbett, T. A. (eds) 1995: *A History of Actuarial Science* (ten volumes of facsimile texts). London.

Hald, A. 1990: *A History of Probability and Statistics and their Applications before 1750.* New York.

Kendall, M. G. 1956: The beginnings of a probability calculus. *Biometrika*, 43, 1–14.

Ore, O. 1965: *Cardano, the Gambling Scholar*. New York.

Pearson, K. 1978: *The History of Statistics in the 17th and 18th Centuries*. London.

Todhunter, I. 1865: *A History of the Mathematical Theory of Probability*. (Reprinted New York, 1949.)

Westergaard, H. 1932: *Contributions to the History of Statistics*. London (reprinted New York, 1969).

Annuity and pension schemes

Davis, A. H. 1934: *William Thorne's Chronicle of St Augustine's Canterbury*. Oxford.

Dunlop, A. I. 1992: *The Scottish Ministers' Widows' Fund 1743–1993*. Edinburgh.

de Moivre, A. 1727: *Annuities on Lives*. London.

Price, R. 1771: *Observations on Reversionary Payments*.

Raphael, M. 1964: *Pensions and Public Servants*. New York.

Sibbett, T. A. 1992: De Witt, Hudde and annuities. *The Actuary*, November 1992, 22–3.

Sibbett, T. A. 1994: A new method for valuing annuities upon lives – a look at Richard Hayes' book published in 1727. *The Actuary*, June 1994, 32–3.

Wagstaffe 1674: *Proposals for Subscriptions of Money &c*. London.

Early economics

Glass, D. V. 1965: Two papers on Gregory King. In D. V. Glass and D. E. C. Eversley (eds), *Population in History*. London.

Hull, C. H. (ed.) 1899: *The Economic Writings of Sir William Petty* (two volumes). Cambridge.

Hutchison, T. 1988: *Before Adam Smith – the emergence of Political Economy, 1662–1776*. Oxford.

Landsdowne, Marquis of 1927: *The Petty Papers* (two volumes). London (reprinted New York, 1927).

Mortality, behold and fear

3

Jillian Evans

Down the years, actuaries have worked together to derive one of the basic elements of their toolkit: a mortality table for practical use in the pricing and valuation of life assurance business. This represents over 150 years of co-operative effort in an otherwise very competitive environment. The practicalities of data collection, the derivation of useful rates, smoothing and projection techniques, and the search for a 'law of mortality' are discussed. Also included are brief sections on sickness data and national mortality statistics.

Taming the grim reaper

In many ways, the actuary can identify with Janus, the Roman god of bridges and doorways, who is often depicted with two heads, looking both forward and back. The actuary looks back to the experience of the past, and uses that as a guide as to what assumptions should be made about the possible incidence of events yet to occur. Often there is no relevant experience from the past and, in carrying out his or her brief, the actuary is forced into a situation very like that of the Israelites in Egypt, of making bricks without straw. In such instances, the actuary will wish to gather the experience as it occurs and to use it periodically to test the validity of his or her assumptions. Such was the case in the earlier days of life assurance as we know it today. In 1775, William Morgan, actuary of the 'Society for Equitable Assurances on Lives and Survivorships' made the very first valuation of a life assurance company. As part of the valuation he compared the actual mortality experience (the actual death claims paid) with the expected experience (the claims that would have occurred had the mortality assumptions underlying the premiums been borne out in practice.)

Let us step back a little and see how this links in with the very earliest manner of the operation of life assurance. As we saw in chapter 2, life assurance was at first usually offered on a one-year basis, frequently with the same premium being paid by all. Even where insurances were designed

Figure 3.1   William Morgan, the first insurance company actuary.

to operate for a period of years, there appears to have been little appreciation of the nature of the risks that underlay promises that were made and
how they might be related to the premiums charged. Although the concept
of a life table had been around for some time, the step from that to the idea
of a mortality rate, or the chance that an individual of a given age will die
within a year, developed much later.

The breakthrough came with one James Dodson, a mathematician of
London. Ironically, the story goes, the impetus for Dodson to develop his
system of offering assurances for the whole of life with a level annual
premium payable throughout (but varying according to age at entry), was
his failure to secure a policy with the Amicable Society on the grounds that
he was too old! At least there appears to have been some appreciation of
the fact that taking all- comers at identical premiums, whatever their age,
might not be the best way to proceed. Central to Dodson's thesis was the
build-up and investment of funds in the early years of a policy, where

mortality rates are light, in order to meet the increasing cost of claims as the lives matured. Thus it was that a petition went to the Privy Council in 1757 with a view to establishing the 'Society of Equitable Assurances on Lives and Survivorships' mentioned above, based on the premium table that Dodson had produced. The mortality rates underlying the premiums were based on the Bills of Mortality for the City of London for the period 1728–50. It was to be five years before the Society finally came into being and, sadly, Dodson did not live to see his ideas come to fruition. There were certainly obstacles along the way; in 1761 a report by the Attorney General and Solicitor General on the petition declared at one point 'the success of this scheme must depend on the truth of certain calculations taken upon tables of life and death, whereby the chance of mortality is attempted to be reduced to a certain standard: this is mere speculation, never yet tried in practice, and consequently subject, like all other experiments, to various chances in the execution'. The long battle to persuade the legal profession of the validity of actuarial evidence was just beginning. Incidentally, the choice of the title 'Actuary' for the chief executive of the new Society is believed to have been derived from the title of the recorder to the Roman Senate, *actuarius*, by an antiquary, Edward Rowe Mores, who was closely involved with the formation of the Equitable. It was later adopted by the other companies to describe those holding a similar position. The job covered a multitude of activities, far more than the actuary of an insurance company covers today, and for the past two centuries or so actuaries have been seeking to explain to the outside world exactly what is done by those who hold this curious-sounding title.

William Morgan's first valuation revealed a substantial surplus, the distribution (or otherwise) of which is related elsewhere. The essential point that concerns us here is that Dodson's rates, although thought by some to be too light at the time, were, in fact, too heavy: he had expected rather more claims to have been paid out than had actually been the case. The search was therefore on for a mortality table that would reflect more accurately the experience of the Society, a concern of actuaries ever since.

After much thought and discussion, a table based on the bills of mortality for Northampton was felt to be the most suitable for the purpose in hand and was adopted as the new basis for premium calculation and valuation. The table had been constructed by Dr Richard Price, a Unitarian Minister and Fellow of the Royal Society, who became an acknowledged expert in matters connected with life assurance and carried out a number of investigations on the bills of mortality of different towns. The premiums required for insurances using the new table being lower than those using the old table, the question arose as to what, if anything, should be done to assist the existing policyholders. The debate, essentially about equity between different generations of policyholder, is a fascinating one but, again, not one for this chapter.

Between 1762 and 1800 there was little development of life assurance in the UK, but from the turn of the century there was an explosion of activity: many new companies were formed and many of today's household names can be traced back to that period. The actuary of each company had the same problem: What mortality table should be used for premium calculation and valuation? At that time there was no savings element in the policies offered. They simply provided protection by sharing the risks of premature death (insurance policies) or against the vagaries of survival (annuities). The mortality experience was therefore the main determinant of profit or loss to the company. What better when you have a problem than to share it? Therefore, in 1838, a committee of eminent actuaries met at the London Coffee House and resolved unanimously:

1. That, in the opinion of the Meeting, it is desirable that the different Assurance Offices should from their records contribute the requisite data to a common fund, to afford the means of determining the Law of Mortality which prevails among Assured Lives.
2. That such a Law of Mortality, fairly determined, would prove generally useful, especially to the Life Offices themselves, and the numerous class of persons availing themselves of these Institutions.
3. That persons professionally engaged in similar investigations are most likely to draw correct conclusions from existing data, and to classify the same into forms showing the same rate of mortality among Assured Lives.

As a result of their deliberations, 17 offices contributed data relating to a total of 83 905 policies. The sex of the policyholder was known for 40 616 of the lives assured and the policies were also classified into Town, Country and Irish. The data were thoroughly investigated and the mortality rates deduced from the experience were compared against those from the Northampton and other tables, including tables that had been derived (and published) from the experience of the Equitable. The tables were published in 1843 and represent the first of a long line of tables based on pooled experience, reaching down to the present day. On this first occasion, only the crude rates (the actual rates derived from the experience) were shown, together with expectations of life calculated therefrom;

although, subsequently, a keen individual by the name of Jenkin Jones published a series of monetary functions (including compound interest) for assurances and annuitants, based on the table. The production of the basic tables (not the monetary functions) was financed by contributions from 58 offices, who in return received a free copy of the tables.

Five years later, in 1848, the Institute of Actuaries was formed. The next set of tables based on pooled experience was produced under the aegis of a special committee of the Institute, convened for the purpose. The committee was joined in its deliberations by a committee of the Faculty of Actuaries in Scotland, the first example of joint operation by the two bodies. A circular from the (Institute) Council to offices was concluded thus: 'The Council cannot doubt that you will concur with it in thinking that the interest and value of the results to be obtained will fully justify the labour of extracting the particulars of the policies'. The committee was anxious to keep its demands for detail reasonable, on the grounds that offices were more likely to contribute if to do so were not made too onerous – a wholly admirable sentiment. Twenty insurance offices responded to the call and 160 426 data cards were submitted, one for each policy in the investigation. Not all offices recorded the sex of the insured so, in those cases, the sex was determined by the name of the insured. The presence of duplicate policies (that is, more than one policy on the same life) was thought to be a problem that could distort the results, so great pains were taken to eliminate such cases; this was relatively simple within a single office but more difficult between offices. The elimination was done by matching names of the insured. This led to certain problems among members of the peerage, where policyholders could move through several subsidiary titles, as relatives died, and appear to be different individuals, while all the time they were one and the same. The cards for each sex were sorted into healthy lives, diseased lives (those charged an additional premium on health grounds) and other extra risks. The committee investigated whether, age for age, the mortality rates varied according to the duration the policy had been in force; or, put another way, whether lives accepted as healthy at the start of their insurance, and therefore likely as a group to suffer fewer deaths than a similar group picked at random from the population containing a mixture of healthy and diseased lives, maintained that superiority over time. In the event, the committee concluded that 'the benefit of selection is lost after the fifth year of insurance'. The tables were published in 1869, with separate sets of mortality rates for both healthy and diseased lives of each sex. There were also tables for males and females combined; unisex tables have been around for a long time. Monetary functions were produced for healthy males, healthy females and diseased males. These included single life assurance and annuity functions, plus joint life and last survivor annuities, at a variety of rates of interest. The labour involved in the production of these tables was phenomenal, and was all down to the dedication and industry of one man, Mr Peter Gray, to whom the committee offered fulsome (and totally merited) praise for what was indeed a *magnum opus*.

Appended to the tables when published was a note on a comprehensive scheme of notation, settled by a special committee of actuaries, after long and careful consideration of the subject which, it was hoped, would facilitate advances in the study of life contingencies and promote exactness of thought and expression. Thus another stone in the foundation of the profession was laid.

Between 1869 and 1924 several further tables, based on pooled experience, were published as a need was perceived. Each was overseen by a joint committee of the Institute and the Faculty and each was financed by contributions from the offices. However, in 1912 two eminent actuaries, Elderton and Fippard, produced a paper that led to a radical change in the way in which life assurance mortality investigations were conducted. Hitherto, investigations had been carried out by observing the progression through time of cohorts of policyholders, recording the numbers of policies issued and counting the deaths as they occurred in each policy year. Elderton and Fippard put forward the idea that the method used to find rates of mortality for the population as a whole from the records of deaths and census data could equally well be applied to other populations (such as the population of individual towns or other community groups). By extension, it could be used to investigate the mortality rates of a population consisting of holders of life assurance or annuity policies. Under this method, the mortality rate for a given age, over a given year, is the ratio of the deaths at that age during the year to the mean population over the year. Provided that the population is reasonably stable over the year, an estimate of the mean population can be found by averaging the numbers at the beginning and the end of the year. From here, it is a short step to collecting annual returns of deaths over the year and the number of policies in force at the end of the year. By utilizing the 'in force' returns from the previous year as the starting 'in force' for the current year, a rolling annual investigation could be set up. Returns would then become part of each contributing office's annual routine, so that a continuous watch could be kept on the experience as it changed over time and new tables produced as the need arose, without the need for periodic special projects and the resources that they required. There were moves to set up a continuous investigation on the lines described. However, the First World War intervened and the project was shelved.

In 1923, a committee that was already investigating the experience of annuitants, based on data for the years 1900–1920, was asked to look into the experience for assured lives. This was the spur to the setting up of a continuous investigation: collection of data on a rolling annual basis was started as from 1 January 1924. The Continuous Mortality Investigation Bureau (CMIB) was up and running. The first standard table based on data collected entirely by the new Bureau was published in 1934. The present structure of the Bureau dates from 1931, when the Councils of the Institute and the Faculty decided to set up a Joint Committee to oversee the actual analysis of the data, to take responsibility for the publication and interpretation of the results of the researches, and to produce standard tables as and when deemed necessary.

At the start, data were collected for three classes of business; namely, whole-life and endowment assurances, immediate annuitants and children's deferred assurances. The investigations for whole-life and endowment assurances and immediate annuitants still continue. The next major class was to be added in 1948, when data collection began for pensioners in schemes insured by life offices. Since then, new investigations have been added from time to time as the market has developed and a need has been perceived. In 1997, data are collected for 16 different classes of business from over 50 offices, covering, by volume, the majority of the market. The labour of collecting, scheduling and amalgamating the data and carrying out the necessary calculations was, in the early days, immense. It was carried out by a succession of diligent individuals employed to toil away, first, in a tiny room under the eaves at Staple Inn Hall, and later tucked away in Barnards Inn, both off High Holborn. The word 'individuals' is used advisedly, each in their own way was a character in the true sense of the word. Perhaps they needed to be in order to survive unscathed the shattering boredom of their (largely unnoticed) activity. The advent of computerization in 1975 transformed the task and also allowed the Joint Committee to explore fully the data at their disposal, and to be far more sophisticated in both data analysis and in the derivation and production of standard tables.

The rough with the smooth

Once the data for any particular investigation has been collected and analysed and a series of observed mortality rates have been calculated, the question arises as to how best to convert these rates into a form that can be used in practice. Observed rates, even from very large experiences, do not normally progress smoothly from age to age. Simple logic would, however, suggest that mortality rates do progress smoothly and, if the population under observation were infinitely large, a set of smooth rates would be found. Also, premium rates or annuity values based on a smooth set of rates will themselves progress smoothly and therefore be easier to justify for use in the marketplace. The art of drawing such a set of smooth rates from the crude observations is known as 'graduation'. The answer to the question as to how smoothness should be defined is still up for discussion, and the arguments can range from the practical to the esoteric. The obverse of the smoothness debate is that of fidelity to the observed data. It is no use producing a set of rates smoothed to perfection if, in the process, undulations in the crude rates which reflect genuine features of the population under observation are obliterated. For example, there is a genuine 'accident' hump in male mortality rates in the late teens and early twenties in the UK; this needs to be retained in any life table that purports to reflect the mortality rates to be expected in that population.

The actual process of graduation can be carried out in a number of ways, which fall into three broad categories; namely, *graphical, summation* and *parametric*. Under the *graphical* system, the observed rates are plotted on a graph and a curve drawn following the general shape of the observations. Rates are read from the curve and are then refined by hand polishing to produce a smooth series. The method is useful where the data are sparse and do not justify the effort of more complex methods.

In *summation*, values at a given point are calculated by combining the observed value at that point with its neighbours on either side, using some predetermined weighting. This produces a series in which the graduated rates are very close to the observed rates; it is really only suitable for large experiences where the ungraduated rates already progress reasonably smoothly and, because of the numbers of deaths involved, are considered statistically to be a good estimate of the underlying expected rates.

However, by far the most popular method of graduation of assured lives data (and census data from 1951 onwards) has been the *parametric*, the fitting of a mathematical curve to the observed experience. The first such table to be so graduated was the table for healthy males mentioned earlier. The formula used was a relatively simple one, which had been put forward by William Makeham, who had adapted it from a law of mortality proposed by Benjamin Gompertz in 1825 (of which more later). The Makeham and Gompertz formulae continued in use well into the early years of the twentieth century. However, Gompertz himself recognized that a simple formula cannot truly represent mortality rates over the whole of life and suggested fitting curves to different parts of the age range and blending the results at the points of meeting. Since then, others have joined the search and derived different families of curves which have been tried and tested in their turn.

The law of life?

In the early days of the actuarial profession, there was a genuine belief in some quarters that there was a natural mathematical law that underlay human mortality. Benjamin Gompertz carried out his researches using the Northampton Table and put forward the theory that 'a law of geometric progression pervades, in an approximate degree, large portions of different tables of mortality'. He justified this philosophically by suggesting that it is possible that death may be the consequence of two generally coexisting causes: the first was chance, without previous disposition to death or deterioration; and the second deterioration, or an increased inability to withstand the forces of destruction. William Makeham built on this two-pronged approach, as it were, and adapted Gompertz' law by showing the 'chance' element as a constant, independent of age, and the 'deterioration' element as the original Gompertz geometric progression. Subsequent practitioners have concentrated mainly on finding either a curve that best fits the data under review or proposing a 'family' of curves that can (with different parameters) fit a number of different experiences. At the same time, statistical theory has moved away from the idea of the life table as a deterministic concept towards modelling techniques in which survival is regarded as a random variable. While some may regard this as esoteric, it can be extended to link up with multiple state modelling, which is a powerful tool in predicting ranges of outcomes over future time periods, with applications in areas well outside the realm of mortality studies.

It may be that the search for a law that encompasses all the changes and chances of this mortal life was doomed to failure. Each experience studied could only be a snapshot, taken at a particular moment in time and subject to very specific influences. However, the wistful feeling that there should be more to it than that is summed up in a remark made during a discussion in 1953: 'it might be a fruitless search, but to find a way of expressing something in a mathematical form is always interesting and, whatever philosophy they might make up, I am sure that actuaries and statisticians will go on doing it and will even enjoy their disappointments'.

Since then, others have approached the question from new angles. One such approach has been to study the distribution of lengths of life, which has in time led on to the consideration of theories of ageing and whether there is a biological maximum to the human lifespan. Oddly, this was also considered by Gompertz, who wrote in his original paper of 1825 that 'it would not follow that the non-appearance on the page of history of a single circumstance of a person having arrived at a certain limited age, would not be the least proof of a limit to the age of man; and further, not neither profane history nor modern experience could contradict the possibility of the great age of the patriarchies of scripture'. On an individual basis, the fascination with one's allotted span is an abiding one. There will be many who would echo the words of the psalmist: 'Lord, let me know mine end and the measure of my days'. Of course, for any one individual, the measure of life is the great unknown. Perhaps the individual being should be regarded as the ultimate random variable. In a curious way, that is not so far from the thinking behind modern statistical theory.

All sorts and conditions of men

In the UK, apart from assured lives, the other main data source for mortality statistics is derived from the national registration of deaths and the decennial censuses. There have been censuses in Great Britain every ten years from 1801 (except in 1941, when Britain was at war). Up to and including that held in 1831, they were little more than a head count, with summary totals being sent to the authorities. However, the censuses of 1841 in England and Wales and 1861 in Scotland are regarded as the first 'modern' censuses. They followed the establishment of the General Register Office (GRO) for England and Wales in 1837 and for Scotland in 1855. In these censuses, forms for completion on the census day were delivered to each household by specially recruited enumerators, who were responsible for collecting the forms, seeing that they were completed correctly and transferring the information thereon to schedules which were then sent to the GRO for analysis. The amount of planning for those massive exercises was phenomenal, down to the finest detail. For example, in the 1841 census, included in the instructions from the Registrar General was a note to the effect that each enumerator should be given a lead pencil for use in carrying out his duties. Apart from the lead pencils, the system has remained virtually unchanged to the present day. The information collected in the 1841 census was fairly simple, but the 1851 census saw the introduction of questions on occupation, and further questions have been added over the years.

From that time on, the census reports have become important social documents, detailing many aspects of the lives, health and living conditions of the population. English Life Tables, based on the census returns and deaths registrations – the latter beginning in 1837 following the Births and Deaths Registration Act – have been produced from the earliest days of the GRO. English Life Table Number 1 was based on the census returns for 1841 and the deaths for the same year. During the second half of the nineteenth century, further life tables were constructed, based variously on the census for a given year or combination of years and the deaths over varying (fairly lengthy by later standards) periods of time. From that based on the 1911 census to the present day, the practice has been to use the census for a single year and the deaths for the three years straddling the census year. English Life Table Number 9 and all subsequent tables have been produced by the Government Actuary, whose own Department, acting as consultant to the government of the day, was set up in 1919.

In 1841, expectation of life at birth was 40 years for males and 42 for females. This figure, however, is affected by the very high infant mortality prevalent at that time – one in six babies failed to reach their first birthday. If the effect of this is eliminated, the expectation becomes 47 for males and 48 for females. In the last decade of the twentieth century, the expectation for either sex is in the upper seventies. Most of the change has been due to the massive reduction in infant mortality and the virtual eradication of the lethal infectious diseases, which affected children and adults alike. This lengthening of the expected span is, of course, to be welcomed. Parents no longer expect to lose their children in early childhood; children expect to have their parents alive during their growing years; and levels of general health and well being are far higher than they were 150 years ago. Yet this very longevity produces its own problems. Old age frequently brings dependence upon others for assistance in the basics of daily living, and degeneration through the ageing process can mean that longer life is not necessarily active, or even particularly meaningful, life. The debate on how we cope with this is one for society as a whole, but when it comes to

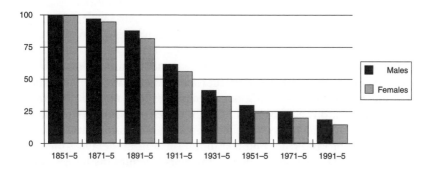

Figure 3.2 Mortality improvement in England and Wales (standardized population).
Source: compiled from *Population Trends*, volume 48, and English Life Tables No. 15, 1990–92. Office for National Statistics, Crown Copyright reserved.

the practicalities of assessing what the problems are, and devising and costing out ways in which to address the situation, the actuary has much to offer.

Through a glass darkly

The availability of long-term series of data, such as those gathered by the CMIB, allows not only the taking of a 'snapshot' at a particular moment in time, but also the study of long-term trends. These in turn can be used as pointers to estimate rates of mortality for future years. For the actuary, if mortality rates are continually reducing, it is essential to allow for the possible continuance of this reduction when costing pension annuity business. In the case of assurances – that is, the payment of a sum on death – if fewer people die over a certain period than have been allowed for the calculations, less than expected is paid out in death claims, and a 'mortality profit' is made, which can be added to the company's reserves or shared out among the policyholders. However, if annuities – that is, a series of payments in return for a consideration – are sold and people live longer then expected, a loss will be made and the business will not be viable. One of the first manifestations of this problem was in connection with annuities sold in the early 1800s by the British Government in an attempt to reduce the National Debt. The considerations were based on the mortality rates in the Northampton Table which, as we have already seen, postulated rates that were much heavier than were justified by subsequent experience. The annuities were therefore being sold at a loss and consequently were not reducing the National Debt. The first Actuary to the National Debt Office was charged with the task of investigating the experience and producing tables that were more appropriate to the task in hand.

The first annuity tables to actually make some (limited) allowance for expected future improvements in mortality were based on insurance company data for 1900–1920. Subsequent tables have refined the projection methods, and the more recent sets of tables prepared by the CMIB have incorporated tables of projected rates by age and calendar year. With the latest set of tables, a computer program was made available that allowed annuity rates to be calculated for years well into the future at any desired rate of interest and incorporating, if desired, adjustments to the base mortality rates before projection in order to reflect more fully the experience on which the actuary is working. We have come a long way from the pencil and paper, and the hours of tedious burning of the midnight oil, required of our predecessors.

In sickness and in health

Apart from the study of mortality, the other area of abiding interest has been the study of morbidity (sickness). As is described in chapter 4, cash benefits during sickness were paid by friendly societies, which flourished in the second half of the nineteenth century, and also in the first half of the twentieth century when they provided the channel for State sickness benefits.

A couple of insurance companies have offered sickness and accident benefits since the 1880s, but it is only since 1946 that life assurers have become really involved in such business through the offering of permanent health insurance, otherwise known as 'long term disability insurance'. These schemes provide a benefit when income from employment stops through sickness, and are arranged either on a group basis by companies for their employees or on an individual basis, mainly by the self-employed. Actuaries involved in setting premium rates and reserves for this business found themselves in the position of their predecessors in the early days of life assurance, over a century before, in that there was no standard table that was felt to be representative of the experience with which they were dealing. Believe it or not, although sickness data was available from the National Insurance scheme, and experience data was available from North America, the table actually used by many of the offices writing the business was that of a large friendly society (The Independent Order of Oddfellows, Manchester Unity), based on their experience of 1893–97 (suitably adapted to reflect the office's own experience, of course), which was the most recent major pooled experience of its kind. Accordingly, following an initiative by the Life Offices Association and the Associated Scottish Life Offices, the CMIB undertook a pooled investigation with a start date of 1 January 1972. Seventeen offices offered to submit data. (The number 17 somehow has a strange resonance for actuarial investigations.) As with the mortality investigations, data is returned on a rolling annual basis, with separate sections for data from group schemes and for individual policies. As it has been gathered in, the experience has been compared with that shown in the Manchester Unity Table.

The Manchester Unity tables were based on a relatively simple technique of counting the weeks of sickness benefit paid in the year and relating that to the numbers paying contributions over the year. In the late 1980s and early 1990s, much theoretical work was carried out, from which emerged a more complex system of analysis of the basic elements that result in the overall picture as it emerges; for example, the chance of falling sick, the chance of recovery from sickness after varying time periods, the chance of dying after falling sick, and so on. Complex multiple-state models have been built up, by means of which the effects, individually and combined, of the different elements can be traced. In conjunction with the theoretical models, sets of experience rates, drawn from the CMIB data pool, for use with new techniques have been calculated and published.

Seek and ye shall find

For over 150 years, actuaries from different companies, all in competition with each other, have seen the benefit of working together to pool information in order to produce something that each can use as he or she sees fit in the conduct of the day-to-day business. In this instance, the whole is quite clearly greater than the sum of the parts.

   When this activity started, there was virtually no information available and a need was perceived. Today, there is almost too much information. In almost all areas of human activity, people and events are counted, coded and categorized. Yet one has to ask whether the best use is being made of all this data which is being collected. Are there too many individual wheels being reinvented, all slightly different? Or, more seriously, is information just being collected (possibly as a by-product of another activity) and not being systematically analysed, and are important clues not being found?

Further reading

Benjamin, B. and Soliman, A. S. 1994: *Mortality on the Move*. London.
Continuous Mortality Investigation Bureau. Reports from 1934 to date.
Nissel, M. 1987: *People Count: a History of the General Register Office*. London.
Ogborn, M. E. 1962: *Equitable Assurances*. London.

Friendly societies

4

Lawrence Eagles

Before the National Insurance scheme, wage-earners insured each other against loss of earnings from sickness or old age by forming friendly societies. This is the story of the development of friendly societies in the UK, from their origins in the seventeenth century through the period of their greatest social and financial importance (1919–45) to the present time. Although the usefulness of actuarial advice received early official recognition, it was only as societies found that actuaries could help them to solve the financial problems that they faced, that they came to regard their advice as essential. Originally, actuaries were concerned with the accumulating societies, which built up funds from level contributions, but evolving actuarial techniques developed to assist with the financial control of any friendly society.

Beginnings

The names of many traditional friendly societies, such as Oddfellows, Druids or Shepherds, convey images that seem remote from the world of financial institutions. They also seem remote from day-to-day concerns. Yet, prior to the twentieth century, the only way in which the wage-earner could provide against loss of earnings in sickness or old age was through becoming a friendly society member and insuring on a mutual basis with other members. However, in many societies, mutual insurance was only part of the reason for joining. In the early societies, the friendly, fraternal aspects were of equal importance. The focal point for the society would be its regular meetings, usually at an inn, where contributions would be paid in and the officers advised of those due benefits. The privilege and obligations of members to each other was often stressed by adopting solemn initiation ceremonies or meeting rituals, backed by reference to a mythical past: thus the Druids claimed a history back to the ancient Britons and the Foresters claimed that Adam was the first Forester. Every society would have an annual feast day with a formal meeting and dinner, and possibly a church service and procession. It is these aspects of the friendly society that these names recall, aspects that can still be important, especially the sense of real mutuality.

Clubs that provided sickness and funeral benefits were found in the UK as early as the seventeenth century, but only became of real importance in the second half of the eighteenth century. The first actuarial work on friendly society finance dates from the same period. Dr Richard Price, a Presbyterian minister and mathematician, who was one of the promoters of the Equitable Life Assurance Society, published a paper deriving contributions for sickness benefits from a theoretical basis.

These early societies were of a strictly local character. The insurance benefits were typically sick pay, throughout life, of 6s. to 10s. a week (which may be compared with average weekly wages for artisans and labourers of about 13s.) and a funeral grant of £5 to £10, which was financed by levies. Contribution rates were uniform for all ages at entry, at around 9d. to 1s. per month. Mitigating the obvious unsoundness of this system, since the cost of sickness clearly increases with age, was the feature that the maximum age at entry was often as low as 40.

Many early societies operated on a yearly cycle, dividing any surplus funds at the year end between the members in cash. It is useful to make an initial broad distinction between such 'dividing societies' and the 'accumulating societies', which sought to build up funds to provide the benefits on a more permanent basis, since it was to these latter societies that actuarial techniques were first applied. Indeed, nineteenth-century actuaries considered dividing societies to be of little interest, and in fact not susceptible to actuarial analysis; however, twentieth-century actuaries have developed techniques to analyse the finances of a dividing society.

A legal framework

Whatever the type of society, it had no special legal status. It was simply treated as a partnership. The problems of fraud and corruption that this could produce became apparent as the number of societies increased, and led to the first Friendly Societies Act in 1793.

The primary motive of this Act was to encourage friendly societies, since they gave the working man an alternative source of funds when sick, rather than claiming on the parish. Societies that registered under the Act had to have all rules and amendments approved by the Justices at Quarter Sessions. In return, registered societies were able to sue and be sued, and thus obtain security for their funds. Registration was both voluntary and discretionary, and it has been suggested that only one-half of societies made use of it. The Act was therefore not altogether successful, and legislative efforts continued over the next century, many being experimental in nature.

A Bill introduced in 1818 made the bold provision that five public valuers be appointed to examine tables and rules. This was, perhaps, the first official recognition of a role for the actuary in the friendly society area, but the Bill never became law.

The Act of the following year left out the public valuers, retained approval of rules and tables by the Justices, but added that they should not 'confirm or allow any table of payments or benefits, or any rules dependent upon or connected with the calculations thereof, until it shall have been made to appear to such justices that the said tables and rules are such as have been approved of by two persons at least, known to be professional actuaries or persons skilled in calculation'. Equally, if the society dissolved, a certificate was required from two actuaries. The Act also contained several provisions regarding investments, in particular the right to place money with the National Debt Commissioners.

However, the requirement for actuarial certification unfortunately proved premature, since there were neither sufficient numbers of actuaries nor any relevant data for them to work from. This was recognized in the Act of 1829, which abolished the provision for actuarial certification, but introduced quinquennial returns of sickness and mortality to be supplied to the clerk of the peace for transmission to central government. Rules now had to be confirmed by the barrister appointed by the National Debt Commissioners to certify the rules of savings banks, an official who was later to become the Registrar of Friendly Societies. From 1834 onwards, the quinquennial returns were also effectively to the Registrar (so titled from 1846). In 1840, societies effectively had a limit of £200 placed on their sums insured on death, to prevent insurance companies registering as friendly societies. The permitted aims of a registered society were defined as follows:

> providing by contribution, on the principle of mutual insurance, for the maintenance or assistance of the contributors thereto, their wives or children, in sickness, infancy, advanced age, widowhood or any other natural state or contingency, whereof the occurrence is susceptible of calculation by way of average, or for any other purpose which is not illegal . . . .

It is, however, worth noting that the most rapidly growing types of society at that time were still not able to register, because they were regarded as secret societies and, as such, as a cover for potentially illegal activities. These were the affiliated orders, which were federations of local branch societies, each branch being independent as regards benefit funds and liabilities, at least to start with, but linked by having the same secret rituals and ceremonies at meetings, and some sort of overall governing body. Initiation rites stressed the privilege of membership: they were often dramatic, as in the Foresters, where before 1845 initiation took the form of a trial by combat.

The two most prominent orders (which remain so today), the Independent Order of Oddfellows (Manchester Unity) and the Ancient Order of Foresters, both originated around 1810, and by 1850 had some 300 000 members between them. The average size of the local branches was nevertheless small, at around 100 members. It was clearly undesirable that members of such societies had no legal protection for their funds, as a number of scandals showed, and from 1850 an order or a branch thereof was permitted to register. Registration was further encouraged by the Act of 1855, which abolished all fees for registration. It also required any society that offered a fixed annuity or a fixed superannuation benefit to have those tables certified by the actuary to the National Debt Commissioners. The legal framework so established basically remained unaltered for the next 20 years.

The first sickness tables

By this time, there were enough actuaries to make a significant contribution to the growing movement. The first attempt to analyse real sickness experience for friendly societies was made by the Highland Society of Scotland and published in 1824. The data was tabulated in decennial age groups, the average number of weeks of sickness in each group was calculated, and then individual rates for each age were obtained by a crude interpolation. The rates derived are in general lower than those shown in subsequent investigations, and when applied to construct contribution rates gave results that were to prove too low. The reasons for these low rates were, first, that data was submitted on a voluntary basis, so that only the best managed societies responded, and also that the interpolation method was faulty, underestimating rates by up to 20 per cent.

A set of tables based on English experience appeared in an actuarial textbook on friendly societies published in 1835. The sickness rates are significantly higher than those of the Highland Society, but are still relatively light above age 35. This is not surprising. It is now known that sickness business is subject to selection effects that can last for 15–20 years, and since the maximum age at entry was low, the membership at older ages was still very select.

Tables actually derived from the quinquennial returns to the Registrar (for the years 1836–40) were published in 1845. The experience was divided into rural, town and city districts; separate investigations were made for England and Scotland, and there was some analysis by occupation. Both sickness and mortality rates were derived. This shows the increasing sophistication of actuarial analysis. Comparing the English and Scottish experiences, the English societies showed heavier sickness rates but lighter mortality, which increased relative contribution rates still further. The basic methods for deriving contribution tables for sickness benefits devised by nineteenth-century actuaries continued to be used for similar insurance until the present decade.

New types of society

The type of society in which actuarial advice seems to have been sought as a matter of course was the patronized county or district society. These developed in the same period as the 'order' societies, but are largely confined to the semi-rural South of England, whereas the orders all had their roots in the industrial North. The distinguishing feature of these county societies was that the membership consisted of two groups, honorary members and benefit members, the management of the society being controlled by the honorary members, who were usually prominent local gentry or clergy. As a result, these societies normally took advantage of registration, made good use of investment with the National Debt Commissioners at guaranteed rates of up to $4\frac{1}{2}$ per cent per annum and were generally well managed. In addition to the sickness and funeral benefits, they also offered deferred annuities. Originally, these were compulsory, since actuaries advised that there should be a definite benefit in old age, but this was later dropped under competitive pressures. The rules could also provide for regular actuarial investigations. Contribution tables were normally calculated by an actuary, and would be graduated by age at entry. Even though the rates themselves were on average too low (the Highland Society experience was often used as a basis up to 1850) and the progression by age too shallow, this was still an improvement on the rule-of-thumb flat scales employed by most local societies (including the order branches).

Other societies developed which were more analogous to insurance companies, and hence ready to make use of actuaries. The ordinary large (or general) societies eliminated the club aspect entirely, in order to attract the more highly paid workers, craftsmen, clerks, shop keepers, and so on. Management was centralized, and contributions were collected and benefits paid either through agents or through Post Office orders. The main advantage claimed was efficiency, management expenses being in some cases only about 6 per cent of benefits paid. The benefits offered were more substantial. The most prominent of these societies was the Hearts of Oak, which offered subscriptions that were unrelated to age, but which only accepted new entrants between the ages of 18 and 30, so that the rates could be justified actuarially.

Also with centralized management, the collecting burial societies were aimed at those who could not afford the full benefits offered by other societies, but at least wanted to avoid the ignominy of a pauper's grave. Their business consisted almost entirely of issuing whole-life insurances for premiums of a halfpenny or a penny a week, collected from door to door. They were thus very similar to industrial insurance companies, with which they should be grouped for the purpose of actuarial analysis. The main problems facing the actuary to such an organization were to make adequate provision for the very high level of expenses and the substantial numbers of lapses.

Actuaries and the orders

The financial basis on which the local or branch society was established was beginning to show its limitations. The uniform scales employed were deficient in at least two respects. In most cases, the initial relation of contribution to benefit had been determined without any statistical justification, and without any specific provision for management expenses. If these were not kept under control, the society could – and many did – run out of funds. Even if the expenses were controlled, and the initial rate was adequate for the benefits, as the membership aged the rate became progressively less adequate unless there was a continuous recruitment of new members at or below the ages at entry of the initial members, so that the average age remained stable. This also caused many societies to fail.

New members alone did not ensure stability and continuity. It was not unknown for new members to try to secure their own position by reducing the benefits of older members, or even expelling them. A further problem was that the basic causes of potential failure were not well recognized. With funeral benefits of, typically, £10 on the death of a member and £5 on the death of his wife, but sickness benefit at the full rate of 10s. per week, societies generally considered that the main risk to their funds was excessive numbers of deaths, even though actuaries could demonstrate that excess sickness claims and long life were the most likely source of financial strain.

Small local autonomous societies probably were never really in a position to obtain proper advice, but as the orders grew their leaders became concerned to put their finances on a sound basis, and to use actuarial techniques. Indeed, some of these leaders were actuaries, amongst the most notable being Henry Ratcliffe, the general secretary of the Manchester Unity.

Although, in origin, each order was a loose federation of financially independent units, there was in each case some sort of central body. The history of the development of an order essentially displays the resolution of the inherent conflicts between complete local autonomy and the needs of the order as a whole for financial stability and progress. In each case, local autonomy has been progressively relinquished, but the pace of development was very different in the different orders. This process advanced most where actuarial advice was most accepted.

As the number of branches in an order increased, for administrative reasons they were formed into districts (some branches choosing not to join the district). In order to provide some common financial element to the branches of a district, the funeral benefits (which were wrongly considered to most need protecting) would be reinsured into a district fund, usually financed on a per capita basis. In due course, this produced its own problems as it transferred funds from expanding branches with young members to contracting branches with older members. However, it started the process of inter-branch financial links and associated administrative returns, while not affecting the branch's right to set its own contribution tables. This was the next focus for central regulation, and owed much to actuarial advice.

The Manchester Unity was the first order to take action in this area. The 1840s was a period of considerable turmoil in the Order. By 1842, it was estimated that there were over 3500 branches, but in 1843 alone 225 closed for lack of funds. This led the central committee to call for returns of funds and membership from each branch, in order to construct sound tables. Branches that failed to do so were suspended from the Order. Two important reforms were introduced in 1845: first, management funds were to be separated from benefit funds and, second, branches could still fix their contributions and benefits, but they had to be such that each halfpenny per week contribution provided 1s. per week sickness benefit and £1 at death. These rates, which met with considerable opposition because they represented a real limitation on branch autonomy, were still inadequate – nor were they graduated by age – but they were a useful first step. The sickness and mortality experience of the Order was collected over the years 1846–48 and analysed by Henry Ratcliffe to provide a sound basis for rating. Graduated rates were derived from this experience and adopted as recommended rates in 1853, although branches were not compelled to introduce them.

The Manchester Unity was thus the first of the orders to accept tables based on actuarial principles as standard. Progress in the other orders was slower; for example, the Foresters expanded later and their branches retained greater autonomy. They experimented with graduated rates in the 1850s, but did not seriously attempt to make them the norm until the 1870s, by which time five-yearly valuations on actuarial principles had become compulsory.

Actuaries and valuations

In addition to enabling actuaries to calculate appropriate rates, the development of sickness and mortality tables – based on relevant experience – also enabled actuarial valuations, comparing the present values of assets and liabilities, to be undertaken. The valuation interval was usually five years. This enabled action to be taken in the event of a deficiency, to deal with the problem by adjusting benefits and/or contributions before it led to the collapse of the society.

In fact, in many early valuations, in contrast to those of life insurance companies, a deficiency was the usual result. This was because many contribution scales had no scientific basis, and even where rates were actuarially calculated they were often based on inadequate experiences. A surplus was generally treated as providing a useful buffer, and only later did actuaries consider the problem of its equitable distribution in depth.

Actuaries recognized that the problem of dealing with a deficiency was avoiding undue adverse selection. An increase in contribution rates alone, especially if it led to rates greater than the rates at which healthy members could obtain cover as new members of other societies, would simply produce selective lapsing. It was considered better to reduce sickness benefit at the longer durations, which would not immediately affect younger, fitter members. This reinforced the pattern of benefit that had appeared in many societies for the full rate of sick pay to be payable only for a limited period (often 6 or 12 months) during any one episode of sickness. After that period, the rate of sick pay was usually reduced to one-half, either for the remainder of the episode, or until a further reduction came into effect.

The importance of actuarial valuation was recognized in the Friendly Societies Act of 1875, which followed from the recommendations of a Royal Commission. Registered societies were required for the first time to submit quinquennial valuations of assets and liabilities, as well as quinquennial returns of sickness and mortality, and annual returns of income and expenditure. Dividing societies were exempted on the grounds that their mode of operation was not susceptible to actuarial analysis. So also were two types of society, deposit societies and Holloway societies, combining savings and insurance, which developed around this time. These were to become of considerable importance, and will be discussed later.

For the accumulating societies, regular valuations on actuarial principles were now a requirement, although the valuer did not have to be an actuary. Each branch of an order was valued separately, and the practice developed of spreading branch valuations over a five-year rolling cycle. The main problem revealed by order valuations was that different branches were in very different financial positions. This, of course, partly resulted from each branch having its own contribution rates, but even where standard tables had been introduced, at first they made no adjustments for risk factors, such as hazardous occupations, which would have very different incidence between branches. Actuaries became concerned about these factors as more sophisticated analysis of experiences was undertaken. Each branch would be valued on tables of sickness and mortality that broadly reflected its own experience, and at a rate of interest corresponding to the average yield achieved over the past five years, less a margin. An interest rate of 3 per cent per annum was in some ways a standard, but rates of up to 4 per cent could be used. For comparative purposes, the degree of solvency came to be measured by the ratio of the fund plus the value of future contributions to the value of the liabilities, so that less than 100 per cent indicated a deficiency.

The first order to take actuarial advice to address this problem was, once again, the Manchester Unity. From about 1890, branches at which valuation revealed a degree of solvency of less than 85 per cent had to adopt a scheme of amelioration, through a combination of increases in contributions and reductions in benefits. In return, assistance was provided by the Order as a whole taking over part or all of the liability for older members and financing that liability through a charge on branches in surplus. Similar schemes were adopted at a slightly later date by the Ancient Order of Foresters and some other orders. At first, these measures were not very effective, but they later led to ambitious and successful schemes of actuarial management of such imbalances, which ultimately resolved the problem.

The practice of a rolling cycle of branch valuations was to make it increasingly difficult to collate the experience of an order as a whole over a certain period. The last major investigation was carried out by Sir Alfred Watson, as actuary of the Manchester Unity, into the experience over the years 1893–7. Great attention was paid to the accurate recording of the data, which was put through a two-way analysis, by occupation and by area. The methods adopted were followed by nearly all UK actuaries until about 1990. The experience itself was so comprehensive that it was used as a standard to be adjusted up to, and even after, life office experiences on permanent health (sickness) were published by the CMIB (see chapter 3).

Friendly societies and National Insurance

It remained the practice in most societies to provide sickness benefits throughout life. The main exceptions to this were some of the county societies and company societies, chiefly found among the railway companies, where the employer gave a subsidy. In both cases, sickness benefit ceased at age 65 or 70, to be replaced by a pension. Actuaries had been pointing out to societies that above age 75 or so it was almost impossible to distinguish sickness from the general decline of old age, and valuing sick pay at those ages as a pension for the lowest rate. Tables were devised for extra contributions to convert sick pay from age 70 to pension, but there was little interest from members before the 1912 National Insurance Act.

An important class of benefit always seem to have been provided by a per capita levy: these were medical aid benefits, under which a member was entitled to the services of a doctor and possibly help in paying for medicines prescribed. These benefits were therefore exempt from valuation.

Also exempt were deposit and Holloway societies, which combined savings and insurance. In a deposit society, members' contributions were first credited to a common fund, from which a proportion of sickness benefits were paid, the balance being paid from the member's own deposit account. Any surplus in the common fund at the end of the financial year was apportioned to members' deposit accounts, to which interest was credited. Members could also make direct contributions to their deposit accounts. Sickness benefit only continued as of right until the member's deposit account was exhausted; thereafter 'grace pay' could be allowed for a period from the common fund. A member could make withdrawals from his deposit account as long as a balance remained equal to one year's contributions. Thus it was practically impossible for such a society to become insolvent. On the other hand, a member's total sickness benefit entitlement at any time was a multiple of his deposit. Another major distinguishing feature of this type of society was that membership was open equally to males and females; in other societies at that time, membership would be single sex.

The Holloway society (devised by George Holloway, MP for Stroud in the 1880s) aimed to provide for both sickness and pension from a single series of contributions. The contribution depended on attained age and increased year-by-year from age 30 to age 65, when both sickness benefit and contributions ceased. The original contribution rates were actuarially calculated from the Manchester Unity 1866–70 experience, and included a substantial margin. At the end of each year, the excess of contributions paid over claims and expenses was divided to member's individual surplus accounts, pro rata to their sickness benefit rate. No reserve was retained, but the society had the right to claw back up to two year's surplus allocations to meet any drain on the funds. At age 65 a member was entitled to withdraw the surplus account and could use it to purchase a pension. Actuarial valuation was deemed unnecessary, because a substantial part of the funds was divided each year to members' accounts.

The Friendly Society Act of 1896 consolidated and replaced the 1875 Act, but did not significantly alter the financial regulation of societies, which was to remain largely unchanged for a century. Societies were now covering a significant part of the working population. In 1910 there were 26 773 societies (of which 20 580 were branches of orders) with 6 622 716 members. The finances of societies were improving as a result of the developments discussed earlier. The major cause of concern for societies had become the discussions in Parliament and elsewhere of some sort of compulsory national insurance scheme, discussions from which many friendly society managers saw a real threat to the movement. However, following the introduction of means-tested Old Age Pensions in 1908, the Chancellor of the Exchequer proceeded to formulate a plan for national insurance, consulting amongst others the National Conference of Friendly Societies (which then represented mainly the accumulating sickness societies). The resulting arrangements set out in the National Insurance Act 1911 provided for the administration of the State scheme mainly through 'Approved Societies', which were separately administered State sections of existing societies. Approved Societies had to provide sick pay of 10s. per week (for men, and 7s. 6d. for women), payable for the first 26 weeks of sickness, excluding the first three days, and reducing thereafter to 5s. per week. There were also medical aid benefits and limited unemployment benefits. No sickness benefits were paid after age 70. The main class of employed contributor paid 4d. per week, the employer 3d. and the State two-ninths of the benefits. Societies were required under section 72 of the 1911 Act to submit schemes for 'continuing, abolishing, or altering such benefits as respects those of its members who became insured persons and for adjusting their contributions accordingly'. However, any scheme was not to prejudice the solvency of the society, and in general societies benefited where members did opt for a reduction. Most members opted to maintain their voluntary sickness cover, as in many cases benefit levels had not been increased as real wages increased.

The National Insurance Act led to fundamental changes in the nature of societies. In order to retain members, societies needed to be seen to operate an approved section, but there was a minimum requirement of 5000 members for approval. This caused many small local societies to affiliate with an order and become branches of it. More important was the fact that the National Insurance Act led to fundamental changes in the nature of the membership. Those joining the State section purely for the State benefits were unlikely to take any interest in other aspects of membership. For the first time, there were large groups of members, even in the orders, who did not want to be involved actively in their society. On the other hand, the administration of the State side was complex, and societies' central staff were increasingly absorbed in it.

Friendly societies in their heyday

In the years immediately after the end of the First World War, there was also other evidence that members were looking at a more personal financial contract with societies. The societies that showed the greatest growth in membership in this period were the deposit and Holloway societies. While the number of members of all societies (other than collecting societies) only increased from some 6.6 million in 1910 to 7.5 million in 1928, the membership of deposit and Holloway societies rose from some 0.4 million to 1.4 million over the same period. In response, accumulating societies started to introduce tables with a savings element. These ranged from establishing deposit or Holloway tables, to tables devised by actuaries on more traditional principles; for example, allowing an additional contribution to provide a lump sum at the age at which sick benefit ceased, with a return of premiums on prior death.

Actuaries were also increasingly being consulted by the non-accumulating societies over aspects of their finances. Some of these had set up separate accumulating sections, mainly to fund death benefits, which required valuation, but actuaries were now being asked to advise in general on new tables, and also to undertake valuations of the whole society. Thus it was increasingly recognized that the actuary had a vital role to play in the proper financial control of any society.

In the event, section 72 of the 1911 Act did not lead to much actuarial activity, but the provisions of the National Insurance Act did produce fundamental changes in the pattern of benefits offered by societies, over and above the move towards a savings element. The fact that State sickness benefits ceased at age 70, combined with the existence of the means-tested Old Age Pension, made the provision of lifetime sickness benefits increasingly inappropriate, since any incentive to return to work was greatly diminished. Most of the larger societies adopted new tables for new entrants, with sickness benefits ceasing at age 70. This limited the financial problem of worsening claims above that age to existing members. However, actuaries also urged the provision of an annuity from the age at which sickness benefit ceased, perhaps at half-pay, as part of the package. This continued to generate little enthusiasm from societies, because it was felt to lead to contributions that new members might consider excessive. When the State pension age was reduced to 65 in 1925, this sentiment was reinforced. Actuaries therefore considered less costly alternatives, such as the provision of a lump sum at cessation of sickness benefit, or retaining the old lifetime tables, but with an annuity of equivalent value substituted for the sick pay after age 65 or 70. Valuation surplus sometimes enabled this annuity to be increased from time to time, for existing members.

By the 1920s, society valuations were in general showing much improved results, mainly as a result of improved yields. Societies continued to invest mainly in mortgages or government securities, on which the rates of interest increased significantly after 1914. The resulting interest surpluses enabled actuaries advising orders to carry through measures not only to eliminate branch deficiencies, but also in some cases to restore benefits and contributions to original levels, where they had previously been reduced. In other cases, surpluses funded the adjustments to deal with the situation after the 1911 Act. For example, one large general society introduced new tables with sickness benefit ceasing at age 70, leaving existing members with lifetime benefits in a closed section. That section also provided a death benefit, which had been funded by levies, a method no longer appropriate in a closed fund. A regular contribution was substituted for the levies, and was partly funded by emerging surplus.

As mentioned above, valuations were not confined to accumulating societies. The growth of the non-accumulating societies caused the Registry of Friendly Societies to become concerned about their overall financial stability, and in some cases to request valuation. Actuaries no longer argued that this was not possible. The focus of valuation was not solvency and surplus as such, but whether the framework of benefits and contributions was coherent; for example, in a deposit society, whether the current proportion of contributions transferred to the common sick fund could be maintained.

Friendly societies in the age of the welfare state

The period between the world wars represented the peak of the social and financial importance of societies in the UK. This was brought to an abrupt end by the enactment after 1945 of a comprehensive scheme of national insurance, covering almost all of the population, and centrally administered. From 1948, the approved sections were disbanded, and their functions taken over by the Ministry of National Insurance. The contribution provided by those sections to general management expenses of societies ceased. Societies also lost many of their best staff, who were recruited by the Ministry to run the new national scheme.

The existence of that scheme in itself acted to reduce the attractiveness of the societies' traditional sickness benefits and to inhibit recruitment of new members. Many societies suffered an immediate substantial loss of members, followed by a continuing gradual decline. Membership of societies, other than collecting societies, had reached a peak of about 8.7 million in 1945: by 1959 it had fallen to 6.1 million. It is to be noted that this decline was most conspicuous in the case of the orders, which had focused on the traditional core benefits. The deposit and Holloway societies, and other societies offering savings and insurance benefits, were much less affected, as were the collecting societies.

The one area in which societies were given some additional scope was life assurance. The limit of £200 on sums assured on death, which was in force from 1840, had been increased to £300 in 1908, but it was increased again to £500 in 1948. Societies continued to be exempt from income tax, so there was the possibility of enhanced life or endowment business. Friendly society insurances were traditionally whole life, but collecting societies and some of the other societies had started writing endowment assurances, both with and without profits, on the same lines as insurance companies in the early part of the twentieth century. The position post 1945 gave this development fresh impetus; indeed, a number of societies introduced such tables for the first time. The collecting societies had always followed insurance company practice in employing agents to sell business, and other societies started to adopt this approach to some extent, although there was a great reluctance to move away from recruitment of new entrants by existing members, the 'member get member' philosophy.

The Trustee Investment Act 1961 gave societies the power to invest in equity investments for the first time. In addition to investments permitted by societies' special powers, broadly investments in public funds, land and secured loans (including mortgages), societies could make authorized trustee investments. These were divided into narrow-range investments, government stocks and secured deposits, and wider-range investments, fully paid UK stocks and shares of UK companies that had paid dividends on all their shares in each of the previous five years and unit trusts. If societies wanted to make wider-range investments, they had to apportion moneys invested in authorized trustee investments 50 : 50 between narrow-range and wider-range. Although the conditions now seem very restrictive, this gave societies significantly greater investment possibilities.

In the early 1960s, a very small number of new societies were formed to take advantage of the totally tax-free status of friendly society assurances on a single premium basis. This practice was prohibited by the Finance Act 1966, which introduced qualifying rules for tax-exempt assurances, the most important of which was that there must be regular premiums payable for a period of at least ten years or until prior death. The same Act gave societies powers to set up taxable assurance funds, taxed in the same way as mutual insurance companies, to write sums assured of up to £2000 per member (£3000 in the case of mortgage protection business). These limits on taxable sums assured were progressively increased, until they were abolished altogether in 1984.

The move towards life and endowment business helped to slow the decline in membership in societies that seriously pursued this option. It also arrested in those cases the decline in the real level of contributions under the pressure of falling membership and inflation. This was a very serious problem for societies that failed to find new sources of business, since the margins to cover fixed costs were continually being eroded. The problem was compounded by the fact that many societies did not update the money values of their benefits, even in the face of the inflation of the past three decades. There were, of course, exceptions – notably amongst the Holloway societies – but there was a dangerous trend away from realistic benefits.

All of these factors meant that an increasing number of societies, including branches of orders, were faced with the alternatives of winding up or merging. The main problem facing the actuary in the valuation was often the funding of management expenses. In order to safeguard the interests of members, it was important to make a recommendation to close or merge, before all of the benefits were eroded. In 1928 there had been 18 489 registered branches of orders and 2353 other societies, excluding collecting societies. The corresponding figures in 1980 were 3818 and 424. On the other hand, total funds, which had been £100 million in 1928, were £550 million in 1980.

New beginnings

In 1974, existing legislation was consolidated in a new Friendly Societies Act. Of more significance was the Finance Act of the following year, which increased the limit for tax-exempt sums assured to £1000 for societies not transacting taxable business. A number of societies were formed to offer basically ten-year regular premium endowments, which they marketed actively. As a result, they became a focus of growth in the movement. Their contracts did not embody any special actuarial features: their distinguishing characteristics were overall simplicity, with a minimum of variations allowed, and front-end loading to cover initial costs and commission. The advantages of the tax-exempt societies increased in 1980 when the limit on the sum assured was raised to £2000, but ended in 1984 when, in addition to abolishing life assurance premium relief, the Finance Act brought in a common tax-exempt limit of £750 for all societies. Nevertheless, several of them had become strong forces in the movement, which continued to grow. The other kind of new society being established was the partnership society, set up to provide pensions for partners, and often to hold the property assets of the partnership.

The factors that have dominated the financial management of societies in recent years have been the European Community Insurance Directives and the Financial Services Act 1986. Both have operated in the same direction, moving society modes of operation closer to those of insurance companies, and this tendency has been further reinforced by the new framework for societies established by the Friendly Societies Act 1992.

The first EC life Directive applied to all organizations in the Community that were writing long-term business with annual premiums in excess of 500 000 ECU. It was therefore clear from its adoption in 1979 that a number of societies would be included. The implementation of the Directive was extensively discussed with representatives of societies and with actuaries. The basic requirement of the Directive was an annual valuation and demonstration of solvency. At that time no society was required to be valued more often than once every three years, and there was no formal solvency test. Societies and their actuaries considered that there were particular problems with the increased frequency of valuation and the resulting increase in actuarial and other costs. A further problem was that a number of societies likely to be affected were exempted from valuation.

Finally, there was the question of whether or not Orders should be consolidated for regulatory purposes. In the event, no major concessions were achieved, except that societies that came under the Directive were automatically authorized to continue business.

The terms of the Directive were implemented by the Friendly Societies (Long Term Insurance Business) Regulations 1987. These initially applied to only 37 societies (including four collecting societies) but these societies wrote over 95 per cent of the long-term business of all societies. These societies were required to submit an annual actuarial valuation return. Orders were to be regulated on a consolidated basis. The regulations for valuing assets and liabilities were very similar to those for insurance companies. As a result, the professional position of the actuary with regard to the society was strengthened, and became closer to that of the Appointed Actuary of an insurance company. In fact, Directive societies must now have an Appointed Actuary.

An interesting corollary of the Directive was that it permitted transfers of business between any bodies recognized under it. Transfer of engagements from a friendly society to an insurance company had always been permitted, but now transfers in the reverse direction became possible, and the first actually took place in 1990.

The Financial Services Act had a much wider immediate impact. This had been clear from the time it was first mooted. The Chief Registrar of Friendly Societies wrote in his 1985 Report that 'The legislation may prove to be a watershed for the movement. It will distinguish those societies which wish to continue writing "investment" business and so appear to have the management and sales capability to do so to the standards now required from those who prefer to concentrate on their traditional benevolent, social and philanthropic role'. Special concessions were given to those societies that decided to stop writing new business, and some 40 per cent of societies took advantage of them.

Compliance with the Act has changed societies in several directions. Setting up the necessary administration has proved costly, especially in management time. The procedure for compliant sales has made 'member get member' sales methods increasingly difficult, so that societies are increasingly having to adopt professional sales methods. Finally, it has caused societies to consider the range of products offered, to ensure that this corresponds to the sales requirements.

With these changes, the legislative framework for societies was increasingly archaic. A Green Paper entitled 'Friendly Societies: A New Framework' appeared in 1990, and the proposals were basically implemented by the Friendly Societies Act 1992. Under this Act, the insurance business for which a society may be authorized is any class of long-term business, or general business classes 1 and 2, accident and sickness. All societies are required to be authorized to write new business. A status of 'incorporated society' has been introduced, under which, for the first time, a society is recognized as a legal entity. Incorporated societies are no longer subject to the Trustee Investment Act, and they can own subsidiary companies with a range of permitted objects. All incorporated societies writing long-term business must have an appointed actuary, and submit annual valuations. Indeed, all societies must be valued by an actuary every three years, even if the only business is General Business.

Actuaries have been advising friendly societies on their finances since the movement first started to develop a serious financial aspect. The contribution that they could make received early official recognition, but it took longer for societies as a whole to accept actuarial advice wholeheartedly. In the heyday of the movement, when societies played a major role in social insurance, actuaries were advising across the whole range of societies. Today, with a return to an emphasis on individual provision where possible, the actuary has a more formal and closer link to the society.

Further reading

Geddes, P. and Holbrook, J. P. 1963: *Friendly Societies*. Cambridge.
Gosden, P. H. J. H. 1961: *The Friendly Societies in England, 1815–75*. Manchester.
Hardy, G. F. 1886: *The Institute of Actuaries Messenger Prize Essay on Friendly Societies*. London.
Watson, A. W. 1912: *Friendly Society Finance Considered in its Actuarial Aspect*. London and Cambridge.

Actuaries and life insurance 5

Ronald Skerman

The foundations of scientific life insurance were laid in 1762 when a life insurance risk, which increases with age, was covered by periodic level premiums, and the first 'actuary' was appointed. Since then, actuaries have seen the provision of financial security to policyholders as their first duty. Safety margins were included in premiums, because the future cannot be foreseen, and profits therefore arose. Actuaries were involved in calculating those profits and in ensuring that they were fairly distributed between policyholders. Initially, these profits were divided using the concept of a pooled fund, sharing the overall return irrespective of the incidence of premium payments on each policy. This concept has become diluted over the years: sharing now depends on the incidence of premium payments, but pooling still occurs since fluctuations in profits are smoothed.

Actuaries have always been involved in the regulatory supervision of life insurers. Initially, this was limited to providing accounts and returns that showed the value of the insurers' assets and liabilities, with an explanation of how these values were determined. After 1945, new statutory requirements defined the principles on which assets and liabilities should be valued. Each life insurer had to nominate an 'Appointed Actuary', whose duties would include the continuous monitoring of the insurer's finances. The actuarial professional bodies instructed Appointed Actuaries on their duties in the light of the statutory requirements, including having regard to the reasonable expectations of policyholders. Thus the professional bodies came to participate in the regulatory system.

Actuaries have also co-operated in measures to ensure consumer protection, in assessing realistic (as distinct from statutory) profits, in valuing the business on the books of an insurer for shareholders, in valuing an insurer in a takeover, in demutualizations, and in discussions on allocating the 'inherited estate' between shareholders and policyholders.

From the 1760s to the 1980s

As Jillian Evans has explained in chapter 3, the foundations of scientific life insurance in the UK were laid by the Equitable Society founded in 1762. The initial, seemingly simple, concept was the provision of life insurance – covering a risk that increases with age – by level periodic premium payments. The practical application of this concept has challenged actuarial thought throughout the development of life insurance. This chapter describes how actuarial thought arising from this concept developed. From the outset, it was apparent that actuarial advice was necessary to determine premium rates. It was envisaged that holders of policies would share in any profits that might arise and in any losses incurred. Actuarial advice was necessary both to determine the amount of the profit or loss and how it should be shared between policyholders.

Since the early days of scientific life insurance, actuaries have played an essential part in its development, through both mathematics and the exercise of actuarial judgement. Mathematical formulae have been developed for a wide range of contracts, for life assurance, for annuities, and for individual and group pension business. If the future could be accurately foreseen, it could be incorporated into these mathematical formulae to determine premium rates and profits exactly. The reality is very different. The future rates of return on investments, rates of mortality and rates of expense incurred by insurers can only be estimated. Options in benefits under contracts and in investments, and in income from equities and properties, make both benefits and investment income uncertain. Actuarial techniques can reduce the uncertainties but actuarial judgement is nevertheless necessary in determining assumptions as to the future to incorporate in the bases for calculating premium rates and profits. Actuarial judgement in these matters has as its essential background the need to avoid the insolvency of the insurer. From the first days, actuaries acted as advisers to insurers and, increasingly, as members of their management. Later, they also assisted the regulatory authorities in formulating and operating a regulatory system designed to protect customers (that is, policyholders) and to safeguard their interests.

The pooled life insurance fund

Underlying life insurance well into the twentieth century was the concept of a pooled life assurance fund for each insurer, into which all income would be paid and from which benefits would be met. The rate of return on investments from this (normally expanding) fund would vary as new investments were made and as existing investments were re-invested at the different current market rates of interest ruling from time to time. All contracts would share in the return on the investments of the pooled fund, which would be influenced by its rate of expansion. Thus the terms on which each premium under a contract were invested would not depend only on the market rate of return on new investments at the time at which the premium was paid. If a sudden rise occurred in market rates of return, the rate of return on the fund would respond only gradually, and premiums received would initially be credited with a lower rate of return than the current market rate – and vice versa if a sudden fall in market rates of return occurred. Thus premiums invested in assets representing a life insurance fund were effectively invested on different terms from investments in, for example, the stock market. The concept of the pooled life insurance fund was successively weakened as life insurance developed.

The need for actuarial professional bodies

The premiums charged by the Equitable, and by most other life insurers who entered the market in the nineteenth century, were determined by an actuarial calculation, so that the value of future premiums discounted to the dates of issue of contracts should be sufficient to provide the discounted value of benefits and of the insurer's expenses. Discounting took into account prudent estimates of future rates of return on the investments of the life insurance fund, of future rates of mortality and of expenses. Premiums generally proved more than sufficient to cover the benefits guaranteed under the contracts. The business was therefore profitable and there was much discussion among life insurance actuaries as to how profits should be assessed and distributed between policyholders. The need for actuarial professional bodies was felt, and so the Institute of Actuaries was formed in England, as was the Faculty of Actuaries in Scotland, in the mid-nineteenth century.

Valuation of liabilities

Contracts under which a single premium was paid formed an insignificant proportion of the business: the main concern of actuaries was with contracts under which level periodic premiums were paid. Because, under most contracts, a level premium was charged for an increasing risk, a fund was built up in the early years of a contract which would be needed to meet claims in later years when the policyholder was older. Much of the actuarial discussion in the late nineteenth century concerned the valuation methods and bases to be used to determine the liabilities of an insurer under life insurance contracts, for comparison with the value of its assets in order to determine profits. In simple terms, these liabilities are the discounted value at the valuation date (allowing for the return on investments and for mortality) of the benefits payable in the future under the contracts, less the premiums that will be available for investment after providing the expenses incurred by the insurer. This simple statement says nothing about the treatment in the valuation of the margins in premium rates which, it is hoped, will produce profits in the future. If only the estimated future expenses are deducted from future premiums, these margins will be discounted to the valuation date and will reduce the liability. Their discounted value will therefore increase current profits unrealistically and they will not be available to contribute to profits in the future as future premiums are paid.

Net premium and bonus reserve methods of valuation

Two methods of avoiding this capitalization of margins in future premiums were developed and discussed by actuaries: either to exclude them from the premiums discounted in the valuation and at the same time to take no direct account of the estimated future profits which they would produce (the net premium method), or to include the discounted value of both items in the valuation (the bonus reserve method).

Under the net premium method, the premium valued is the net level yearly premium calculated on the actuarial bases of interest and mortality used in the valuation, with no allowance for expenses. This net premium has no direct relationship with the premium received. Moreover, if the rate of interest used in the valuation basis is changed, so is the net premium valued, whereas the premiums paid in future on existing business will not change. This does not represent quite as great a divergence from reality as might at first sight be apparent. If, say, the actuary considers that there will be a permanent reduction in interest rates, this means that the cost of providing the benefits guaranteed under the contract will increase and the premiums needed to support them will be greater. Thus the net premiums used in the valuation should be higher and the valuation rate of interest should be lower. The changes in net premiums as valuation interest bases change do not accurately reflect what would be appropriate but move in the right direction. It is clear that, if the valuation rate of interest is reduced to a low level, the net premiums valued may be increased to such an extent that, when compared with the premiums payable, they may be insufficient to provide the margin to cover estimated future expenses. In this event, net premium reserves can be increased by reducing the net premiums valued to provide a margin sufficient to cover future expenses.

Because the net premium valued is calculated on the valuation basis, the liability when a contract is issued is zero – discounted future net premiums are equal to discounted future benefits. The net premium valued is level throughout the duration of the contract, because it ignores the incidence of expenses. It was soon realized by actuaries that, because expenses incurred by insurers at the time of issue of a contract were greater than subsequently, the use of a level net premium throughout the duration of a contract was unrealistic. In 1863 Dr Zillmer, a German actuary, proposed that the net premium valued should be suitably reduced in the first or early years in recognition of this fact and, in compensation, should be increased in subsequent years to be greater than the pure net premium. This method had two disadvantages. It could result in liabilities under contracts having negative values in the valuation in the very early years of an insurance contract; in other words, they would be treated as assets unless, as is usual, these negative values were eliminated. Also, the method resulted in lower valuation liabilities in total, and thus required lower financial strength for an insurer than an unadjusted net premium valuation.

Under the bonus reserve method of valuation, both the margins in premium rates which will produce profits and the estimated future profits are taken into account. The premiums valued will be the premiums payable including profit margins, after deducting estimated future expenses, and the benefits valued will include the estimated value of future bonuses to policyholders reflecting profits. After a good deal of actuarial discussion, distribution of profits by permanent additions to sums assured (reversionary bonuses) became widely accepted. These additions were calculated in proportion either to the original sum assured (simple bonuses) or to that sum assured increased by bonuses added to date (compound bonuses). It was necessary to decide what rate of bonus should be assumed in the bonus reserve valuation. Various acceptable practical solutions to this problem have been advanced, but none can claim to be above criticism. For example, should the future bonus rate be taken to be constant? If interest rates have fallen and remain lower for some time, the future yield on the life insurance fund will reduce gradually and so should bonus rates. Should these reducing bonus rates in the future be taken into account in the valuation? Because the bonus reserve method provides explicitly for expenses in the future, it implicitly takes into account the higher level of initial expenses, because it values gross premiums that allow for them and is thus comparable to a Zillmerized net premium valuation.

The cash value of a reversionary bonus increases as the contract continues. In order to harmonize the valuation basis with the reversionary bonus system, distributable profits must emerge in increasing sums in

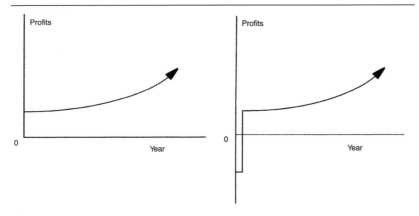

Figure 5.1 Profits arising in each year from a traditional with-profit endowment assurance (reduced interest basis). Left, net premium valuation; right, fully Zillmerised net premium valuation or bonus reserve valuation.

terms of cash as contracts continue. This can be achieved in a net premium valuation by a reduction in the valuation rate of interest, the reduction being greater for a compound bonus than for a simple bonus at the same rate of bonus. If valuations on the Zillmerized net premium method using a reduced interest basis and on a bonus reserve method were made on bases approximating to those on which premiums on the business in force had been calculated, the emergence of profits would be similar.

A comparison of net premium and bonus reserve valuations

Net premium method

Sum assured *plus* accrued bonuses *less* future net premiums* (on valuation basis)

Bonus reserve method

Sum assured *plus* accrued bonuses *plus* future bonuses* *plus* future expenses* *less* future gross premiums*

*Discounted to valuation date at same rate of interest

Developments until the end of the Second World War

The nineteenth century saw vigorous growth of the life assurance industry, on sound basic actuarial principles. Actuarial discussions on major matters of principle were concentrated particularly in the period 1850–75. Thereafter, until the beginning of the Second World War, professional knowledge and practice was consolidated and refined. Premium rates were developed on more scientific methods. Mortality data became much more reliable, expenses were analysed more thoroughly and provision could be made for them more accurately in premium rates. Margins to provide future simple and compound reversionary bonuses could be included in premium rates. The main source of variations in bonus rates became variations in the return on investments. For a long period, except during the two World Wars, there was relative stability in the rate of return on investments – only a very small proportion of investments were in equities and the well established method of net premium valuations associated with reversionary bonuses was broadly satisfactory.

The net premium method of valuation is concerned almost entirely with the value of liabilities. Its only link with the assets is through the relationship between the rate of return on the assets and that used in valuing the liabilities. The interrelationship between assets and liabilities in all its aspects was not given much consideration and the actuary had little influence over the insurer's valuation of the assets. Variations in that value did not normally immediately affect distributable profits. Assets were valued at purchase prices less investment reserve funds. Realized investment profits were credited to an investment reserve fund and realized losses were drawn from it. The amount of the investment reserve fund was deducted from the value of assets on the valuation date.

By the use of prudent actuarial bases in calculating liabilities and by refraining from writing up asset values to market values, hidden reserves were built up in the published values of assets and liabilities. A sharp reduction in interest rates provides an example of the use of these reserves. The actuary would consider it prudent to reduce the rate of interest used to value the liabilities, which would increase as would asset values. A transfer of an amount broadly equal to the increase in liabilities would be made from the investment reserve account to the insurance fund. Similarly, a transfer from the life insurance fund to the investment reserve account (and thus from the value of the assets) would be made if the rate of interest used to value the liabilities was increased. In either case, the published profit for the year would be little affected.

Prior to the Second World War, there were two periods during which financial markets were seriously disturbed. The first was during the First World War, when market prices of fixed interest securities fell and gross yields rose from 4 per cent in 1913 to around 5 per cent in 1918, with a severe increase in income tax that kept net yields down. There were also additional costs of death claims arising from the war and the subsequent influenza epidemic. Most insurers did not declare a bonus in one or more years. Interest rates rose further after the war, but by 1927 had reverted to 1918 levels. The second serious disturbance followed the international depression of the 1930s, during which interest rates fell to below 3 per cent gross. Insurers did not consider that this called for any departure from the well established reversionary bonus system, but there was great reluctance to reduce bonus rates from what were then unsustainable levels – which may mark insurers' recognition that declared bonus rates create expectations in the minds of the policyholders. This dilemma was relieved at the beginning of the Second World War, which provided clear justification for special measures, including reductions in bonuses, because the return on investments remained low and the future was uncertain. Not only were bonus rates reduced but they were made payable only on claims arising in the ensuing year (known as interim bonuses). Bonuses added in earlier years as permanent (reversionary) additions to sums assured were unaffected. At the end of the war, actuaries were free to recommend the resumption of reversionary bonus declarations operating from the beginning of the war at rates appropriate to the low rates of return on assets then prevailing and their assessment of the future.

Overseas business: departure from the pooled life insurance fund

The concept of the life insurance fund as a single pool of assets did not fully survive the development of business from overseas branches of UK insurers. When business was transacted in the UK, the same scale of premium rates applied throughout, except where extra risk was involved. When UK insurers established branches overseas, it was desirable (if not compulsory) to invest resulting funds in local currency, where suitable investments were available to match liabilities expressed in local currency. Local investments influenced the return on the investments of the life insurance fund, but it did not seem fair to allow this to affect the profits allocated to policyholders in other countries. Premium rates for overseas business were therefore calculated to reflect estimated future local experience with regard to mortality, interest and expenses. The provision for bonuses made in the premiums was initially intended to provide a uniform bonus rate for all business throughout the world. By the end of the Second

World War, it had become clear that changes in rates of return on investments in different countries were different (both in timing and extent), and the uniform world-wide bonus rate was replaced by bonuses differentiated between countries, thus reflecting local experience. The assets of the life insurance fund were notionally allocated by the insurer to reflect investments held against the business in each country and the return from these assets; and the local mortality rates and local expense levels entered into the determination of bonus rates, as well as of premium rates, in each country. However, the assets were not formally segregated, and policyholders world-wide could look to the life insurance fund as a whole for their security.

Developments following the Second World War

The end of the Second World War marked the beginning of a period in which life insurance presented problems and opportunities not previously encountered by actuaries. By 1945 or so, premiums for new business were scientifically calculated with provision for reversionary bonuses (simple or compound) appropriate to each insurer. Most insurers transacted a fairly small proportion of business on a non-profit basis. If this was financed by life insurance funds, with-profit policyholders could justifiably share in the profits or losses therefrom. If a company financed this business from shareholders' funds, the profits or losses could properly go to shareholders.

The overall level of the with-profit premiums of an insurer was not normally changed significantly over time. Relatively minor adjustments might be made to reflect changes in mortality and expense rates. Changes in rates of return on assets were reflected by changes in bonus rates. If, however, an insurer considered that its overall level of premium rates and bonuses was inappropriate in the market in which it operated, it would revise its overall level of premiums for new contracts and, if the change was significant, would open a new series of contracts with bonuses suitably differentiated from those under the original series. Assets corresponding to the new series would not be segregated.

New business strain

Most insurers used an un-Zillmerized net premium valuation basis. This meant that new contracts imposed a financial strain on profits, while business written earlier would release each year part of the strain created when it was written. If the fund was stationary, strains and releases would broadly balance and the fund would benefit from investment income on the excess of the full net premium liabilities over Zillmerized liabilities. If, however, the fund was expanding rapidly, the strain from new contracts would exceed the release of strain from existing business, and a net strain might arise which could reduce distributable profits. This did in fact occur in the highly inflationary 1970s, but its effect was masked by the high rates of return on assets, which increased profits. New business strain could reduce profits so much that actuaries might advise insurers to reduce the volume of new business of certain classes, particularly of non-profit business.

Fair distribution of profits

In the postwar period, discussions on the fair distribution of profits continued. Profits were related largely to the return on investments, mortality and expenses, so that it would be fair to share them for each contract in relation to their sources. However, this was impracticable. Moreover, it would leave unsolved the problem of how to deal with other factors affecting distributable profits (for example, new business strain and non-profit business). Furthermore, policyholders had been led to expect reversionary bonuses. Fairness had been defined as leading to an equality, when a contract commenced, between the discounted value on a realistic basis of benefits, including profits, and premiums (less expenses). In changing conditions, particularly with regard to the rate of return on investments on a pooled insurance fund, this equality could not be achieved in practice through the simple or compound reversionary bonus system. The effect on bonus earnings of a change in the rate of return on investments was greater for existing business than for new business. On the other hand, the uniform reversionary bonus system produced acceptable results in practice when changes were gradual and moderate. It was used generally by insurers and had become accepted by policyholders. It therefore survived in the early postwar period.

The interrelation of assets and liabilities: 'immunisation'

Actuaries became increasingly interested in changes in asset values. Initially, these occurred largely in consequence of changes in the rate of interest on fixed interest investments, because the proportion of investments held in equities and properties was small. It had long been realized that the length of term of the assets should be related to that of the liabilities if the effect of changes in interest rates on the financial strength of an insurer was to be minimized. At the same time, assets and liabilities had tended to be regarded as two separate elements, assets being the responsibility of the investment manager and liabilities the responsibility of the actuary. In the early 1950s, papers were published that went back to basics and led to a much fuller realization of the interrelationship between assets and liabilities. A paper by Redington recognized that the business on the books of a life insurer at any valuation date would produce two series of payments, which could be described as follows:

- liability outgo (the net outgo in future years from existing business – that is, claims and expenses less premiums), which may be either positive or negative, and
- asset proceeds (interest plus maturing investments in future years from existing assets)

If it is assumed that funds are invested in fixed-interest securities, and that assets earn a uniform rate of interest whatever their length of term, a term can be found for the asset proceeds such that changes in the rate of interest change the value of the liability outgo and the asset proceeds by an equal amount. For a redeemable security, the length of term of the asset proceeds is less than the unexpired term to redemption, because the former takes into account the income from the security over its term as well as the redemption proceeds. An insurer so matched may be said to be 'immunised' against changes in interest rates. Such 'immunisation' is theoretically possible except where the business is very immature, in which case the term of the liability outgo could be infinite. An alternative view was expressed that liability outgo should not take into account premiums payable in future years or benefits provided by them. Changes in asset values would then be compared with changes in the liability for benefits secured by premiums paid prior to the valuation date.

In practice, however, the assumptions made do not apply, in particular because of investments in equities and properties from which future income is uncertain, but assumptions can be made as to how this income will change in future. 'Immunisation' as defined does not indicate the investment policy that should be adopted when choosing the length of term of the assets. With suitable assumptions as to future income from equities and properties, and as to other uncertainties, it gives an indication of a norm that would insulate the financial strength of the insurer's existing business from changes in the rate of interest. Adoption of a norm would mean that financial strength would be unaffected not only by losses but by profits arising from such changes. Investment policy would seek profits, and should lead to investments of terms either longer or shorter than the norm, depending on whether interest rates were thought likely to fall or rise in the future. The essential principle of 'immunisation' is that asset proceeds and liability outgo form two cash flows which must be treated consistently in valuation. The same principle should underlie a realistic bonus reserve valuation: assets and liabilities should be valued using consistent rates of interest. If an insurer were 'immunised' on the basis first described, it would not mean that changes in a published net premium valuation liability would be the same as changes in the value of assets used in conjunction with it. Net premium valuations are less sensitive to changes in interest bases than are bonus reserve valuations involving a given rate of future bonuses.

The 'estate'

It was increasingly realized that the choice of the method of valuation, and of the valuation basis for an insurer's liabilities, should depend on the purpose of the valuation. The net premium method, in conjunction with a cautious valuation of assets, had for a very long time served two purposes: the maintenance of a sound level of financial strength of an insurer (with margins in the valuation of assets and liabilities) and an appropriate emergence of profits from year to year, reflecting changes in the experience. It did not, however, attempt to measure the financial strength of an insurer, nor the changes occurring in it from time to time. Such quantification can best be achieved by a bonus reserve valuation on realistic bases, with assets and liabilities valued on consistent bases. Realistic assumptions for estimated future mortality and expenses would be used. The long-term interest yield for gilt-edged securities that is current at the valuation date could be used for the interest basis, assuming that where the return on other assets differs from this, the difference is due to the risk content in the income from them. The use of this rate of interest could be regarded as consistent with valuation of the assets at market value. The maintenance of the current rate of bonus could be assumed in the valuation. The excess of the value of the assets at market values over the value of the liabilities at the valuation date, sometimes called the 'estate', is an indication of the financial strength of the insurer over and above that needed to provide reasonable bonus rates to policyholders in the future.

There is no single agreed basis for the evaluation of the 'estate'. For example, equities and properties can be valued assuming that the current level of income will be maintained or that income from them will increase at a fixed rate. Different rates of future bonuses may be assumed. If the 'estate' is calculated each year on consistent bases, the insurer will know how it varies from year to year as conditions, including the market rate of interest, change. This is a guide to steering the financial strength of the existing business of the insurer and is probably more important than the absolute level of the 'estate'.

Large increases in equity dividends and market values

After the Second World War, the proportion of largely with-profit life assurance funds invested in equities and properties increased substantially, because these investments were seen as likely to produce better returns than fixed interest securities. This change in investment policy led to what was eventually a radical reappraisal by actuaries of the determination of distributable profits and their allocation between policyholders.

In the early postwar period, the dividend yield on equities was greater than that on fixed-interest securities. This did not call for any modification of the uniform reversionary bonus system (simple or compound) used by the great majority of insurers. It implied the existence of a risk content in income from equities and properties, which might not be taken credit for when determining distributable surplus.

Distribution of part of the increase in the market values of equities

The large increases in equity dividends in the mid-1950s reflected economic recovery from the war and the end of dividend restraint. These increases significantly increased current profits of life insurers, but not to the extent that special action was felt necessary. The increase in income from equities and properties also increased market values, but this had no effect on the published balance sheets of insurers, where assets were shown at values that were not written up to reflect market values. Insurers were not required to disclose the market values of their assets, but these changes in their values created a problem which had soon to be faced. This problem, which called for decision in the early 1960s, was as follows: how were policyholders to benefit from the rise in the market values of equities and properties? The net premium method of valuation had nothing to contribute to the solution of this problem, since it called for transfers from the increases in asset values into revenue to increase distributable profits. There were two aspects of the problem:

- How much should be transferred?
- How should the amount transferred be shared among policyholders?

In order to decide how much should be transferred, it was necessary to examine the overall financial strength of the insurer. This could be done by evaluating the 'estate' on various assumptions as to the value of equities and properties. A cautious assumption at each valuation was that the income would remain at its then current level. Less cautious assumptions might assume future growth in income at chosen prudent fixed rates. Still less cautious was to value assets at market values. Depending on the outcome of the examination of the level of the 'estate', it could be decided by how much the 'estate' should be reduced to provide an increased bonus rate in the current year and to steer the 'estate' in changing conditions.

'Terminal' bonuses: further departure from the pooled fund

The problem of how to share the sum transferred from asset values gave rise to various possibilities. Three possibilities were advanced in a paper published in 1959:

1. To declare a rather larger reversionary bonus than had been declared before the surge in asset values. This would still leave a substantially higher 'estate' and would disadvantage existing policyholders, particularly the older ones who would benefit little from the change in asset values.
2. To declare a substantially higher reversionary bonus, which could be justified by the level of the 'estate'. This would favour existing policyholders but would call for increased premiums from new business, if the increase was to be maintained.
3. To declare a normal reversionary bonus together with a special reversionary bonus for the period. This would enable existing policyholders to benefit from the surge in asset values and would not call for increased premiums for new business.

This last possibility was the preferred course, but it left the problem of how the special bonus should be determined for each contract. The possibility of sharing the appreciation in relation to the liability under each contract (or an approximation thereto) was discussed, because the value of assets is related to liabilities. This led to consideration of a further possibility – that of declaring a terminal bonus on claims occurring in the ensuing year without any commitment in relation to subsequent years (as would arise with reversionary bonus), and to relate this bonus to the duration for which a contract had been in force since the appreciation occurred. This solution recognized that the values of equities and properties could fall as well as rise, and that it would therefore be prudent to declare an addition to sums arising as claims in the ensuing year only (a 'terminal' bonus). This did not exclude the possibility of declaring some part of the benefit of these increases in capital values as increases in sums assured ('reversionary' bonuses). The transfer from asset values would be determined by the cost of the special bonus declared in the current declaration. Special bonuses dependent on the period since the appreciation occurred would represent a major departure from the concept of a pooled life insurance fund in which all contracts would share profits on a uniform basis.

The early 1960s saw the main movement of insurers into the declaration of special bonuses, some declaring terminal bonuses. The upsurge of dividends and equity prices continued. The gap between the dividend yield on equities and the interest yield on gilts changed from being positive to become negative – the 'reverse yield gap'. This created a new problem for actuaries. Insurers and their investment managers, who were sometimes actuaries, were convinced that in the long term investment in equities would, because of their assessment of future growth in dividends and capital values, be more advantageous to insurers in the long run than investment in fixed interest securities. But was that investment policy advantageous to policyholders? There was a view that increases in dividends and capital values should not enter into profits distributable to policyholders before they were received. This would mean that, until dividends had grown to reach the rate of return obtainable on fixed-interest investments when the equities were purchased, the income from investments distributable to policyholders would be less than if fixed-interest securities had been purchased. On this view, an investment policy considered advantageous to the insurer would not for some years be advantageous to policyholders. When deciding how much capital appreciation should enter into distributable profits, insurers were therefore led to assess the 'estate' by including the value of equities, discounting future dividend income, on the assumption that it would increase at a prudent rate, and assuming the maintenance of an appropriate rate of terminal bonus. Steering the 'estate' to decide bonus declarations including terminal bonuses resulted in smoothing changes in values of equities and properties rather than reflecting changes in their market values immediately. How much smoothing was achieved was a matter for each insurer to decide and, in the 1970s when equity values were still increasing (except in 1974), the smoothing process meant that distributed capital appreciation lagged behind appreciation in market values.

'Super-compound' bonuses

The rapidly changing income from investments caused further discussion of the fairness of the uniform reversionary bonus system in sharing profits. The main changes in profits arose from changes in the return from investments and, if this was to be shared between policyholders in relation to their contributions to it on a pooled basis, sharing should be in relation to the liabilities under their contracts. To share in relation to the value of sums assured (simple bonuses) or sums assured plus accrued bonuses (compound bonuses) produced, by comparison, too much benefit in the early years of a contract and too little at later durations. This is particularly so with the simple reversionary bonus system. The bonus scale can be made steeper as the duration in force of the contract increases by the use of what became known as 'super-compound' bonuses, where the bonus on accrued bonuses is at a higher rate than that on the sum assured. With a suitable rate of super-compound bonus, sharing can approximate to sharing in relation to liabilities.

Super-compound bonuses became widely used, but underlying the system was the danger of misuse by creating hopes of future bonus rates – and thus policy proceeds – which would not be fulfilled. The steeper the bonus scale, the greater should be the margin between the interest rate used in a net premium valuation of liabilities and the rate implicit in the premiums. However, valuation bases in use did not seem adequately to reflect this. The possibility of misuse arose also with terminal bonuses when no specific provision for future bonuses was made in published accounts. In order to illustrate the benefits that a policyholder might receive under a with-profit contract, it became customary to quote the results that would arise if the current reversionary and terminal bonus rates were maintained. These illustrations would include the high (possibly super-compound) bonus rates that were applicable when a contract reached maturity, and also terminal bonuses. Business was expanding rapidly and, combined with discontinuances, this meant that the average duration of the business on an insurer's books might be quite short. Insurers were not therefore currently experiencing (and therefore meeting) the high cost of bonuses when contracts neared and reached maturity which would arise if expansion (and discontinuances) were at lower rates. There was no clear demonstration that insurers would be able to meet this cost and, for new business, the rate of return on investments needed to maintain current reversionary and terminal bonus rates rose to levels that were unlikely to be achieved over the term of the contract.

Equity-linked life insurance

For a long time after life insurance was developed, competition was not a dominant factor. Insurers competed with each other but, as insurance became increasingly regarded as a savings medium, it began to face competition from other savings media. A life insurance contract could be seen as being a combination of a means of saving and a decreasing term assurance making up the difference at any time between the accumulated amount saved and the amount payable on death should a claim arise.

In a period of rapid appreciation of equity values, unit trusts, which enabled savers to obtain immediately the full benefits of capital appreciation, became popular. The underlying concept was different from that underlying the pooled life insurance fund, in that each amount applied to purchase units was invested at the market yield ruling at the time of investment. By the beginning of the 1960s, a few insurers had developed life insurance contracts with level yearly premiums which, in effect, enabled a unit trust type investment to be combined with a decreasing term assurance, so that the whole contract satisfied the definition of a life assurance contract, and qualified for income tax relief on its premiums in the same way as a traditional life insurance contract. The favourable returns on equity investments, taking both dividends and capital appreciation into account, resulted in considerable expansion in unit-linked business. By the end of the 1960s there was much discussion among actuaries on the principles that should underlie the calculation of premiums and of liabilities under unit-linked contracts.

The essential principle underlying the contract was that the main part of each premium paid was used to buy units in an equity fund at the price ruling when the premium was paid, and the benefit resulting therefrom would be the value of the units purchased when a claim arose at the price ruling at that time. The contract did not entitle the policyholder to a share in the insurer's profits. The premium under the contract had to provide:

- the decreasing life cover needed to make up the value of the units (at the time at which a death claim occurred) to the sum insured
- the insurer's expenses
- the cost of the investment services
- the cost of any guarantees, such as a minimum payment on maturity
- a margin for insurer's profits

A considerable variety of contracts was developed as the business expanded. Expenses were recovered by deductions related to the premium. In a contract with level yearly premiums, a level deduction for expenses might be made from each premium, in which event a deduction would be made from surrender values (the amounts payable on termination of the contract before maturity) to cover the portion of the new business expenses not recovered by the level deduction for expenses on premiums paid to date. Alternatively, a smaller proportion of the premium in the first year would be invested in units than subsequently, and no deduction would be made from surrender values. A charge in relation to the value of the units purchased to date would be made for investment services. Charges were explicit and originally were totally guaranteed. Later, they might be guaranteed for a limited period only, if at all.

Unlike a holder of a unit trust, a holder of a qualifying unit-linked life insurance is not liable to capital gains tax on its proceeds. This tax is borne by the insurer when assets are realized, as it is for other life insurance business. Benefits under unit-linked insurances are adjusted to meet the estimated discounted cost of this tax. Profits or losses arise to the insurer to the extent that the estimated discounted cost proves to be incorrect. They also arise from the bid and offer prices used for units and, indeed, from any situation in which pricing does not correspond to transactions by the fund in the stock market.

The valuation of the liabilities under linked contracts was discussed by actuaries. Provided that units notionally credited to contracts had been purchased by the insurer, the liability under the unit-linked part of the contract would be the market value of those units. For the contract as a whole, it would be necessary to increase this value by liabilities arising from any foreseen shortfall in future charges, for death and any other benefits and for any guarantees.

Maturity guarantees under equity-linked insurances

In the 1970s, actuaries became increasingly involved in the problem of a proper charge for a guarantee of the maturity proceeds of a unit-linked contract and the liability to be recognized for this guarantee. A typical maturity guarantee was of the total amount deemed to be invested in units. A working party was set up by the Institute and Faculty of Actuaries in 1977 to consider what would be a suitable method and basis for calculating this liability, it being noted that the premium charged for the guarantee must take into account the need to finance it. There would be a much greater variability in claims under these guarantees as asset values change from time to time than there would be under traditional contracts. The working party sought a stochastic time series model that could simulate equity price movements and dividend yield changes with charac- teristics similar to those observed in the past. An acceptable risk of the liability proving inadequate was identified, from which the level of the liability to be recognized was calculated. Most offices granting maturity guarantees had not set up liabilities on as strong a basis as the working party suggested. The report served as a warning against readily granting maturity guarantees and they became less common.

During the 1970s, there was increased competition between unit-linked contracts, under which the policyholder benefited (or suffered) from changes in asset values immediately they occurred, and with-profit contracts, under which these changes were smoothed by insurers to the extent that each insurer considered appropriate. Returns on equities taking income and capital appreciation together were generally very favourable, but the sudden large fall in equity values in 1974 caused concern to holders of unit-linked contracts and faced insurers with the problem of whether to reduce terminal bonuses under traditional contracts and, if so, to what extent. Insurers generally held strong 'estates' at the time and did not consider it necessary to make large reductions in terminal bonuses, at least unless and until the reduction in equity values should prove to be lasting. In fact, equity prices soon recovered but the uncertainty created by the fall in 1974 may well have made insurers more cautious than was later seen to have been necessary in their smoothing process of bonuses under traditional with-profit contracts. Thus, by the 1980s, 'estates' had grown to levels higher than were needed to provide adequate financial strength for insurers and their policyholders, and competition with unit-linked contracts which benefited immediately from the recovery became more difficult. A different approach to the determination of bonuses under with-profit contracts was considered necessary, based on what became known as 'asset shares' and encouraged by the introduction of a new type of with-profit contract that bridged the gap between unit-linked and conventional with-profit business.

Unitised with-profit contracts

Other market developments suggested the need for new types of contract that differed from traditional with-profit contracts. Pension business expanded, particularly after legislation in 1988 increased the opportunities for insurers to provide Personal Pensions, premiums under which tended not to be regular or level. Sales of unit-linked contracts suffered after the stock market declines in 1987 and 1990. New insurers (who could not match the financial strength of the long established traditional with-profit insurers) needed a contract that would enable them to compete while making limited demands on capital. The new type of contract became known as the 'unitised with-profit' contract. In essence, units of benefit are purchased by each premium paid in accordance with a scale. Premiums are in effect treated as single premiums and contracts participate in profits in relation to the units of benefit purchased to date. By contrast, under traditional with-profit contracts, premiums are paid to secure a defined benefit when a claim arises on death or maturity, and

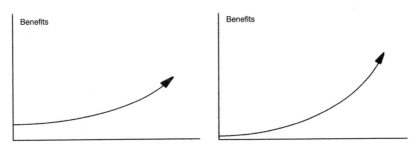

Figure 5.2   A comparison of benefits secured on a claim arising under a traditional (left) and a unitised with-profit (right) contract.

participation in profits is related to that defined benefit. Premiums paid under 'unitised' contracts can be increased or decreased from time to time, and single and regular premiums can be accepted under the same contract. A wide variety of contracts is possible and choices are open to insurers on:

- the benefits that should be provided – the contracts are often designed to provide a fund that will be used to purchase a Personal Pension
- whether only permanent bonuses (analogous to reversionary bonuses) should be added periodically or whether terminal bonuses should also be added
- whether and, if so at what rate, accumulation of the invested part of the premium should be guaranteed for units purchased to date, whether any guarantee should apply also to future premiums and whether any guarantee should be achieved by adding bonus units to those already secured or by increases in the price of units
- whether expense charges should be explicit, or implicit by being a charge on bonus rates.

There was a general tendency to minimize guarantees. It was usual to guarantee the return of the amounts invested on surrender or on a claim. Charges were not usually guaranteed in respect of future premiums or sometimes in respect of premiums already paid. Unless it was provided that any deficiency or surplus in the charges would be met by or would benefit shareholders, they would affect profits and policyholders would bear their proportion. Contracts usually included the right of the insurer to make a market value adjustment on claim or surrender payments to reduce the normal benefits (number of units times current price) to amounts not exceeding the market value of the assets supporting the contract. Few insurers seem to have applied such an adjustment to all contracts at a given time but it has been applied more widely on an individual basis.

Although large volumes of 'unitised with-profits' business were written, statutory regulations and professional guidance were not designed to be suitable to this type of business, but must be complied with as far as they are applicable to it. Methods of valuation for its published liabilities have been the subject of discussion within the profession. The methods must differ depending on the benefits and guarantees provided.

'Asset shares': a further significant departure from the pooled fund

'Asset shares' may be defined as the accumulation at an appropriate rate of return on investments of the premiums paid under a contract less deductions for expenses, tax, mortality risk and other benefits, including guarantees and transfers for shareholders (for proprietary insurers) plus or minus allocations for miscellaneous profits or losses. The rate of return on investments used in the accumulation would take both the income and changes in capital value of the insurer's life fund into account. 'Asset shares' thus represent retrospective accumulation based on the past experience of the insurer. The rate of investment return may be based on a notional asset mix appropriate to the insurer, the overall return on its non-linked assets or, more usually, the return on assets notionally allocated to with-profit business. The total amount to be committed for bonuses would be determined having regard to the steering of the financial strength of the insurer treating 'asset shares' rather than bonus reserve liabilities as the liability under with-profit contracts.

'Asset shares' for individual contracts are used as a guide to the total benefits (including bonuses) payable when a claim arises. They are also often used as a guide to surrender values. 'Asset shares' used as a guide to total distributable profits and to bonus rates are usually based on a smoothed return on investments. Unitised with-profit business can be treated in the same way as traditional with-profits business when determining 'asset shares' and smoothing the effect of changes in the rate of return on investments on bonus rates. They may be calculated using the actual investment return on the assets of the unitised fund.

To use unsmoothed 'asset shares' as a guide to bonus rates under with-profit contracts would involve an almost complete departure from the philosophy of a pooled life insurance fund. To determine an 'asset share' for an individual contract in effect hypothecates to the contract that part of the assets of the fund which represents the accumulated net contribution of the contract to the fund. Contracts would not share in profits from the return on the investments of the whole fund. To base bonus rates on smoothed 'asset shares', as is usual, involves the use of the life insurance fund as the source of smoothing and, to this extent, the concept of the pooled fund survives. The basic concept of with-profit life assurance as a savings medium has become much closer to that underlying unit-linked insurance and unit trusts.

Unitised with-profit contracts are similar to unit-linked contracts, but the smoothing process used to determine bonus rates means that they produce less variable benefits on claims arising from time to time. To relate bonus declarations closely to 'asset shares' requires regard to be had to the incidence of payment of premiums in determining the terminal bonus scale. A scale appropriate to level premiums would be no more than a rough approximation for variable premiums. It would be possible to combine a scale for level premiums (based on year of entry) with a scale for single premiums (based on year of payment) which would be applied to departures from level premiums.

Statutory regulation

This is a suitable point at which to describe the activities of the actuarial profession, which has always co-operated with the regulatory authorities to ensure the development of life insurance on sound lines, so as to provide both security and fair treatment to policyholders. In the period after the Second World War, co-operation became particularly close and the development of the profession cannot be separated from the development of statutory regulation. From the 1960s onwards, the supervisory authorities increasingly felt the need to prescribe standards for life insurers. This need was accepted by actuaries, who increasingly entered into partnership with the authorities in defining standards.

In the earliest stages of the development of life insurance, there was no statutory regulation. However, a small close-knit group of actuaries discussed their duties and this ensured that the insurers advised by them adopted sound practices. After the mid-nineteenth century, some insurers found themselves in financial difficulties and a few ceased to write business. In order to provide security to policyholders, the Life Assurance Companies Act 1870 was passed. This required, *inter alia*, the annual publication of revenue accounts and balance sheets and, periodically, of an actuarial investigation into the insurer's financial condition, including a valuation balance sheet and a statement of the business in force, in some detail. This reflected the principle known as 'freedom with publicity'. There was no control over premium rates or valuation bases for liabilities or assets. The Assurance Companies Act 1909 replaced the 1870 Act without radically changing its 'freedom with publicity' basis, and the 1958 Act consolidated earlier Acts and included a requirement, where the insurer also transacted non-life insurance, that the actuary should certify that in his belief the liabilities under long-term business did not exceed the assets of the long-term business fund shown in the long-term balance sheet.

The returns to the supervisory authority were made public and were available for scrutiny by the actuarial profession and by others. This was regarded as an important feature of the system of supervision. It relied heavily on the integrity and competence of the profession. Disclosure of information in relation to the assets and their valuation was less full than in respect of liabilities. The returns were further amended in 1968 but, although it was required that the accounts as a whole should give a true and fair view, the market value of assets was not required to be disclosed. A certificate was required as to whether or not the value of the assets was in total equal to the amounts shown in the balance sheet. Although market values did not need to be disclosed, the returns provided information as to the income from them, broken down by type of investment. The returns required the actuary to comment on the extent to which account had been taken of the nature and term of the assets available to meet the liabilities valued.

A statutory minimum solvency standard

Side by side with the development of legislation and requirements for statutory returns, actuaries were discussing the principles that should be adopted in order to establish a minimum solvency standard (that is, a minimum standard of financial strength) for life insurance business. This standard would aim at providing a minimum margin of safety that would ensure that the financial failure of an insurer was highly unlikely. Moreover, it was clear by the 1960s that, if full freedom for insurance business was to be achieved within the European Union, the standard prescribed in the UK would have to be recognized as valid in the other member states. A net premium valuation on a prescribed basis was usually required by them. A net premium valuation was preferred to a bonus reserve valuation for the UK solvency standard. It is capable of clear legal definition, whereas a bonus reserve valuation would present much greater difficulties of definition, particularly in relation to the rate of future bonuses to be assumed. A paper published in 1965 set out five principles which, it was considered, would provide a suitable underlying basis for a statutory minimum solvency standard:

1. The liabilities should be valued by a net premium method or another basis that produced stronger liabilities. This would ensure that margins in with-profit premiums that were expected to produce bonuses in the future were not taken into account in the premiums valued. (If they were, the reasonable expectations of policyholders would not be fulfilled in the future.)
2. An appropriate Zillmerized liability would be acceptable in order to allow for initial expenses. (A maximum degree of Zillmerization would be prescribed at a lower level than would be likely to be justified by the level of new business expenses of an insurer.)
3. Adequate margins over the current rate of expenses should be kept in the valuation of future net premiums to provide for future expenses. (If liabilities were valued at a low rate of interest, net premiums – particularly under non-profit contracts – might not provide a sufficient margin in comparison with premiums payable, and should be suitably reduced in the valuation.)
4. Appropriate recognized tables of mortality should be employed.
5. The valuation of liabilities should be at rates of interest lower than those implicit in the valuation of the assets, as indicated by the yield on the life insurance fund after taking taxation into account.

A further provision was added later:

6. That liabilities should be not less than guaranteed surrender values or the values of any other options available under contracts.

An insurer would be considered to meet the standard if the value of its assets, taken at not more than that shown in the balance sheet, was at least equal to the liabilities of the insurer, including actuarial liabilities determined in accordance with these principles. Only in exceptional circumstances could assets be shown in the balance sheet at more than market value. The standard would involve testing the financial situation of the insurer at the various rates of interest which would be earned on the fund from time to time, and was therefore more effective than a single test based on a single rate of interest.

In an OECD working party set up in 1967, the UK concept of a solvency standard based on the interdependence of the rate of interest used for valuing liabilities and that implicit in the valuation of assets was put forward. The working party concluded that the method did not seem to lend itself to general application in Europe but that, in principle, it was valid where the conditions permitting its use were fulfilled. The membership of the working party included a representative of the Government Actuary's Department and an actuary advising a UK insurer.

The duties of an actuary advising a life insurer

A greater level of understanding and agreement developed within the profession in the postwar years as to the duties of an actuary advising a life insurer in the UK. A paper published in 1973 described the main duties as evaluating the likely financial consequences of various courses of action open to an insurer, and thus assisting the formulation of judgements on policy, making recommendations as to the bases to be used in calculating premium rates and assisting in the periodic valuation of liabilities and assets. The actuary should also advise on the profits to be distributed and on how they should be shared between policyholders and, where applicable, shareholders. The actuary should also explain his or her activities to others – to the insurer so that informed decisions could be taken and, as appropriate, to the public, in particular to policyholders and prospective policyholders. Information would also be supplied as required under insurance control legislation to the regulatory authorities. It was stated that the adoption of the six principles described above for the minimum solvency standard should ensure that the financial soundness of an insurer should not be in doubt. Valuation in accordance with these principles would not, however, quantify the financial strength of the insurer as represented by the 'estate', which could be assessed as the excess of the realistic value of the assets over the value of the liabilities, including appropriate future bonuses using a bonus reserve valuation. The vulnerability of the 'estate' to changing conditions could be judged by the results of valuations of assets and liabilities on various bases, including valuation of equities and properties as the discounted values of future income on different assumptions as to their rate of growth. These valuations would enable the actuary to advise the insurer not only on the level of the 'estate' but also on its trend over the years, thus indicating whether it is tending to increase or decrease.

The actuary should advise the insurer not only on the determination of the amount of the distributable surplus, so as to achieve a satisfactory degree of fairness between one generation of policyholders and another, but also on how that surplus, including transfers from capital appreciation, should be shared between policyholders. He or she should also advise on the maintainability of the declared bonus rates.

In the 1970s, there was increasing pressure for the greater disclosure of the financial strength of insurers to inform policyholders (and prospective policyholders) and their advisers and also to inform present (and prospective) shareholders and financial analysts. The author of the 1973 paper said that it would be undesirable for a single figure to be disclosed to the public as an indication of the level of the 'estate'. To publish a range of figures on different assumptions would cause confusion. It would be better for an independent actuary to use the returns supplied to the DTI to evaluate the 'estate' on bases of his choice. There was some pressure for the disclosure of the true profits of a life insurer, which could be taken as the change over a year in the 'estate'. Such an assessment would be considerably more a matter of judgement than for most other types of business. It would, however, be possible and perhaps desirable to quantify major factors (for example, new business strain) that were causing published profits to differ from realistic profits.

Security for holders of life insurance policies issued in the UK was underpinned by the Policyholders Protection Act 1975, under which some 90 per cent of the contractual benefits under such contracts are guaranteed should an insurer fail to meet its liabilities; but the guarantee does not necessarily apply if an actuary certifies that the insurer has offered excessive benefits for the premiums charged. The guarantee is met from a fund provided by levies on life insurers.

Professional guidance to actuaries advising life insurers

In 1975, following problems that arose for a few insurers as a result of the fall in stock market values in 1974, the professional actuarial bodies in the UK thought it desirable to issue, for the first time, guidance to actuaries advising life insurers as to their responsibilities. This step was not universally welcomed, because some considered that actuaries should be free to exercise their professional judgement as to these responsibilities. The guidance, issued in 1975, was on general principles and, to be effective, compliance was necessary with its spirit as well as with its letter. Not surprisingly, the guidance was later amplified and clarified.

The role of the Government Actuary's Department

Side by side with these developments, the Government Actuary's Department had, since its formation in 1919, continued to develop its role in the supervision of insurance. At the beginning of the 1970s, life insurance supervision still relied largely on the insurer's actuary to value the liabilities, and to ensure that the assets of the life fund were sufficient in value to cover them and to give a fair return to with-profits policyholders. Because of the prudent approach of actuaries to valuation, no solvency margin was required. The Government Actuary's Department judged whether appropriate methods were used and whether the valuation was sufficiently prudent.

The Appointed Actuary and professional guidance

In the early 1970s, there was rapid growth in the formation of new life insurers with moderate capital. The need was felt by both the supervisory authorities and the profession to strengthen the status of the insurer's actuary. This was achieved in an Act of 1973 which introduced the concept of the Appointed Actuary, who would be identified, to advise the insurer and continuously monitor its financial position. An Appointed Actuary must possess a Certificate issued by the Faculty or Institute of Actuaries to the effect that the holder is a Fellow of the Faculty or Institute, is aged at least 30, has appropriate practical experience and is an appropriate person. This last requirement is similar in effect to the 'fit and proper' requirement for directors of insurance companies. Guidance issued by the Institute and the Faculty of Actuaries on the responsibilities of the Appointed Actuary has been modified from time to time in the light of experience, as have statutory regulations under the Insurance Companies Act. Regulations under the Insurance Companies Act 1981 prescribed minimum standards for the assessment of actuarial liabilities in accord with the six principles described earlier, suitably elaborated. Assets must be shown in the balance sheet at market values but investment reserves may be held and distributable profits need not be based on market values. An example of the elaboration of the six principles was the introduction of a test of the resiliency of the insurer to financial changes, assuming an immediate rise or fall in the rate of interest or a sudden substantial fall in equity and property prices. The prescribed solvency standard does not represent a standard of financial strength recommended to insurers by the authorities but, rather, defines a minimum standard. If an insurer should not satisfy the standard, intervention by the regulatory authorities would follow, with a view to rectifying the situation.

The Regulations required insurers to have regard to 'policyholders' reasonable expectations'. These have neither been defined nor tested in the Courts. Clearly, they include contractual benefits. Beyond this, they depend in part on expectations created by the insurer. It is to be expected that under with-profit contracts they would include a proper share in profits.

The main provisions of the Guidance Notes issued by the Institute and Faculty on the responsibilities of Appointed Actuaries involved in life insurance require them to be satisfied that the financial condition of the insurer is at all times satisfactory. In particular, their responsibilities are defined as follows:

- To ensure, as far as is within their authority, that the business is

operated on sound financial lines and with regard to policyholders'
reasonable expectations.

- To be sure that he or she has or has access to appropriate knowledge
  and practical experience relevant to the insurer.
- To advise the DTI, after informing the insurer, if the insurer pursues a
  course of action or is faced with a situation that creates a material risk
  to the adequacy of the life insurance fund.
- To advise the insurer of his or her interpretation of policyholders'
  reasonable expectations.
- To certify, when carrying out the periodic investigation into the
  financial condition of the insurer, including a valuation of its liabilities, that the relevant Guidance Notes have been complied with.
- To ensure, as far as is possible, that the insurer will not make or
  promise an allocation of profits from a life fund before considering his
  or her observations or recommendations.
- To have regard to all aspects that might affect the financial position of
  the insurer's life business, including contingent liabilities.
- To be satisfied that the premiums being charged for new business are
  appropriate, taking into account all relevant factors; and, for unit-
  linked contracts, to be satisfied with procedures for unit pricing.
- To be satisfied, in the light of periodic actuarial investigation, as to the
  financial condition of the existing business, having regard to the
  liabilities and the corresponding assets, their interrelationships and
  the resilience of the financial position of the insurer in all reasonably
  foreseeable circumstances. When assessing liabilities, he or she must
  have regard to policyholders' reasonable expectations, must make
  adequate provision for future expenses of continuing the existing
  business and must decide the rates of interest to be used (having regard
  to the existing assets and the rate of return at which future investment
  will be possible and to the relationship between the length of term of
  the assets and that of the corresponding liabilities).
- To advise the insurer of the restraints on its investment policy that are
  necessary to protect policyholders if he or she considers that its
  investment policy is, or could become, inappropriate, having regard to
  the nature and term of its liabilities.
- To advise the insurer of the limits within which the insurer must act in
  relation to events under the control of the insurer, to avoid the
  possibility of insolvency or failure to meet policyholders' reasonable
  expectations. He or she must also consider factors outside the control
  of the insurer which could lead to insolvency and act as he or she
  considers necessary.
- To report in writing to the directors on the results and implications of

actuarial investigations and on the maintainability of any recommended allocation of profits to policyholders.

Thus the insurance regulatory system in the UK depends on a combination of legislation, Guidance Notes from the Institute and Faculty on the responsibilities of Appointed Actuaries and on the actuaries advising or involved in the management of life insurers. The actuarial profession has thus combined with the supervisory authority to ensure good standards of supervision and of conduct by insurers.

The Insurance Regulations 1994 defined the bases for the valuation of liabilities under life business and embodied requirements for the provision of solvency margins in accordance with the EEC Life Establishment Directive, and a Guidance Note for Appointed Actuaries on these Regulations was issued. Guidance was also given on the interpretation of the criteria for the minimum statutory valuations. The requirements for the minimum solvency margins did not necessarily result in an increase in liabilities, because certain implicit margins in liabilities could be used to cover them.

Investment 'derivatives'

In recent years, a new problem has arisen for Appointed Actuaries because of the increasing use of investment 'derivatives' such as futures, forwards, options and swaps by life insurers as an aid to managing their risk exposures: their use carries with it the possibility of these exposures being mismanaged. An advisory Guidance Note was issued in 1994 to actuaries providing an actuarial opinion on liabilities, which has regard to the nature of assets covering them. The Insurance Companies Act 1982 (as amended in 1994) requires insurers to have systems of 'sound and prudent management' over all of their activities, including the use of derivatives. The Guidance Note advises actuaries to be satisfied that suitable controls exist regarding derivatives and describes the steps that they should take to assess whether such controls exist. The Appointed Actuary should also consider whether suitable reserves or provisions exist in respect of the insurer's derivatives controls.

The Faculty and Institute announced in 1996 the introduction in 1997 of an examination for 'An Advanced Certificate in Derivatives: the Mathematics, Principles and Practice'.

The present regulatory system

Except for the Guidance Note on derivatives which is *advisory* (that is, recommended practice) the Guidance Notes to Appointed Actuaries are *mandatory* (that is, a practice standard) in relation to the Code of Conduct of the profession, which means that a material breach of them would provide strong prima facie evidence of unprofessional conduct and a ground for a complaint against the member under the disciplinary procedures.

The Government Actuary's Department also continues to participate in the regulatory arrangements, and may question an Appointed Actuary in order to establish whether the requirements of the Regulations and the Guidance Notes have been satisfactorily met.

The successful operation of the system of regulation, which may appear to be complicated, depends on co-operation between the supervisory authorities, the Government Actuary's Department, the actuarial profession, Appointed Actuaries and insurers. It is not practicable to express in statutory Regulations all that is required in actuarial investigations without imposing unduly restrictive controls. Professional guidance that amplifies and clarifies statutory regulations should be helpful to Appointed Actuaries in defining their responsibilities. The system imposes some restraints on the freedom of Appointed Actuaries but, on the other hand, it strengthens their position in relation to the insurers advised by them, because the Appointed Actuary has to certify in the insurer's returns to the supervisory authority that, in discharging his responsibilities, the Guidance Notes have been complied with. The Guidance Notes are helpful to the Government Actuary's Department because, without them, the Department would be likely to be involved in unnecessary questions to Appointed Actuaries as to compliance with the Regulations. Acceptance of the system by Appointed Actuaries and insurers, and co-operation with the spirit as well as the letter of the Guidance Notes, is essential to the effectiveness of the system. Any significant moves to test the limits of what the system will permit could endanger it.

International activities

Since the 1960s, the international activities of actuaries concerned with life insurance have increased, initially through OECD working parties and later through meetings of supervisory authorities in the European Community, concerned, *inter alia*, with Directives affecting life insurance. The European Insurance Committee, which represents European insurers, has actuaries as members of its working parties concerned with life insurance. An actuarial Consultative Group was formed in 1978 to represent the profession in the European Union. Both the Committee and the Group have access to the European Commission, which thus enables them to express their views.

Co-operation between Appointed Actuaries and auditors under the Insurance Companies Act 1982 and the Companies Act 1995 is necessary even though the Appointed Actuary has no defined role under the Companies Act. Discussions took place with the accountancy profession, as a result of which an understanding was reached of the respective responsibilities of Appointed Actuaries and auditors. A Guidance Note indicating best practice was issued to Appointed Actuaries in 1980, the latest revision being made in 1997, referring to Reporting Actuaries.

Information to present and prospective policyholders

On the legislation front, interest has turned increasingly to the subject of supplying clients and their advisers with information that would help them to make a more informed choice between the various savings contracts available, and between those providing them. With regard to life insurance contracts, useful information was felt to be desirable on two points:

- the financial strength of an insurer
- the benefits that were likely to arise under a contract when the amount of the benefit was not fully guaranteed from the outset

The Financial Services Act 1986 required an independent financial adviser to give an investment client, including the holder or prospective holder of an insurance contract, 'best advice'. Intermediaries thus found it necessary to consider the financial strength of a life insurer, with regard to both security and future bonus prospects, before recommending its products to clients. Investment analysts were interested in financial strengths and dividend prospects when assessing the values of the shares of proprietary insurers writing life business.

The obligation to disclose the market value of an insurer's assets in accordance with Regulations under the Insurance Companies Act 1981 prompted some intermediaries to make comparisons between insurers of ratios of the market value of insurers' assets to the value of their liabilities, believing this to be a good guide to an insurer's strength. This ratio is, however, only part of the story. The Appointed Actuary, in determining the published value of the liabilities, has the primary aim of controlling the release of profits, usually by the use of a net premium valuation. The bases used in this valuation – and the decision whether, for example, to use a Zillmer adjustment – will depend on many factors; in particular, the policy of the insurer with regard to bonus declarations. Some of the strength of the insurer is thus held in the prudent valuation of the liabilities and is not disclosed.

Discussions have taken place within the actuarial profession on the consequences of the need arising from the Financial Services Act 1986 for intermediaries to give the investor or prospective investor 'best advice'. A paper published in 1988 led to a wide-ranging discussion on what further information could usefully be supplied by insurers to assist intermediaries and prospective policyholders to choose between insurers. It was felt that no single figure for each insurer would provide a suitable guide to relative financial strength and prospects for bonuses in the future. For example, if figures for the 'estate' based on bonus reserve valuations were published, who would choose the valuation bases to be used? If it were to be individual Appointed Actuaries, there would inevitably be different approaches to the choice of bases for different insurers, and the resulting figures would not be closely comparable. It would be difficult, if not impossible, for a standard basis to be defined for the calculation of the 'estate' which would be suitable to all insurers, given their differing mixes of business and different investment policies. Moreover, the publication of a figure at a given time does not solve the problems of the person who is seeking information. He or she is concerned with the strength of the insurer throughout the period for which a policy is operating, and this may be influenced by changes in the future, including those caused by the insurer's reactions to future changes in the investment market and the insurer's rate of expansion in comparison with that of other insurers. The discussion concluded that, rather than concentrate on a quantitative evaluation of the current strength of an insurer, it would be more valuable to intermediaries and prospective policyholders to give fuller information about with-profit contracts and the insurer's policy on bonus rates.

It had for some time been recognized that an illustration of the amount payable on a claim arising under a with-profits life insurance contract, which assumed the indefinite maintenance of current bonus rates, would not give a reliable indication of the outcome of a contract currently being issued; this was especially so in the 1980s, when interest rates decreased and bonus rates seemed likely to reduce. Quotations of amounts payable under contracts currently becoming claims were factual, but were open to the objection that past experience and performance could not be relied upon as an indication of what would be achieved in the future by contracts currently being issued.

Regulations arising from the Financial Services Act require indications to be given of the outcome of contracts becoming claims based on two prescribed rates of interest. This would show the extent to which the outcome would depend on the rate of return on investments in the future and would enable the recipient to estimate what the outcome would be at a rate of return of his or her choosing. The illustrations are now required to use the rates of expense and mortality of the insurer concerned. Actuaries have been involved in determining these rates, and an advisory Guidance Note was issued, which was revised in 1996. In order to provide more information, an insurer must now issue (to anyone requesting a copy) a guide regarding its with-profits contracts. The guide includes an indication of how bonus rates are determined. Guides made available cover various aspects to various degrees of precision:

- *Fairness* is usually described in general rather than in explicit terms.
- *Smoothing* is usually described without explicit information as to how it is achieved and its extent.
- *'Asset shares'* are mentioned explicitly by some insurers, but others refer to bonuses being based on profits earned over the duration of the contract. Few are explicit as to the assumptions underlying the calculation of asset shares.

Few guides refer at all to the importance of the financial strength of the insurer in determining bonuses.

The information in with-profits guides therefore falls far short of that given by the Appointed Actuary when advising the insurer on bonus declarations. This is understandable not only because of competitive considerations but also because information published on this subject must be made understandable to the recipient if it is to be of assistance to him or her. With bonus systems as they stand in 1997, this represents a challenge to actuaries. The adoption of 'asset shares' as the basis of bonus rates may have reduced the difficulties of explanation. Some say that unitised with-profits contracts make explanation less difficult, but this has been disputed.

Surrender values

Under a contract involving a savings element, an amount is payable (a surrender value) if the contract is terminated before it becomes a claim by death or maturity. Surrender values under life insurance contracts have for a long time been a source of complaint by policyholders. Nowadays, specimen surrender values have to be supplied to prospective policy-holders. There have been two grounds for complaint. Surrender values are low in comparison with premiums paid in the early years of a contract – nothing at all may be payable in the very early years. Commission and expenses involved in putting a contract on the books are high in relation to those in later years. The costs of setting up a contract may well be related to the whole cost of the selling organization, and it has been asked whether the expenses of unsuccessful attempts to sell should be charged directly (as new business expenses) against contracts written, or be regarded as part of overhead expenses. Also, surrender values may be low in comparison with sums paid on claims on completed contracts if little or no credit is given for terminal bonuses. Significant improvements have been made recently by the payment of surrender values close to 'asset shares' for contracts near to maturity, with improvements at earlier durations also.

From the 1980s to 1997

Profit testing for new types of contract

Actuaries have continued to develop their activities as advisers to life insurers and as participants in their management. More intense competition induced insurers to adopt more sophisticated methods involving actuarial participation when considering the introduction of new types of contract. In particular, in order to ensure that capital was used as effectively as possible, the suitability of a new contract involved considering its profitability, marketability, competitiveness, financing, the cost of guarantees and the administrative systems required. Premiums for a possible new contract would be determined on the basis of estimated future experience having regard to these factors.

The rate of return on capital (the risk rate of return) that was desired would be decided having regard to the risks presented to the profits of the insurer by the contract. In order to choose between the relative efficiency in the use of capital by different contracts, they would be tested by a process called 'profit testing'. Possible criteria for these tests are as follows:

- *Net present value*. The discounted value at the risk rate of return of estimated future profits produced by the contract on the published valuation basis. The contract that produces the highest result is the most attractive to the insurer.
- *Internal rate of return*. The rate of return at which the discounted value of estimated future published profits is zero. The insurer should prefer the contract with the highest rate of return.
- *Discounted pay-back*.The duration in force for a contract at which estimated published profits that have emerged have a discounted value of zero at the risk rate of return. This indicates the time it would take

for the insurer to recover its capital investments with interest at the risk interest rate. An insurer with limited capital may prefer the contract with the shortest pay-back period.

The approach would be the same whether capital was provided by shareholders or from within the life insurance fund.

'Immunisation' and asset/liability management

A paper published in 1984 widened consideration of 'immunisation' to the selection of an investment portfolio matched to any set of liabilities. The paper used a statistical model that took account of the statistical variance in the rates of interest and inflation; as distinct from the 1952 paper, which used a deterministic approach that assumed no variance. Some actuaries have become increasingly involved in asset-liability management – the selection of an investment portfolio that is best suited to the liabilities, whether of a life insurer or a pension fund.

'Dynamic solvency'

The importance of forward planning led actuaries in the 1980s to become interested in 'dynamic solvency'. The traditional concept of a solvency standard relates only to the business currently on the books. 'Dynamic solvency' is based on forward projections of the cash flow of the insurer, including the flow from future new business, consistent with its business plan, to test whether it will have sufficient assets in future years. Making various additional assumptions as to future development and experience will enable the susceptibility of the insurer to adverse changes to be assessed. An advisory Guidance Note was issued in 1996 regarding the Appointed Actuary's responsibility for reporting to the insurer on its financial condition, including dynamic solvency testing.

Value of a life insurer to shareholders

In the 1980s, interest increased in assessing the value to shareholders in a proprietary life insurer of its existing business and in estimating realistic shareholders' profits from year to year. This information was considered to be valuable to financial analysts as well as to shareholders. The value of the existing business to shareholders may be assessed as the sum of net assets relating to life business held outside the life insurance fund plus the discounted value of the shareholders' share of future surplus on the published valuation basis, based on forward projections of the insurer's life revenue accounts. Calculation may be by one of two methods:

1. *The embedded value method.* The projections use realistic assumptions. Allowance for risk is made within the discount rate.
2. *The accruals method.* Influenced in its development by accounting principles, this method reflects accumulated profits based on risks borne and work done at each stage of a contract. The forward projections of revenue accounts make allowance for risk through margins in each of the main factors; for example, investment return, mortality, expenses and discontinuances. A realistic discount rate is used.

In practice, the profits and shareholder balance sheet values produced by the two methods can be very similar and, indeed, some insurers adopt a hybrid approach in which some risk is reflected directly in the projection parameters while some is contained within the discount rate.

The difference between the value to shareholders at the end of the year from that value at the beginning, after allowing for any dividend payments made, represents the realistic profit to shareholders for the year. At present, each insurer is free to determine the value of its existing business to shareholders using the method and bases of the its choice. Thus, assuming consistency of method and bases from year to year, the results should indicate changes and trends in the value of the business of an insurer to shareholders, but cannot be relied upon to provide a comparison of realistic values between insurers.

Takeovers

As the result of recent takeover bids, actuaries have been involved in the valuation of a life insurer for purchase, the so-called 'appraisal value'. The 'appraisal value' includes the value of existing business to shareholders, including the value of profits from future premiums as may be obtained from the 'embedded value' approach. It also includes (as a major item in most cases) the estimated value to shareholders of new business that will be written in the future. The assessment of the 'embedded value' may properly be regarded as an actuarial responsibility. The valuation of profits from future new business depends very much on the development of business, which is for the interested parties rather than actuaries to assess. Given the rate of development that is foreseen, the actuary can value these profits. Not surprisingly, in a disputed takeover, different embedded values result from actuarial valuations made by actuaries advising the two parties, and markedly different values of profits from future new business are produced. Discussion within the profession on recent takeovers has shown the need for careful consideration to be given to the professional duties of actuaries in takeover situations.

'Demutualizations'

Actuaries have also been involved in 'demutualizations', the conversion of a life insurer from ownership by its policyholders to ownership by shareholders. This can be achieved by compliance with the requirements of the Insurance Companies Act 1982, which governs the transfer of business from one insurer (the mutual insurer) to another (the proprietary insurer), which would involve the Appointed Actuary, an independent actuary and the Government Actuary. The Appointed Actuary is concerned to ensure that the solvency and financial strength of the insurer are maintained and that reasonable expectations of policyholders will be satisfied. The independent actuary must report on the scheme of transfer and give his opinion on its likely effects on the life policyholders. The Government Actuary advises the statutory regulators, whose main concern is the protection of the policyholders' interests. The independent actuary and the Government Actuary should consider not only the satisfaction of policyholders' reasonable expectations, but should also examine the fairness of the share in the 'estate' of the mutual insurer which it is proposed should be allocated to policyholders of the mutual insurer as their recompense for giving up their ownership of that insurer. An advisory Professional Guidance Note was issued in 1990 on the role of the independent actuary in the transfer of life insurance business in accordance with the Insurance Companies Act 1982.

'Inherited estate'

As long as the assets representing the life insurance fund were regarded as a pool and while the profits from that fund were, for proprietary insurers, shared between policyholders and shareholders in accordance with their Articles of Association or established practice, the question of attributing part of the assets to policyholders and to shareholders did not arise. 'Asset shares', which in effect identified the accumulated contributions of with profit policyholders to the fund, led insurers and actuaries to consider the allocation of the 'estate' between policyholders and shareholders. The 'estate' became known as the 'orphan estate', but later it was thought that it would be better described as the 'inherited estate'.

It was recognized that, in order to quantify the 'inherited estate', the liabilities to with-profit policyholders should include provision for their reasonable expectations with regard to bonuses.

'Asset shares' were used as a measure of the liabilities under with-profit contracts in preference to a bonus reserve valuation, and would be increased as necessary to provide for the possibility that they were not adequate to provide policyholders' reasonable expectations. The 'inherited estate' was quantified as the excess of the value of the assets over the obligations to policyholders, shareholders and creditors. It might originate from:

- shareholders' capital
- retention of surplus to stabilise bonus rates, to ensure solvency, and to finance future expansion and allow greater investment freedom
- under-distribution of surplus, because of caution or reluctance to distribute surplus too quickly
- low surrender values

Where the division of profits is not otherwise defined by the Articles of Association or elsewhere, it can be argued that, in the allocation of the 'inherited estate', shareholders should benefit from capital injected into the fund and from sources of retained surplus not attributable to with-profit policyholders.

With regard to the balance of the 'inherited estate', it can be questioned whether it is satisfactory to allocate it on an arbitrary 90 : 10 ratio to policyholders and shareholders, because this would mean distributing profits created by one generation of policyholders to their successors. Against this, it can be argued that, although the claims of policyholders for a larger share may be tenuous, this does not enhance the entitlement of shareholders. Clearly, the particular situation of each insurer must be taken into account when apportioning the 'inherited estate'.

A few applications have been made to the supervisory authorities for approval of arrangements to apportion the 'inherited estate'. The authorities have indicated that:

- they considered that the proportions of policyholders' and shareholders' interests are unaffected whether or not the surplus is distributed
- they would expect a 90 : 10 proportion to be used as the basis for apportionment unless there was clear evidence that a different proportion was appropriate

The authorities have indicated that they would require a report from an independent actuary on any proposed apportionment, including an opinion on the influence of the various factors affecting the reasonable expectations of policyholders and on the appropriateness of the proposed arrangements having regard to them.

To attribute part of the 'inherited estate' to shareholders would not necessarily mean that it could be transferred out of the life insurance fund, because this would affect the interests of policyholders. Only interest income on the shareholders' allocation might be distributable to them.

Conclusion

The foregoing account shows that actuaries, through their use of mathematics combined with judgement, have been indispensable to the development of life insurance. Their activities have covered an expanding field, including determination of premiums for an increasingly wide range of contracts, the financial investigation of assets and liabilities of insurers, the steering of their financial strength and the assessment of realistic profits.

With regard to mathematics, it has been recognized that changes in factors relating to experience entering into actuarial formulae reflect not only changes in the average values of those factors but also fluctuations about those average values. The probability of a given fluctuation reduces as its magnitude increases. Large adverse divergences from average values at the time of an investigation into an insurer's financial position would have a significant effect on the results, and should be taken into account in conjunction with the probability of their occurrence, however small that might be. This procedure had long been recognized in statistical mathematics but it involved a large volume of calculations. Computers have made these calculations practicable, and they have become increasingly used in actuarial calculations where they could yield useful results. At the same time, various approximate methods used by actuaries to reduce the burden of calculations have become less used as computers have facilitated exact calculations.

The manner in which actuarial judgement has been employed over the years has also changed. The constant objective of actuaries in this field has been to encourage the development of the insurers that they advise, by enabling them to provide contracts that are attractive to policyholders while, first and foremost, ensuring the financial soundness of insurers so that policyholders will have confidence that their contracts will be honoured and their reasonable expectations met.

At first, there were only a few life insurers and the actuaries advising them formed a small close-knit group that shared a similar outlook, and used their judgement in a similar and prudent way. A few failures of insurers led to the need for legislation, the underlying principle of which was freedom to exercise professional judgement, but subject to an obligation to reveal how it had been used. This freedom was far from absolute. It was strongly influenced by discussions within the profession on sound standards, and by the fact that the way in which an actuary used his or her judgement would be published and could be judged by his or her peers. Control, in the main, depended on self-regulation.

Over the years, the life insurance industry has become a major medium for savings and protection. The actuarial profession has expanded and inevitably become less close-knit. It is not surprising that the regulatory authorities felt that judgement aimed at ensuring the soundness of life insurers should be subjected to some restraint. This was not opposed by the profession. A system of control was introduced, supported by Guidance Notes that ensured sound practice. It imposed some restraint on actuarial freedom but, at the same time, enhanced the standing of an actuary advising a life insurer, and put him or her in a stronger position to resist pressure from the insurer. It did not fetter the use of actuarial judgement so as significantly to inhibit the growth of the life insurance industry.

More recently, 'consumerism' has became a matter of greater public concern and pressure has been applied to ensure that good advice is given to prospective policyholders. Legislation aiming to achieve this has extended beyond actuarial responsibilities and has raised problems that are difficult to resolve satisfactorily. 'Best advice' to a prospective policyholder who seeks a good return from a life insurance contract is likely to be to effect a with-profits or unit-linked contract. If this advice is taken, the customer inevitably sacrifices a guarantee of the return that will be achieved from the contract. Although information can be given about the contract and about the insurer, it is not possible to quantify in advance the outcome of a contract involving uncertainty. It is a challenge to insurers and their actuaries to identify information relevant to that outcome which would be of assistance to prospective policyholders, but nothing can remove all uncertainty as to the outcome.

To keep this chapter to a reasonable length, it has only described how actuaries have participated in the development of life insurance in the UK. Actuarial judgement elsewhere has been flexibly restrained, particularly with regard to the determination of premium rates and liabilities under contracts.

Further reading

Premium rates and assessment and distribution of profits

Bailey, H. H. 1878: The pure premium method of valuation. *Journal of the Institute of Actuaries*, 21, 115.

Bayley, G. V. and Perks, W. 1952: A consistent system of investment and bonus distribution for a life office. *Journal of the Institute of Actuaries*, 79, 14.

Coutts, C. R. V. 1907: Bonus reserve valuations. *Journal of the Institute of Actuaries*, 42, 173.

Cox, P. R. and Storr-Best, R. H. 1962: *Surplus in British Life Assurance*. Cambridge.

Elderton, W. P. 1930: Fair distribution of bonus. *Proceedings of the Ninth International Congress of Actuaries*, 158.

Fisher, H. F. and Young, J. 1965: *Actuarial Practice of Life Assurance*. Cambridge.

Haynes, A. T. and Kirton, R. J. 1952: The financial structure of a life office. *Transactions of the Faculty of Actuaries*, 21, 141.

Lyon, C. S. S. 1988: The financial management of a with profit long term fund – some questions of disclosure. *Journal of the Institute of Actuaries*, 115, 349.

Needleman, P. D. and Roff, T. A. 1995: Asset shares and their use in the financial management of a with profits fund. *British Actuarial Journal*, 1, 603.

Ogborn, M. E. and Bayley, G. V. 1954: Participation in profits as a means of securing stability in life assurance funds. *Proceedings of the Fourteenth International Congress of Actuaries*, 2, 112.

Ranson, R. H. and Headdon, C. P. 1989: With profits without mystery. *Journal of the Institute of Actuaries*, 116, 301.

Redington, F. M. 1952: Review of principles of life office valuations. *Journal of the Institute of Actuaries*, 78, 286.

Skerman, R. S. 1954: Surplus funds as a means of securing the stability of a life office. *Proceedings of the Fourteenth International Congress of Actuaries*, 2, 134.

Skerman, R. S. 1957: The application of actuarial principles to the transaction of overseas life business. *Journal of the Institute of Actuaries*, 83, 73.

Skerman, R. S. 1967: The assessment and distribution of profits from life business. *Journal of the Institute of Actuaries*, 94, 53.

Sprague, T. B. 1857: On certain methods of dividing the surplus among the assured in a life assurance company, and on the rates of premium that should be charged to make them equitable. *Journal of the Institute of Actuaries*, 7, 61.

Suttie, T. R. 1945: Equity in bonus distribution. *Journal of the Institute of Actuaries*, 73, 37.

Wise, A. J. 1984: The matching of assets to liabilities. *Journal of the Institute of Actuaries*, 111, 445.

Statutory solvency standards

Bews, R. P., Seymour, P. A. G., Shaw, A. N. D. and Wales, F. R. 1975: Proposals for the statutory basis of valuation of the liabilities of long-term insurance business. *Journal of the Institute of Actuaries*, 102, 61.

Daykin, C. D. 1992: The developing role of the Government Actuary's Department in the supervision of insurance. *Journal of the Institute of Actuaries*, 119, 313.

Fine, A. E. M., Headdon, C. P., Hewitson, T. W., Johnson, C. M., Lumsden, I. C., Maple, M. H., O'Keefe, P. J. L., Pook, P. J., Purchase, D. E. and Robinson, D. G. 1988: Proposals for the statutory basis of valuation of the liabilities of linked long-term insurance business. *Journal of the Institute of Actuaries*, 115, 555.

Johnston, E. A. 1989: The Appointed Actuary. *Journal of the Institute of Actuaries*, 116, 27.

OECD Working Party Report 1971: *Financial Guarantees Required from Life Assurance Concerns.*

Skerman, R. S. 1965: A Solvency standard for life assurance business. *Journal of the Institute of Actuaries*, 92, 75.

Actuarial practice

Skerman, R. S. 1973: The work of a life office actuary in the United Kingdom: recent developments and a look into the future. *Journal of the Institute of Actuaries*, 100, 33.

Group life and pension business

Edey, J. 1956: A system of distribution of surplus for participating deferred annuities. *Journal of the Institute of Actuaries*, 82, 179.

Fellows, D. E. 1972: Insured group pension plans and ancillary benefits. *Journal of the Institute of Actuaries*, 99, 19.

Contracts linked with investment values

Anon. 1980: Report of the Maturity Guarantees Working Party. *Journal of the Institute of Actuaries*, 107, 101.

Bailey, W. G. 1962: Some points on equity-linked contracts. *Journal of the Institute of Actuaries*, 88, 319.

Grant, A. T. and Kingsnorth, G. A. 1966: Unit trusts and equity-linked contracts. *Journal of the Institute of Actuaries*, 93, 387.

Laker, R. J. and Squires, R. J. 1985: Unit pricing and provision for tax on capital gains in linked assurance business. *Journal of the Institute of Actuaries*, 112, 117.

Squires, R. J. 1974: Unit-linked assurance: observations and propositions. *Journal of the Institute of Actuaries*, 101, 1.

Unitised with-profits business

O'Neill, J. E. and Froggett, H. W. 1993: Unitised with profits – Gamaliel's advice. *Journal of the Institute of Actuaries*, 120, 415.

Squires, R. J. and O'Neill, J. E. 1990: A unitised fund approach to with-profit business. *Journal of the Institute of Actuaries*, 117, 279.

Valuation of a life insurer

Burrows, R. P. and Whitehead, G. H. 1987: The determination of life office appraisal values. *Journal of the Institute of Actuaries*, 114, 411.

O'Brien, C. D. 1994: Profit capital and value in a proprietary life assurance company. *Journal of the Institute of Actuaries*, 121, 285.

Demutualization or takeover of a life insurer

Needleman, P. D. and Westall, G. 1991: Demutualisation of a United Kingdom mutual life insurance company. *Journal of the Institute of Actuaries*, 118, 321.

Salmon, I. L. and Fine, A. E. M. 1990: Reflections on a takeover of a United Kingdom insurer: a case study. *Journal of the Institute of Actuaries*, 118, 59.

Occupational and personal pensions   6

Stewart Lyon

The idea of setting up occupational pension schemes with clearly defined entitlements to benefits grew out of a tradition of *ex gratia* pensions, granted by enlightened employers to long-serving employees. The establishment in the early eighteenth century of an embryo 'pay as you go' scheme in one section of the public service, and in 1743 of the first soundly financed occupational pension fund (for widows of ministers of the Church of Scotland), is described in chapter 2. Subsequently, schemes were established for rather special private-sector companies such as the East India Company and the Bank of England. From the 1840s onwards, pension funds and other types of pension scheme were instituted by the railway companies and other utilities, and by some large employers in the financial, manufacturing and retail fields.

Public-sector schemes

The pattern for the best occupational schemes was set in the public sector by the Superannuation Act 1834, as revised by the Superannuation Act 1859. These Acts applied to the Civil Service. The first introduced a maximum pension of two-thirds of actual final salary after 45 years' service; the second shortened that period to 40 years, with an accrual rate of 1/60th for each year of service, and reduced the normal retirement age from 65 to 60. Later on, the rate of accrual of pension was reduced by a quarter, to 1/80th, in return for providing a lump sum at retirement of 3/80ths of final salary for each year of service. There have been many amendments during the past 50 years, including basing benefits on the best year's salary in the last three years of service, adding for new entrants a contributory widow's or widower's pension at half the rate of a deceased member's own pension, and increasing pensions in line with price inflation under the provisions of the Pensions (Increase) Acts. Since 1972, power to make and operate schemes for the Civil Service has lain with ministers, instead of being governed by statute.

Spouses' pensions apart, Civil Service pensions are non-contributory.

They are also unfunded ('pay as you go'), the emerging benefits being a charge on general tax revenues. Most other schemes in the public sector, including those for the police, firemen, teachers and National Health Service staff, are also unfunded, although their members are required to contribute. However, in the case of teachers and the NHS staff, their employers also have to contribute at rates determined and periodically reviewed as if a fund were being built up to provide the pensions. Benefits are broadly in line with the Civil Service scheme, although differing in some important details; for example, it may be optional to take a lump sum in place of a quarter of the pension. For the police and firemen, pensions accrue at an accelerated rate, so that the maximum of two-thirds is reached after 30 years.

In contrast, schemes for employees of local government are funded. Some authorities established their own schemes by Act of Parliament, but the first general Act was the Local Government and Other Officers' Superannuation Act 1922, which enabled local authorities to set up schemes without special legislation. The Local Government Superannuation Act 1937 made the establishment of such schemes compulsory and defined both the benefits to be provided and the contributions to be paid by employees; only authorities with their own-Act schemes were exempted.

Taxation and the development of private-sector schemes

Before 1921, although tax relief could be obtained on the contributions to pension funds by both employees and employers, the practice of different tax offices was inconsistent. However, it was usual for income tax to be payable on the excess of investment income over pensions in payment. This tax was preventing funds from paying adequate pensions after the inflation of the First World War and, since 85 per cent of pensioners were reckoned to be below the income tax threshold, it seemed unfair that any tax should be paid on a fund's investment income. The provisions of the Finance Act 1921 therefore gave the Inland Revenue power to approve the benefits of pension funds set up under irrevocable trusts, subject to certain conditions, which included a maximum pension of two-thirds of final salary. Approved funds would be exempted from tax on investment income, but pensioners would be liable to income tax on their pensions to the extent that their income exceeded their personal tax threshold. In addition, tax reliefs on contributions were confirmed.

The new legislation helped to stimulate the growth of private pension funds, as they came to be called. By 1930, more than 1200 funds had been approved under the 1921 Act, and by 1936 nearly 1900. Increasingly, and especially by large employers, the provision of pension benefits was seen as a desirable aid to recruitment. However, at this time many employers, particularly the smaller ones, were reluctant to go to the trouble of setting up and administering a trust fund, and of appointing an actuary to advise on the level of contributions and how the assets should be invested. In the late 1920s, a market began to develop for simpler schemes, with the documentation and administration handled by insurance companies, and benefits on retirement and death in service insured by group deferred annuities and group life assurance respectively. For ease of administration, earnings of salaried employees were normally grouped into a series of bands, although a single band was often used for manual workers. A specified amount of pension would accrue for each year spent in a particular band, and a specified lump sum would be payable on death in service while in the band. In no sense was there a contractual relationship between the pension at retirement and an employee's final salary, although the absence of a direct link did not become a matter of overriding concern until postwar inflation began seriously to erode the value of earlier years' pension accrual.

It has been estimated that by 1936 there were a million members of public-sector pension schemes and 1.6 million in schemes in the private sector, of whom 0.3 million were in insured schemes. In total, this represented about 13 per cent of the workforce. By 1956, the numbers had dramatically increased to 3.7 million in public-sector schemes (the increase being mainly attributable to nationalization) and 4.3 million in the private sector, 2.3 million of them in insured schemes. The proportion of the workforce covered by all schemes had risen to 35 per cent.

A level fiscal playing field

Before 1956, the annuity section of an insurance company's life fund, to which premiums for the deferred annuities effected under insured schemes were credited and from which pensions were paid, was taxed on investment income less annuity outgo in much the same way as private pension funds had been before the 1921 Act. Actuaries pricing the premiums had to allow for this, and insured schemes were therefore at a disadvantage when compared with the cost of a private pension fund. Meanwhile, the Income Tax Act 1952 had consolidated, into section 379, the approval of a private pension fund, while the legislation governing approval of insured schemes (essentially conferring tax relief on contributions) was consolidated into section 388.

Under the 1956 Finance Act, if the trustees of a fund approved under section 379 insured some or all of their pension liabilities, the insurance company was allowed to include the relevant policy in a newly created pensions business section of its life fund, which would not be subject to tax. This resulted in a level fiscal playing field and led to a major exercise by insurance companies to replace schemes approved under section 388 by trust funds approved under section 379. Guided by their actuaries, they reduced their premium rates to allow for the improved tax position, and gave special credit when accrued benefits were transferred from the old scheme.

Under the Finance Act 1956, a facility was introduced for self-employed people, and for employees not in pensionable employment, to effect retirement annuity policies that would have similar tax treatment.

The interface with State pensions

Before 1960, occupational pension schemes had little difficulty in living alongside the National Insurance (NI) scheme. The full NI retirement pension for a single person was little more than one-fifth of the average earnings of a male industrial worker: for a married couple it was about one-third. An employer who considered that the combination of occupational and NI pensions would produce too high an income in retirement could 'integrate' his scheme with the State scheme. Some did so by deducting the full NI pension for a single person, which depended on the payment of contributions throughout working life, from an occupational pension based on the length of a member's pensionable service. Because this could be regarded as unfair to employees with short service, a more usual approach was to treat as non-pensionable a tranche of earnings that could be assumed to be adequately covered by the State pension – for example, earnings up to one and one-half times the NI pension for a single person.

In the late 1950s, for reasons explained in chapter 7, the government decided to depart from wholly flat-rate contributions for National Insurance and express part of them as a percentage of earnings, although within a fairly narrow band. Ministers felt that they could only gain public acceptance of the change if there were some reward for those who paid contributions in excess of the basic rate. The National Insurance Act 1959 therefore introduced, from 1961, a supplement to the basic pension for each unit of graduated contributions, but actuaries were able to demonstrate that the additional pension was appreciably less than an occupational scheme could have provided for the same contributions.

The government was persuaded by organizations representing, advising and insuring occupational schemes that many employers would find it difficult to modify them to take account of a graduated State pension. Also, the result of having to do so would be to reduce the funding of pensions in advance through occupational schemes, particularly those in the private sector, while increasing the State pensions that would have to be financed 'pay as you go' by future contributions or through taxation. Arrangements were therefore made for employers to elect to contract their employees out of the graduated pension. To do this, an employer had to demonstrate that he had a scheme that would provide employees with a pension at least equal to the maximum rate of accrual of the graduated pension, in return for which both he and the employees would be exempted from graduated contributions, but would pay basic NI contributions at a higher rate than would otherwise be the case. The idea was that the net reduction in contributions would be broadly comparable with the commercial cost of replacing the graduated pension forgone, and the increase in the basic contribution rate was decided following discussions in which the Government Actuary and actuaries in the private sector were much involved. The minimum pensions to be provided by contracted-out schemes (known as Equivalent Pension Benefits, or EPBs) did not have to be protected against inflation, because no such protection was being automatically provided for the graduated pensions that they were replacing.

The contracting-out terms were independent of the age distribution of the employees involved (although the terms for men and women were different), and employers were given the right to choose which categories of employees to contract out. This meant that employers could exercise a financial option against the State. Substantial savings could be made by not contracting out older employees, so making the average age of those contracted out lower than that assumed in the contracting-out terms, and also by not contracting out the lowest paid, the cost of whose graduated pensions would be very small. There was therefore an incentive for an employer who did not already have an occupational scheme, or who had excluded some categories of employees from his scheme (for example, manual workers), to set up a minimum scheme for a selected group of employees, designed to provide no more than the EPB at a cost that was less than would be incurred had they participated in the graduated part of the NI scheme. Although this was clearly not the purpose for which contracting-out was designed, many minimum schemes were established which, in time, would provide a base for future expansion.

As an illustration of the explosive growth of occupational pension schemes at this time, it is estimated that while there were some 37 500 schemes in operation in the private sector at the end of 1956, with a total membership of 4.3 million, seven years later there were about 60 000, with a membership of 7.2 million. Of these schemes, 80 per cent had fewer than 50 active members and only 3 per cent had more than 500.

The 1959 Act was only the beginning of a continuing involvement by governments in the provision of earnings-related pensions. Increases in the basic NI pension because of inflation soon forced the government to extend the range of earnings covered by the graduated scheme, so that from January 1964 the future rate of accrual of EPB was increased by one-half. Successive governments attempted to replace the graduated scheme with their own ideas of a more durable scheme, but due to the length of legislative time required to bring about radical change and the lack of political agreement, these attempts proved abortive for more than a decade. The one change that was made was the inclusion in the NI scheme, as a result of the National Insurance Act 1966, of a graduated addition to sickness and unemployment benefit and to some benefits on early widow-hood. This caused an increase in the rates of graduated contributions, and although there was a corresponding increase in the accrual of graduated pension, it was on such a small scale that it was decided not to disturb the contracting-out terms. As a result, even contracted-out employees now began to accrue a minuscule entitlement to graduated pension.

Living with an expansion of State pensions

Changes to State pensions and their implications, both for the economy and for occupational pensions, have been a matter of concern for the actuarial profession during most of the second half of the twentieth century. When the framework of the graduated scheme was being developed, the Councils of the Institute of Actuaries and the Faculty of Actuaries in Scotland submitted two memoranda to the Minister of Pensions and National Insurance. The first drew attention to the growing burden on future generations of contributors that would result from the introduction of a graduated pension financed on a 'pay as you go' basis. The second, while endorsing the principle of commercial equivalence between the reduction in contributions for employees contracted out and the graduated pensions forgone, questioned the durability of a system based on full relief of graduated contributions and a higher flat contribution.

Under the 1966 Act, as already mentioned, contracting-out did not confer exemption from the new graduated contributions for sickness and other pre-retirement benefits, and these contributions counted towards the accrual of graduated pension. Although their scale was minuscule, contracting-out had nevertheless become partial rather than total. It was then a small step to accepting the principle that partial contracting out of any form of earnings-related State scheme was feasible, with a lower rate of earnings-related contribution being paid in return for a reduction in earnings-related pension of broadly equivalent value. F. M. Redington, the actuary most associated with this development, described it as the 'abatement' of a State pension. As a result of intensive discussions with civil servants and ministers, mainly by members of a committee of actuaries that Redington had chaired, the principle was enshrined in the Labour government's ambitious National Superannuation and Social Insurance Bill, which was lost when the government fell at the general election in 1970. Its time came with the next Labour government's Social Security Pensions Act of 1975, which replaced the graduated scheme with a new State earnings-related pension scheme (SERPS). This took effect in April 1978; its scope and the general nature of the contracting-out arrangements are described in chapter 7. Suffice it to repeat here that, for the members of a scheme to be contracted out, a guaranteed minimum pension (GMP) had to be provided that corresponded to the rate at which an employee's SERPS pension would otherwise have accrued (which depended on the employee's age in 1978). The GMP would be deducted from his SERPS pension and, in return, lower rates of NI contributions were payable by both employee and employer, the reduction reflecting the commercial value of the accruing GMP liability for a scheme membership with a typical age distribution. Once again, discussions between the Government Actuary and actuaries from the private sector preceded the prescription of that reduction.

SERPS led to another surge in the growth of occupational pension schemes, not so much in their coverage of the working population (which had stabilized for a number of years at between 11 and 12 million, roughly half the workforce) as in the benefits provided. If their members were to be contracted out, those schemes which still provided pensions related to salary bands had to change them to a final-salary basis. (In theory, they could have followed the SERPS pattern by basing pensions on average career earnings, provided that each year's earnings were continuously revalued by the index of National Average Earnings, but few schemes found it convenient to take this route.) By 1979, 5.5 million active members of occupational schemes in the public sector and 4.8 million in the private sector had been contracted out of SERPS, with only 1.3 million not contracted out, nearly all of them in the private sector. Some four-fifths of members in that sector must therefore have belonged to final-salary schemes, compared with under a quarter in 1966.

NI pensions in payment, including those from SERPS, are uprated

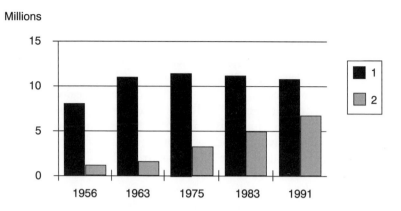

Figure 6.1 Pension scheme members (1) and beneficiaries (2) in Britain.
Source: compiled from Occupational Pension Schemes 1991 – ninth survey by the Government Actuary.

annually in line with increases in the Retail Prices Index (RPI). During the discussions on abatement, actuaries had argued that it would be unsound for schemes in the private sector to undertake to index any benefits that they were expected to provide to replace part of a State pension. The 1975 Act therefore left within SERPS the responsibility for indexing GMPs. However, partly as a result of the availability of index-linked gilts, but more particularly because of a change in attitudes, the private sector has now come to accept a liability for limited price indexation (LPI) of most pensions in payment – namely indexation by the RPI subject to a maximum. In line with this development, contracted-out schemes are required to give LPI at up to 3 per cent per annum to GMPs which accrued betweeen April 1988 and April 1997 when GMPs ceased to accrue, as did residual SERPS benefits for contracted-out employees; instead, salary-related schemes now have to provide pensions which, considered as a whole, are actuarially certified as being at least broadly equivalent to those under a so-called Reference Scheme.

Statutory protection

Until 1973, the only statutory body with responsibility for monitoring the rules and conduct of occupational pension schemes was the Superannuation Funds Office of the Inland Revenue, the main concerns of which were to ensure that, to obtain the permitted tax reliefs, a scheme's benefits would not exceed the limits for approval laid down by statute and that their funding was not excessive. The motivation was thus the protection of the Exchequer, not of the members. The yardstick for the maximum approvable benefits was (and always has been) the Civil Service scheme, although allowing the employer to provide a full two-thirds pension after only ten years (increased to 20 years in 1987).

A new chapter opened with the establishment under the Social Security Act 1973 of a complementary body, the Occupational Pensions Board (OPB), with a membership drawn from the public and private sectors, including representatives of both sides of industry and the various pensions interests, several of these being actuaries. The OPB was initially charged with overseeing a requirement, which took effect in April 1975, for an approved pension scheme to preserve the accrued pension of any member aged 26 or over who left the employer's service after at least five years' membership. Up to that time, most leavers had received no more than a refund of their own contributions. For example, of those in the private sector leaving in 1971 after five or more years of membership, 78 per cent had no pension preserved for them. In the public sector the proportion was even higher, at 87 per cent. In one sense, this was a deterrent to job mobility, for the retirement savings of most of those who did leave were destroyed, but it also provided a temptation for people who needed a lump sum for some other purpose to change their job so as to recover their own contributions. On both counts, it came to be perceived as against the public interest. The new requirement initially allowed employees to take a refund of contributions that they had paid before April 1975, in which case only the pension that had accrued after that date was preserved, but that concession was later withdrawn, and the period after which a pension had to be preserved was reduced to two years.

The OPB also had the wider responsibility of advising the Secretary of State on pension matters which he or she chose to refer to it, and over the next 20 years it produced a number of reports that directly or indirectly influenced the form of subsequent legislation on the equal treatment of men and women, and the protection of pensions and deferred pensions against inflation. The duties and responsibilities of trustees have been laid down in the Pensions Act 1995 – an Act which, incidentally, abolished the OPB and subsumed its function into the Occupational Pensions Regulatory Authority, which has been given wide-ranging powers to intervene in the running of occupational pension schemes. The main reason for trustees being given new powers and responsibilities was the scandal of the abstraction of investments from the pension funds controlled by the late Robert Maxwell, when it appeared that their trustees had little or no power in practice to prevent it.

The funding of occupational pensions

The object of funding the benefits of a pension scheme is to ensure, as far as possible, that when members come to retire the payment of their pensions will not be dependent on the continued existence of the employer, and that for the same reason there is security for the pension entitlements deemed to have accrued at any point of time for members who have not yet retired. From the employer's point of view, funding his obligations enables provision for their cost to be made as they accrue and not deferred until they fall due. He or she will usually prefer the cost to be a stable percentage of payroll. Techniques for achieving these objectives are within the province of the actuary.

In a money-purchase scheme, the employer pays a defined contribution for each employee, in addition to any contribution paid by the employee, and these contributions are invested either in the stock market or in insurance contracts. The proceeds are either directly attributed to individual members or are apportioned between them on an equitable basis, and must mainly be used at retirement to buy an annuity. The employer carries no unknown financial risk, unless he is dissatisfied with the resulting pensions and feels that he has to augment them.

In other schemes, the benefits and any employees' contributions are defined, and the employer is expected to meet the balance of the cost. Unless the amount of pension accruing each year is defined in terms of current rather than final salary and is purchased under an insurance contract (as was usually the case with the salary-banded schemes, which became obsolete in 1978) the cost to the employer in any one year is not capable of precise determination. Instead, views must be formed on how the scheme's liabilities are likely to develop in the future and at what speed they are to be funded by the payment and investment of contributions. The prospective liabilities are valued periodically by an actuary, who makes calculations that involve assumptions about the future of the membership: for example, how long pensions in payment can be expected to be payable (including continuation to a surviving spouse); when pensions preserved for former employees who have left service will come into payment; how many of the active members may be expected to remain in service until retirement and what their final salaries will be; how many will die in service or retire early and what benefits will be payable in those circumstances; how many will leave service early and what pensions will have to be preserved for them; and what allowance, if any, should be made for new entrants. The actuary bases his or her assumptions on information about the past experience of the scheme and on general knowledge of other comparable schemes. He or she then determines the present (discounted) value of the liabilities, using a suitable assumption about the rate of return that may be expected over the long term on the fund's existing and future investments.

The actuary must then calculate the contribution rate that he or she will recommend for the scheme until the next valuation. Until recently, with the exception of insured schemes, it was most usual for this rate to be determined as the percentage of pay which, if paid until retirement for existing active members, would have a discounted value equal to the present value of the benefits of all members (including pensioners and deferred pensioners), less the present value of the projected future proceeds of existing assets. Future new entrants were ignored. The contribution rate would include any contributions by members and the employer would pay the balance. This approach was known as 'aggregate funding'. Its disadvantage was that it provided no information about the relationship between the existing assets and the accrued liabilities of the scheme.

Since it has become a statutory requirement to demonstrate the security for those liabilities, it is nowadays usual for the actuary to look separately at benefits for past and future service. The present value of existing members' benefits, excluding those for future service, is compared with the present value of the proceeds of the invested assets, and if there is a shortfall the actuary may recommend a special contribution rate for a limited period to eliminate it. The future service benefits to be valued will allow for projected salary increases until retirement, and may either take account of service until pensionable age or limit it to a fixed number of years. Allowance may also be made for future new entrants. The present value of the relevant benefits is then compared with the value of a contribution of 1 per cent of the projected pensionable salaries of the members concerned, payable over the same timescale and on assumptions consistent with the benefits valued, and the recommended percentage contribution obtained by simple division. This approach is known as the 'projected unit' method. A similar approach (based on a fixed term) had been in use for some time for insured schemes, although initially using current rather than projected salaries.

Past generations of actuaries developed sophisticated techniques for estimating the future emerging liabilities of a pension fund. Progression up through salary scales was allowed for, and detailed assumptions were made about rates of mortality, early retirement and withdrawal from the employer's service. The benefits on withdrawal were usually limited to the return of the member's contributions, often without interest. Those techniques, adapted to fit modern conditions such as new legal requirements on the preservation and indexation of pension rights on withdrawal, continue to be used where lifetime career opportunities still exist, particularly in the public sector. However, where employment is less stable and salary scales – where they exist – are often less significant than inflationary or performance-related pay increases, it has become more usual to use a broader brush. For example, rather than specifying actual rates at which salaries and pensions in payment would be assumed to increase in the future, the actuary might express the assumptions, respectively, as x per cent per annum above price inflation and (if pensions were not expected to be fully indexed) y per cent below it. The assumed investment return would also be in real terms, and similarly the discounting rate of interest. However, if actual rates are assumed, what matters is not so much the rates themselves as the consistency of their relationship with an explicit inflation assumption.

If the assets of the scheme are held in the form of insurance contracts, the contributions may be payable as premiums under a with-profits group pension policy and be allocated, net of an expense charge but augmented by bonuses, to secure outright the prospective pension entitlements of the oldest active members, based on their present salaries. Alternatively, they may remain unallocated in a pool which is increased by guaranteed interest and also by bonuses, and is drawn on as necessary to buy annuities for members as they retire. Variations on this theme include 'deposit administration', in which any non-guaranteed additions are entirely at the insurer's discretion but are usually related to its profits, and 'managed funds', in which premiums are translated into units of a pooled fund of assets operated by the insurance company. In effect, these various contracts constitute different forms of investment by the trustees; the actuary will allow for them in his or her valuation but, as in the case of other investments, there is no absolute guarantee that they will always be sufficient to secure the accrued liabilities of the scheme. Exceptions are where trustees choose to insure lump sums or widows' and dependants' pensions that are payable on the death of a member while still in service, or to purchase annuities at retirement, or where an employer sets up a disability income scheme and insures the benefits under a group permanent health insurance policy: in these cases, payment of the agreed benefits is guaranteed.

Because of the increasing emphasis that legislation has been placing on the security not only of pensions in payment but also preserved pensions and the accrued (past service) benefits of serving members, the determination and certification of the degree of security have become an essential part of the actuarial valuation of a pension fund. If there is too little security (the result, perhaps, of actuarial funding assumptions that have not been fulfilled in practice), the Pensions Act 1995 will require the employer to take steps to improve it; if there is too much (because the actuary's assumptions have proved too conservative, perhaps especially in relation to the rate of investment return), the Inland Revenue will require the employer to reduce it by improving benefits, suspending contributions or, as a last resort, receiving a cash refund from the trustees (from which tax would have to be deducted).

A keystone of the 1995 Act is that every scheme that needs to be actuarially funded must have a designated scheme actuary, appointed by the trustees. If the scheme is privately administered, they will usually choose an actuary from a firm of consultants, but if it is operated by an insurance company, an actuary employed by that company is more likely to be appointed. As recently as 20 years ago, the Institute of Actuaries would not accept that an employed actuary could give advice direct to a client of his employer; he was limited to giving his employer advice on how the client's scheme should be funded, and the employer could then pass this on to the client either directly or through a third party as, in effect, advice of its own. Later, it was realized that this could leave the actuary open to pressure from his employer on his choice of assumptions, and that it was also an invitation to those passing on his advice to put a gloss on it that could seriously weaken its impact. It therefore became a requirement for an employed actuary to address funding advice directly to his employer's client and to take personal professional responsibility for its quality, in the same way as an actuary who is self-employed.

Guidance on the form and content of actuarial funding reports was first issued by the Institute and Faculty in 1984 and has been revised on several occasions since then. It also covers the actuarial statement that has to be issued to members with the trustees' annual report, in accordance with statutory regulations introduced in 1986. These regulations require the actuary who last carried out a valuation of the assets and liabilities to summarize the methods and assumptions used in the valuation, and to express an opinion on the security of both the accrued and prospective rights of the members.

Apart from making the appointment of a scheme actuary the responsibility of the trustees, the 1995 Act introduced a requirement for the actuary to monitor the security for accrued rights against a minimum funding requirement (MFR), which is calculated on a statutory basis laid down after consultations between the Government Actuary's Department and the Institute and Faculty. The idea is that if the accrued rights are at least 100 per cent funded as measured by the MFR, pensioners can expect their pension entitlements to be met in full if the scheme is discontinued, while other members can expect to be able to transfer the cash equivalent of their rights to another scheme or to a Personal Pension arrangement.

Surpluses and deficiencies

When he or she values the assets and accrued liabilities, the actuary seldom finds that they are exactly equal. If the difference is small he or she may choose to ignore it, but if there is a substantial deficiency of assets the trustees will be advised on how it should be eliminated. The situation most likely to give rise to a deficiency is when investment growth is lower in relation to the growth in members' earnings than was assumed in the previous valuation. The high inflation of the 1970s and 1980s created such a situation for many funds, and substantial additional contributions had to be made by the employers concerned. Conversely, when the relative investment growth is higher than assumed, the surplus may be large enough for some action to be needed to reduce or contain it; for example, by improving the benefits of some or all classes of members and allowing the employer to suspend contributions until the next valuation. In such a situation, the advice of the actuary is essential in helping the employer and the trustees to decide what to do, bearing in mind the duty of trustees to act fairly as between different groups of beneficiaries.

The assumptions used by the actuary for valuing the assets and liabilities are usually chosen so as to avoid sudden fluctuations between successive valuations, such as would result, for example, from taking assets at market value. The approach is essentially that of a going concern. However, as already mentioned, in his or her role as scheme actuary under the 1995 Act it will also be necessary to monitor the minimum funding requirement, which is concerned with the position on the immediate discontinuance of the scheme. If on that basis there is a deficiency, the employer will have five years to eliminate it – unless it exceeds 10 per cent, in which case the shortfall must normally be made good within 12 months. This provision of the Act will not take full effect until 2002, and it remains to be seen whether it will create pressure on actuaries to change their customary approach to valuation and align it more closely with the MFR basis.

Investments and the matching of assets and liabilities

Before the Second World War, the assets of most pension funds and insurance companies were dominated by fixed-interest securities. A few were prepared to be more adventurous, and invested in ordinary shares in the belief that they would obtain a higher rate of return, although many pension funds were precluded from doing so by the terms of their trust deeds.

Such a strategy is not well suited to the liabilities of final-salary schemes, and this became more widely recognized as inflation began to accelerate in the 1950s. The investment manager of one of the largest funds in the private sector, G. H. Ross Goobey – an actuary – persuaded his trustees to invest heavily in ordinary shares because he believed that they would protect the fund against the inflation of its liabilities and were therefore a more appropriate investment than fixed-interest securities. His policy proved successful, and he became a powerful public advocate of what became known as the cult of the equity. Property also came to be recognized as a suitable investment of pension funds, for much the same reason, although it is less highly regarded by most funds nowadays. In 1997, four-fifths of the market value of the assets of the average non-insured pension fund is represented by ordinary shares (a quarter of them overseas); most of the rest is in fixed-interest securities and only a tiny proportion is still in property.

In recent years, the management of pension fund investments has become an area of keen competition between financial institutions, resulting in trustees' attention being focused on their professional managers' comparative performance, often with too much emphasis on the short term. The Financial Services Act 1986 requires investment management to be regulated and limited to people with requisite qualifications, so it is no longer the province of the trustees or the employer. However, the Pensions Act 1995 placed the responsibility on the trustees for choosing and appointing an investment manager, and for establishing and publishing to the members a statement of investment principles after consulting the employer. They must obtain expert advice about those principles, and should be expected to look to the scheme actuary for advice on whether, because of the present nature of the liabilities or expected future trends, any special constraints need to be placed on the balance of the portfolio between different types of investment. For example, if a scheme has few active members but many pensioners, and does not have a comfortable surplus of assets, it may need to increase its proportion of fixed-interest investments to reduce the risk of failure to meet the MFR in the event of a fall in the equity market. Continuing research is being undertaken by actuaries into methods of modelling the behaviour of the assets and liabilities of a pension fund in different future scenarios.

Personal Pensions

From 1988, the Social Security Act 1986 prohibited employers from making the membership of an occupational pension scheme a condition of either initial or continuing employment. In the same year, the Income and Corporation Taxes Act facilitated the development of a so-called Personal Pension. This replaced the retirement annuity that had been available to the self-employed and those in non-pensionable employment since 1956, although based on similar principles. Contributions to such a pension can be made by anyone under the age of 75 with taxable income from self-employment or from a source of earnings which, with one important exception, must be non-pensionable. The exception is where an employee, although a member of an occupational pension scheme, is not contracted-out of SERPS. In that case, the employee may arrange to contract him- or herself out by effecting what is known as an Appropriate Personal Pension (APP). The Department of Social Security is then required to pay into the APP the rebate of NI contributions that would have been obtained by the employee and employer combined had the occupational scheme been contracted out. This was initially augmented by a 2 per cent 'sweetener', which was reduced to 1 per cent in 1993 and limited to contributors aged 30 and over. (The same basis of contracting-out was also made available in 1988 to pension funds based on defined contributions and providing money-purchase benefits.)

A Personal Pension can be set up under an irrevocable trust or under an insurance contract and, like a money-purchase scheme, the benefits are what can be secured by the investment of an individual's contributions. There are restrictions on how and when the benefits can be taken, and those arising from an APP are called protected rights pensions (PRP); these annuities must be given limited price indexation (initially with a maximum of 3 per cent a year, increased to 5 per cent for funds built up after 1997) and must normally continue at half-rate to a surviving spouse. Their pricing must be independent of the sex and marital status of the purchaser.

The government actively promoted Personal Pensions and they were widely sold by insurance companies and intermediaries, often by persuading members or prospective members of occupational schemes to opt out or, in the case of early leavers, to take the transfer value of a preserved pension and invest it in a Personal Pension. In many cases, such sales conflicted with the requirement under the Financial Services Act for best advice to be given; for example, insufficient attention may have been paid to the fact that the replacement Personal Pension arrangement would not attract any contributions from the employer. Again, in the case of an APP the contracting-out terms looked attractive to younger employees, but they were not always warned that, because of expense charges, failure to maintain a policy in force could result in the accrued PRP being less than the SERPS pension given up. At the time of writing, the problem of identifying and compensating those who have been mis-sold Personal Pensions is proving difficult to solve. Determining the amount of compensation, and in particular agreeing with the trustees of an occupational scheme the terms on which an employee can be re-admitted and put in the same position as if he or she had never opted out, is necessitating much work for the actuaries of the insurance companies involved and for scheme actuaries as well.

The drift towards money-purchase

Final-salary pension schemes were originally designed to reward employees with long service by awarding them pensions related to their standard of living immediately before retirement. They suffer from two disadvantages. The first is that the cost to the employer is uncertain; as we have seen, assumptions must be made about future earnings and investment returns, and in changing financial conditions these can prove to be wide of the mark. The other is that employees who change their jobs usually find that only their service with their final employer qualifies for a pension related to their final pay; pensions for earlier periods of service are preserved in terms of their final earnings with the employers in question. This is likely to remain so even if the value of a preserved pension is transferred into a new employer's scheme. Over the years since 1986, legislation has increasingly required preserved pensions to be revalued up to retirement age in line with the retail price index, with a maximum of 5 per cent per annum compound, but the difference between earnings on leaving one employer, revalued in that way, and earnings on retirement from another employer remains uncovered.

With the breakdown of the concept of a job for life, even in what used to be the safest of employments, and the growth of short-term contracts, many employers are now reviewing whether it is still appropriate to run a final-salary scheme. The changes resulting from the Pensions Act 1995, including the transfer of more power from the employer to the trustees, have increased the attractions to employers of Personal Pension arrangements; the alternative is a money-purchase scheme. In either event (assuming that the employer chooses to contribute towards Personal Pensions), the employer's cost is known, and at the end of a contract an employee will receive the full value of his or her own and the employer's contributions, whereas under a final-salary scheme the benefits that accrue and are funded by what appears to be a uniform contribution rate are actually worth considerably less for a young employee and much more for one nearing retirement.

The trouble is that few people joining a money-purchase scheme or taking out a Personal Pension realize how large a contribution is needed to provide, at the age of 65, a pension of the order of half or two-thirds of final salary, with protection against inflation and a half-pension continuing to a surviving spouse or other dependant. In broad terms, contributions not far short of 15 per cent of earnings, payable for 40 years, would be needed to produce a pension likely to be in that range, although even these would probably be insufficient to cover substantial pay increases close to retirement. Far too many of today's Personal Pension arrangements are limited to investing the very modest rebates available from the DSS for contracting out of SERPS.

The guiding role of the actuarial profession

Actuaries have in the past sounded warnings about the consequences in 25 or 50 years' time if the working generation tried to secure for itself too great a share of the next generation's production. Their anxiety was not limited to earnings-related increases in State pensions which would have to be met on a 'pay-as-you-go' basis by higher contributions from a future working generation. Promises of more generous occupational pensions could also be detrimental to future generations if they resulted in a net cash flow of savings (from an excess of contributions and investment income over pension payments and other outgo) that was greater than was consistent with the economy's demand for new capital. In that case, there would be compensating dis-saving elsewhere as pension funds bought an increasing proportion of the nation's existing financial assets as security for their liabilities to members. In 1997, however, an actuary looking in his crystal ball might have different worries. Seeing the steady erosion of State pensions relative to current earnings, and forecasting a continuing trend away from the high contributions associated with final-salary occupational pension funds, he would be justified in warning of an increasing risk of people retiring in the second quarter of the twenty-first century with seriously inadequate incomes. Steering a course between these extremes is now seriously exercising the minds of politicians as well as actuaries.

Occupational pension schemes are nowadays one of the principal fields for the provision of actuarial advice. The explosive growth in the number of private-sector schemes in the second half of the twentieth century is partially reflected in the number of Fellows of the Institute engaged in private consulting practice in the UK. In 1955, there were 32 (6 per cent of all active Fellows); in 1996, the figure had reached 1116 (42 per cent). Of course, many are involved in different fields of work but, on the other hand, the number of Fellows employed by insurance companies has trebled in the same period, and much of this increase is also to do with the growth of pensions.

The statutory responsibilities now conferred on the scheme actuary (which include reporting to the Occupational Pensions Regulatory Authority any material failure of duty by the scheme's administrators) recognize the major role that the profession has played in the development of soundly funded occupational pension schemes. As with the Appointed Actuary of a life assurance company, whose role has served as a model, a scheme actuary has to possess a practising certificate issued by his professional body.

However, the profession's responsibilities in the pensions field do not end with the scheme actuary. With the attitude of both the State and employers towards pensions being in a state of flux yet again, it must be prepared to give voice to its unique experience and authority in the structural debates that clearly lie ahead.

Further reading

For reference to the work of F. M. Redington, see Chamberlin (1986).

Bacon, F. W., Elphinstone, M. D. W. and Benjamin, B. 1954: The growth of pension rights and their impact on the national economy. *Journal of the Institute of Actuaries*, 80, 141–288.

Chamberlin, G. (ed.) 1986: *A Ramble through the Actuarial Countryside: the Collected Papers, Essays and Speeches of Frank Mitchell Redington, M.A.* London.

Colbran, R. B. 1982: Valuation of final-salary pension schemes. *Journal of the Institute of Actuaries*, 109, 359–416.

Crabbe, R. J. W. and Poyser, C. A. 1966: *Pensions and Widows' and Orphans' Funds*. Cambridge.

Day, J. G. and McKelvey, K. M. 1964: The treatment of assets in the actuarial valuation of a pension fund. *Journal of the Institute of Actuaries*, 90, 104–47.

Dyson, A. C. L. and Exley, C. J. 1995: Pension fund asset valuation and investment. *British Actuarial Journal*, 1, 471–557.

Fellows, D. E. 1973: Insured group pension plans and ancillary benefits. *Journal of the Institute of Actuaries*, 99, 19–67.

Government Actuary 1956–94: *Occupational Pension Schemes Surveys*. London.

Greenwood, P. M. and Keogh, T. W. 1997: Pension funding and expensing in the minimum funding requirement environment. *British Actuarial Journal*, 3, 469–582.

Hannah, L. 1986: *Inventing Retirement: the development of occupational pensions in Britain.* Cambridge.

Heywood, G. and Lander, M. 1961: Pension fund valuations in modern conditions. *Journal of the Institute of Actuaries,* 87, 314–70.

Humphrey, G. T., Langham, F. R., Snelson, R. E. and Sparks, J. D. 1970: Pensions and company finance. *Journal of the Institute of Actuaries,* 96, 189–249.

Johnston, E. A. 1982: The comparative value of pensions. *Journal of the Institute of Actuaries,* 109, 1–38.

Lee, E. M. 1986: *An Introduction to Pension Funds.* London.

Lyon, C. S. S. 1968: Social security and occupational pension schemes. *Journal of the Institute of Actuaries,* 94, 173–253.

Lyon, C. S. S. 1983: Presidential address: the outlook for pensioning. *Journal of the Institute of Actuaries,* 110, 1–15.

Marples, W. F. 1947: An analysis of a pension fund. *Journal of the Institute of Actuaries,* 73, 66–98.

McLeish, D. J. D. and Stewart, C. M. 1987: Objectives and methods of funding defined benefit pension schemes. *Journal of the Institute of Actuaries,* 114, 155–225.

Pingstone, G. W. 1951: Group life and pension schemes including group family income benefits. *Journal of the Institute of Actuaries,* 77, 335–81.

Rhodes, G. 1965: *Public Sector Pensions.* London.

Robb, A. C. 1950: The development of public superannuation schemes. *Journal of the Institute of Actuaries,* 76, 3–37.

Thornton, P. N. and Wilson, A. F. 1992: A realistic approach to pension funding. *Journal of the Institute of Actuaries,* 119, 229–312.

Wise, A. J. 1984: The matching of assets to liabilities. *Journal of the Institute of Actuaries,* 111, 445–501.

Occupational Pensions Board Reports (HMSO, London)

1976: *Equal Status for Men and Women in Occupational Pension Schemes.*

1981: *Improved Protection for the Occupational Pension Rights and Expectations of Early Leavers.*

1982: *Greater Security for the Rights and Expectations of Members of Occupational Pension Schemes.*

1989: *Protecting Pensions – Safeguarding Benefits in a Changing Environment*

Social security and demography

Colin Stewart

A hundred years ago, those who were destitute ended up in miserable conditions in the parish workhouse. Since then, governments have introduced schemes to provide financial support for the elderly, the disabled, widows and orphans and others who were unable to support themselves. Some of the benefits were subject to a means test; others were 'as of right' after contributions paid during working life. For both, the government had the use of financial estimates and other professional advice from actuaries. Since 1919, this support has been available 'in-house' from the members of the Government Actuary's Department.

In 1948, a single comprehensive social security scheme was introduced, covering virtually the whole population of the UK. The contributions charged corresponded (on an actuarial basis) to the cost of benefits to be received by new entrants to the scheme, but this income was needed to meet benefits already in payment, so no funds were built up. In addition to the National Insurance Scheme, the National Health Service was introduced, providing a free medical service, including hospital care. People are now living for much longer than they used to, so that the costs of State pensions and of caring for the elderly are becoming unacceptably high.

Living in dread of the workhouse

In the middle of the nineteenth century, provision by the State for those in need had changed little in 300 years. It took the form of the relief of destitution when it arose rather than its prevention by, for example, promoting savings during working life. Although the system was governed by the Poor Law Acts promulgated by the central government, relief of poverty was seen as the responsibility of the local community, so the system was administered locally and the costs met by taxes assessed and collected locally. 'Outdoor relief' was given in the form of subsidy to those who had homes to live in, and 'indoor relief' in the form of accommodation in an institutional workhouse, where those who were able-bodied were given work to do, as a contribution towards the community that was supporting them.

The aim was to provide conditions rather less favourable than the situation of the lowest class of labourer in work. Incarceration in a workhouse did nothing to restore comfort or self-respect to the victims of poverty, and those on the borderline of poverty lived in dread of it. A hopeful trend was the growing network of friendly societies, run by and for working-class people, which enabled members – and their families – to escape the miseries of the workhouse by providing benefits during sickness, disability and on death. In the 1850s, approximately one-half of men and women over the age of 65 were in receipt of Poor Law relief, of whom some 10–15 per cent were in institutions.

Canon Blackley's proposal for compulsory insurance

Dissatisfaction with the Poor Law was growing. The best known of those proposing reforms was the Reverend Canon William L. Blackley, a strenuous advocate of replacing the Poor Law by a scheme of compulsory insurance that would provide benefits during sickness and in old age. From his observation of the amount of money spent by young persons on drink and tobacco, he had concluded that the great mass of the population were able to provide for themselves. Moreover, he believed that, in principle, compulsory insurance for all was preferable to compulsory taxation of the thrifty to meet the cost of Poor Law relief for those who, for whatever reason, had not made provision for themselves voluntarily.

In 1879, Canon Blackley proposed that every man and woman between the ages of 18 and 21 should be required to pay a total sum of £10 into a national fund, in return for which 8s. a week benefit would be paid during sickness and 4s. a week pension from age 70. A young married woman's husband would be responsible for paying her contributions. Although it was not remarked upon at the time, this would have resulted in a married woman being entitled to benefit in her own right rather than as a dependant of her husband. An actuarial basis was claimed for the £10 contribution rate, but it seems that this figure was based on a figure of £15 used by friendly societies, reduced to £10 by assuming a higher rate of interest than was generally adopted in friendly society valuations, to reflect a presumption that the national fund would be able to invest in higher-yielding mortgages and public loans. There was considerable public support for the kind of scheme proposed by Canon Blackley, but there was opposition from the friendly societies, which doubted the adequacy of the £10 contribution rate proposed and feared that their own schemes would be damaged by the introduction of a compulsory national scheme.

A Parliamentary Select Committee was set up 'to inquire into the best system of National Provident Insurance against Pauperism'. Although a number of schemes were submitted to the committee, the evidence always tended to revert to Canon Blackley's scheme, which was the one that had attracted the most public attention. While giving evidence, a number of prominent actuaries cast severe doubts on the likelihood that a £10 contribution would be adequate to meet the benefits promised, principally because they did not believe that the incidence of claims for sickness benefit from a remote compulsory national scheme would be as low as in a voluntary scheme run by the members themselves locally. Although the figure of £10 purported to have been arrived at by an actuarial calculation, the result was not endorsed by members of the actuarial profession. The committee reported in August 1887, advising against the introduction of a compulsory national scheme. They had concluded that the attendant actuarial and administrative difficulties would be too great and that many people would be unable, or unwilling, to pay the necessary contribution rate.

Consideration of the German system

Actuaries in the UK were aware of developments elsewhere in Europe; in particular, the 1889 German Law of Insurance against Invalidity and Old Age, which followed Sickness and Accident Insurance Laws introduced a few years earlier, and provided compulsory insurance covering the whole of the wage-earning classes.

It was common knowledge that Prince Bismarck was hostile to the capitalist system, and that the new law reflected his determination that the State should monopolize the entire system of insurance and divert it from private enterprises which, in his view, were exploiting the misfortunes of the labouring population. However, that view was not shared in the UK, so it was not surprising that there was widespread opposition to the introduction of a similar regime here, although it was noted that a number of other countries were already following the German example.

Doubts were expressed concerning the reliability of some of the assumptions on which the estimated costs of the German scheme had been based. However, the method used for calculating the contribution rates to be paid by insured persons and their employers to meet their two-thirds share of the costs of the scheme was one familiar to actuaries. The combined contributions paid during the working lifetime of insured persons would exceed their share of the expenditure on benefits in the early years, so that large funds would be built up. Ultimately, the interest on these funds would be sufficient to meet the expected excess of expenditure over contribution income. There was, however, criticism of the fact that the State would be paying one-third of the cost and, in particular, that this would take the form of subsidising benefits only when they came into payment, with no advance funding during working lifetime. Estimates of income, expenditure and of the funds likely to be built up over a period of 80 years had been before the German Parliament when the new law was being considered, so it cannot be said that the decision to introduce the scheme was taken without attention being drawn to the long-term financial implications. These estimates showed that the State subsidy could be expected to increase from the equivalent of £200 000 in the first year to £4 million in the 80th year, but it was clear that the new scheme would make little call on the German government's own resources for many years.

The general view of actuaries in the UK concerning the German scheme was similar to the opinions held earlier on Canon Blackley's scheme. They thought it preferable to continue with the encouragement of voluntary arrangements, and did not think that a compulsory national scheme similar to that in Germany would be acceptable or appropriate in the UK. It was nevertheless recognized that, as a profession, actuaries should keep an open mind on the subject. The nation had derived considerable benefit from the gradual development of friendly societies and other institutions that fostered thrift, and it was possible that, without disturbing that development, a democratic government might be able to build on that foundation and create nation-wide arrangements to the common good. Actuaries should therefore stand ready to offer their unbiased advice on whatever scheme might in due course find favour politically.

Public debate on introducing social security in the UK

Public debate continued on the kind of scheme that might be suitable in the UK, including a 'Committee of Experts' set up by the government in 1896. The experts included three actuaries, who were thus able to exert a greater influence on the committee's deliberations than they could have done as witnesses. The committee's remit was to consider schemes 'for encouraging the industrial population, by State Aid or otherwise, to make provision for old age'. This wording was taken to preclude consideration of schemes that would have been compulsory or to which working people themselves did not contribute.

The UK entered the twentieth century intent on improving the arrangements for the relief of poverty, particularly in old age, but still undecided as to how to set about it. Although the condition of the working classes had improved significantly, there was still a pressing need for change. The proportion of the population over age 65 in receipt of Poor Law relief had fallen to about one-quarter, but there were still about 200 000 elderly persons in institutions. Efforts might have been made to help them directly, by improving the conditions in institutions, but the preferred solution was the elimination of poverty by providing pensions for the elderly. The problem was that any scheme involving compulsory contributions was thought to be unacceptable; any pension scheme paid for wholly by the State was thought to be too costly; and any scheme in which a State subsidy was offered to those willing to contribute to friendly societies or similar bodies would be inadequate, since the Poor Law would have to remain in force to sustain others who had not made their own provision. It was recognized that those on very low incomes would have difficulty in paying even a modest rate of contribution and there would, moreover, always be some whose poverty was attributable to a craving for drink or some other inadequacy, and who would therefore be more in need of care than cash.

Although much emphasis was placed on the needs of the elderly, it was suggested by some actuaries that the priority should be to safeguard those of working age against loss of income following the death, incapacity or unemployment of the breadwinner. Provision of widows' and orphans' benefits was seen as a field that the State might usefully enter without encroaching upon the domain of the existing providers of such benefits. A national scheme providing benefits on incapacity resulting from sickness, injury or disablement would clearly have encroached upon the activities of the friendly societies to a significant extent, but it was envisaged that the existing societies might provide the framework for the collection of contributions and payment of benefits for a compulsory national scheme.

Means-tested Old Age Pensions from age 70

In the event, priority was given to the elderly. The Old Age Pensions Act 1908 provided for the payment of a pension of 5s. a week to all men and women aged 70 and over, subject only to their income from other sources not exceeding a specified amount. However, the means test was much less severe than under the Poor Law so that, in the event, over 600 000 pensions were awarded under the Act. It was suggested that those under age 65 should be required to contribute in advance for their pensions, with the State meeting part of the cost for those above age 40 whose contribution rates would otherwise have been excessive. Since no projections of cost were provided in support of this suggestion, estimates were published later by actuaries indicating the likely magnitude of the State subsidy in the longer term and the build-up of funds. Consideration was also given to the dangers of accumulating very large funds in the hands of a single investor – the State – whose activities would inevitably have a profound influence on the money markets.

Sickness and unemployment benefits up to age 70

The National Insurance Act 1911 provided for sickness and unemployment benefits up to age 70. It provided benefits on incapacity resulting from sickness, accident and disablement, for free medical and sanatorium benefits, and for a lump sum maternity benefit. All employees other than better-paid non-manual workers were required to join. It also provided for unemployment benefits for manual workers in certain industries known to be subject to severe and recurrent unemployment. For the administration of the health insurance scheme, the co-operation of the friendly societies was obtained. Most of the existing societies were persuaded to set up separate sections to deal with the national scheme and, in consequence, its administration was shared by several thousand units known as 'Approved Societies'. Sickness benefit was 10s. a week for men and 7s. 6d. for women for up to six months, followed by 5s. a week disablement benefit, the same rate as the pension payable from age 70 under the 1908 Act.

The financial arrangements were very complicated. The contribution rates paid by insured men and women and their employers were calculated as the rates that would have been sufficient to secure the benefits and pay the costs of administration for 16-year-old entrants. However, these rates were insufficient for all those entering at higher ages at the outset, so the Approved Societies started off with substantial unfunded liabilities. The State therefore undertook to meet two-ninths of the annual expenditure on benefits and administration as it arose, so that only seven-ninths of the joint contributions was required to fund the remainder. The other two-ninths was to be applied towards eliminating the initial unfunded liability over a period of about 20 years. The end result would be that the total liabilities of Approved Societies would be seven-ninths fully funded, with the remainder of the cost being met by the State on a 'pay as you go' basis.

The formation of the Government Actuary's Department

In order to illustrate the financial implications of the proposals in the Bill, the Treasury commissioned an actuarial report on the health insurance provisions and the Board of Trade an actuarial report on the unemployment provisions. Revised actuarial reports were later submitted by the same actuaries to accommodate changes made to the Bill in Committee. A further six actuarial reports examined other questions that arose during passage of the Bill, so that no fewer than ten actuarial reports were prepared informing Parliament about the financial implications of the provisions that they had under consideration. It was perhaps not surprising that, shortly afterwards, an actuary, Alfred Watson, was appointed to the position of Chief Actuary to the National Health Insurance Joint Committee. The financial arrangements for the new Health Insurance Scheme were complicated and the committee felt that there would be a continuing role for actuaries in government, in valuing the Approved Societies and ensuring the satisfactory conduct of the business. Watson soon found himself being consulted by other government departments on a variety of matters of an actuarial nature and, in 1917, he was given the title of Government Actuary, in recognition of his broadening responsibilities. In 1919, the Treasury took matters a stage further by announcing the creation of the Government Actuary's Department (GAD) and notifying all government departments that, in future, all actuarial questions on which they might require advice should be referred to the GAD. Accordingly, when amendments were made in 1920 to the unemployment and national health insurance schemes, both Bills presented to Parliament were accompanied by reports of the Government Actuary on the financial implications.

Contributory pensions from age 65 and widows' pensions

Although it had been suggested that priority should be given to the needs of widows and orphans, it was not until 1925 that provision for them was included in the Widows', Orphans' and Old Age Contributory Pensions Act. The means-tested Old Age Pension payable from age 70 under the 1908 Act had been doubled in 1920. Under the 1925 Act, a pension of 10s. a week from age 65 or subsequently on retirement would be payable as of right to all those who had contributed to the new scheme, to married women over age 65 who had not contributed but whose husbands were

Figure 7.1 Sir Alfred Watson, the first modern Government Actuary.

receiving pensions, and to widows whose husbands had contributed. All those contributing to the Health Insurance Scheme would also be required to contribute to the new pension scheme, and provision was also made for voluntary contributors to join. Curiously, the pension was described as being payable from age 65 to age 70, but continuing after age 70 without a means test to those then receiving pensions. When the Bill was presented to Parliament it was accompanied by a detailed report by the Government Actuary on the financial provisions.

Separation of the pension into two parts, before and after age 70, was also reflected in the contribution rates. The weekly contribution to be paid by insured men and their employers (in equal shares) was calculated on an actuarial basis as the rate that would be required in respect of a new entrant to the scheme at age 16 in order to meet the cost of the benefits to be received by him and his wife or widow up to age 70, assuming, as in the case of the National Health Insurance Scheme, the accumulation of a fund from the contributions paid during working life. However, choosing an appropriate contribution rate for insured women took some thought. Most women would pay contributions for only a few years before marriage and, if all those contributions were to be applied for the benefit of the minority who remained unmarried until retirement, the women's contribution rate would have been very small indeed. It was therefore decided by the government that women should pay half the men's rate, with the result that the contributions of those who gave up work on marriage would be available to meet part of the cost of the benefits that they would receive later as widows or pensioners' wives.

Provision was made in the Act for contribution rates to be increased in 1936, in 1946 and again in 1956. The effect of these increases was that the contributions paid by and in respect of entrants at age 16 in 1926 would, after all, be sufficient to pay for about one-fifth of the pensions which they and their wives would receive after age 70, this percentage increasing progressively for later entrants, until the contributions for those entering at age 16 from 1956 onwards would pay for the whole cost of their pensions throughout life. However, pensions were awarded immediately to many existing widows and persons over the pensionable age, in respect of whom no contributions whatever had been paid. As a consequence, as fast as the contributions were received, they were paid out again to those already entitled to benefit, and a subsidy from the Exchequer was needed in order to keep the account in balance. In the 30 years to 1956, expenditure under the new pension scheme was expected to grow rapidly, and only part of this would be covered by the increasing contributions of insured persons and their employers. The Exchequer subsidy would have to increase as well. However, in the same period, the cost to the Exchequer of paying War Pensions and means-tested Old Age Pensions would be declining, and the net result would be that the total charge upon the Exchequer would remain fairly level.

The Government Actuary's report explained why the income from contributions and from the Exchequer would have to rise significantly in the first 30 years of the new scheme. The principal cause lay many years in the past. The number of births each year had increased steadily throughout the nineteenth century, but had then levelled off. As a consequence, the numbers reaching pensionable age or becoming widows would increase steadily between 1926 and 1956, whereas the numbers leaving school and becoming contributors would show relatively little increase over the same period. If each cohort of new entrants to the scheme had paid a sufficient contribution and those contributions had been put to reserve to meet the accruing pension liabilities, it would not have mattered how few or how many new entrants there had been, as each cohort's benefits would have been properly secured by their own contributions. However, when the cost of pensions has to be met from the contributions currently paid by a younger generation of contributors, the relative numbers in the two generations matter very much indeed. This does not mean that even higher contributions should have been paid and large funds built up. It was concluded that no advantage would be gained by building up a large fund, most likely invested wholly in stocks issued by the government, over the government simply acting directly as guarantor of the scheme in the long term.

Unequal treatment of men and women in National Insurance

In 1940, the pensionable age for women was reduced from 65 to 60. Labour interests had been pressing for some time for a reduction in pensionable ages generally, to alleviate unemployment. Also, many thought it unreasonable that married men, whose wives were usually a few years younger than themselves, had to support two people on a single pension until their wives too reached age 65 and were awarded their own pensions. Spinsters' pressure groups were also arguing that working women had two jobs – one in the home and one in employment – and that they therefore deserved to retire earlier. It is said that those arguments won the day in 1940 only because of the immediate need of the Coalition government to offer a sweetener to Labour for supporting the war effort. As we now know, it has proved very difficult to undo this unequal treatment of the sexes. In the State scheme, it will not be until the year 2020 that the women's pensionable age will be brought back into line with that for men. However, recent decisions of the European Court have not afforded funded occupational pension schemes the same luxury of a leisurely restoration of equal treatment of the two sexes. The transitional arrangements for the State and occupational schemes are thus out of line and, given the interaction between the two, this has produced a situation of considerable complexity.

The Beveridge Plan: State support 'from the cradle to the grave'

There was now in place a variety of schemes dealing with different aspects of social security, developed at different times on largely independent lines. During the Second World War, thought was being given to the problems of reconstruction after the cessation of hostilities, and one aspect of this was the need to rationalize the social security provisions. To that end, a committee set up in June 1941 under the chairmanship of Sir William Beveridge was asked to 'undertake, with special reference to the inter-relation of the schemes, a survey of the existing national schemes of social insurance and allied services, including workmen's compensation, and to make recommendations'. His committee was composed of senior civil servants in those government departments concerned with the existing schemes, including the Government Actuary, who would act in the role of advisers and assessors, Beveridge alone being responsible for the recommendations. The Beveridge Report, including a detailed memorandum by the Government Actuary on its financial aspects, was presented at the end of 1942 and, with a few modifications, formed the basis of the comprehensive social security scheme introduced after the war.

The three existing schemes, with some additions, were amalgamated in 1948 to form a single National Insurance scheme, and extended so as to include virtually the whole population over school-leaving age, including the self-employed and those who were not gainfully occupied. Only those with incomes below £75 a year could choose whether or not to contribute. The standard rate of benefit for insured persons of both sexes, and for widows, was 26s. a week, a large increase from the previous rate of 10s. a week. Calculation of the contribution rates for men and women followed the previous practice of assessing, on an actuarial basis, the rates that would have been sufficient for an entrant at age 16 in a fully funded scheme. However, on this occasion, instead of the women's rate being set arbitrarily at half the men's rate, it was calculated as the rate that would be appropriate for the benefits to be received by a woman who was insured throughout her working lifetime. This produced weekly contribution rates of 10s. 6d. for employed men and 8s. 2d. for employed women. The Exchequer paid about one-fifth of the total contribution and the employee and employer shared the other four-fifths. Lower total rates

Table 7.1 The National Insurance fund (figures in £million).

	1948	1978
Outgo		
Benefits and administration	454	752
Income		
Interest on fund	21	21
Contributions		
Insured and employers	315	314
Exchequer	83	79
Exchequer grant (to balance)	35	338

were paid by the self-employed and non-employed because they did not qualify for the full range of benefits.

The combined funds of the merged schemes amounted to little more than a working balance, so the investment income fell a long way short of making up the difference between contribution income and benefit outgo. The Exchequer was therefore obliged to make additional grants in order to keep the account in balance. The Government Actuary's estimates made at the outset of the new scheme showed that the amount of these grants could be expected to increase substantially in the ensuing 30 years, as shown in table 7.1.

A new Industrial Injuries Scheme was set up to replace the existing statutory Workmen's Compensation Scheme, under which employers had been required to insure their employees against loss of earnings from accidents at work. The new scheme provided benefits related to loss of faculty, as distinct from loss of earnings. Once the residual degree of disability resulting from an accident at work was known, the benefit awarded would reflect the degree of disablement. This would be a cash sum for less than 20 per cent disablement and a pension in other cases. In the case of lung diseases, the degree of disability does not become settled but increases remorselessly, ending ultimately in death. Although actuarial techniques were well able to deal with benefits of both kinds, and a certain amount of information was available about the incidence of injuries and diseases from the operation of the superseded Workmens' Compensation Scheme, there was much uncertainty about the early estimates of the finances of the new scheme and the contribution rate to be charged. In the event, income from the contribution rates decided upon exceeded the outgo on benefits in the early years, although the excess fell gradually as the expenditure on pensions grew. A study of the finances of the Industrial Injuries Scheme presented to an International Congress of

Actuaries in 1964 concluded that, in the event, little had been gained by building up a fund in the early years and that the scheme could reasonably have been financed on a 'pay as you go' basis from the outset, perhaps as a small part of the much larger National Insurance Scheme, which was financed by that method. Some years later, the two schemes were indeed merged.

Three further schemes financed wholly, or almost wholly, by the Exchequer were introduced on the recommendation of Beveridge. An allowance of 5s. a week became payable, irrespective of means, in respect of each child in a family other than the eldest. (Some years later, the scheme was extended so as to include the first child in the family as well.) A safety net provided assistance for persons in need who were not qualified for benefits under the National Insurance Scheme or for whom those benefits were insufficient. Of major importance, both from a social and a financial point of view, was the introduction of a comprehensive National Health Service providing free medical treatment (including dental, ophthalmic, specialist and hospital services) for the whole population, and for the hospitals to be administered by the State. The bulk of the cost of this scheme was to be met by the Exchequer, but a contribution towards it was included in the amount charged under the National Insurance Act, since the medical benefits previously provided under the National Health Insurance Scheme would in future be provided under the National Health Service.

Actuarial studies in demography and population projection

Shortly after Beveridge's report on social security was published, the government set up a Royal Commission on Population to 'examine the facts relating to the present population trends in Great Britain; to investigate the causes of these trends and to consider their probable consequences; to consider what measures, if any, should be taken in the national interest to influence the future trend of population and to make recommendations'. In its turn, the Royal Commission appointed a Statistics Committee to advise it on the statistical aspects of its inquiry. Four of the ten members of the Statistics Committee were actuaries. The report of the Statistics Committee included a number of studies – on aspects of mortality, fertility and marriage – which had been prepared in the Government Actuary's Department and a series of 16 population projections up to the year 2047, based on a variety of assumptions on rates of mortality, fertility and marriage in future years.

Following the comprehensive review of social security conducted by the Beveridge Committee, and subsequently also by the government in examining and implementing Beveridge's proposals, two actuaries who had been closely involved in those proceedings, and also in the work of the Royal Commission's Statistics Committee, wrote textbooks that were published in 1950 and became required reading for students preparing for the actuarial examinations. One book described in detail the very complicated method of calculating the actuarial contribution rates for male and female entrants to the new National Insurance Scheme at the minimum age of 16. The other book examined the characteristics of demographic data and the statistical concepts underlying the analysis of such data, and explained methods of making the kind of population projections required as a basis for making estimates of future social security income and expenditure At the time there were no suitable books on this subject and, given the responsibility placed on actuaries to provide financial estimates for the new comprehensive range of social security benefits, the profession had to devise its own material.

Actuaries have always had a strong interest in population statistics. The formation of the Institute took place at about the same time as the registration of births, marriages and deaths was made compulsory, and the information collected every ten years in national censuses came to include particulars of ages, occupations and family relationships. Nevertheless, there were gaps in the information obtained and in the statistical tables published. The view of actuaries on those inadequacies was discussed in 1901, drawing attention to comprehensive demographic studies that had been published in other countries, notably in France.

Information on fertility and the composition of families was still lacking when the actuarial report on the 1911 National Health Insurance Scheme – which included estimates of the cost of maternity benefits – was prepared. The actuaries concerned were obliged to have recourse to detailed fertility statistics available for New Zealand and to adapt those statistics to the crude measures of overall fertility available in the UK. It was not until 1951 that suitable data for the UK became available, following new requirements introduced under the Population (Statistics) Act 1938. This new information aided understanding of the increase in the birth rate that had taken place shortly after the war, and its subsequent decline. Part of the increase could be seen to have resulted from earlier marriage and earlier childbearing within marriage, and part of the subsequent decline resulted from a reversal of those trends. Family size did not vary nearly as much as cruder measures of reproduction might have suggested. This information was important to those making population projections, who had to choose suitable assumptions for the future. At about this time, in order to avoid different government departments making financial provisions for their departments' interests on different assumptions as to the future, it was decided that all departments were to use 'official' population projections which would be made by the Government Actuary in consultation with the Registrars General in London, Edinburgh and Belfast.

In 1950, the Institute of Actuaries Students' Society set up a Demography Study Group to foster the profession's growing interest in demography. About half of the members were, or had been, directly involved in population studies inside government, but for others it was a personal interest. The members of this group individually made several studies of different aspects of the population both in Great Britain and in other countries, and presented papers to population conferences held under the auspices of various international bodies, such as the United Nations and the Council of Europe, as well as to sessional meetings of the Institute and the Students' Society. The matters addressed in those studies ranged from consideration of population policies in overseas countries where over-rapid population growth was a problem, to tracing the growth of the participation of women in the workforce in the UK and showing how this was related to marriage and to the presence of dependent children in the family. With a growing number of immigrants arriving from former colonies in the West Indies, a study was made of the characteristics of the populations there. In a personal capacity, a number of actuaries have played leading roles in the activities of the Royal Statistical Society and the Eugenics Society.

The book *Demography* attracted interest in academic circles and in other countries. In recognition of this wider interest, the text in later editions was extensively revised and extended in order to increase its usefulness for university students. Also, less reliance was placed on the demography of the UK in the examples chosen as illustrations, and further material was added relating to world population problems. The book ran to five editions and remained in the course of reading for actuarial students for over 30 years.

Coming to terms with inflation

The 1946 National Insurance Act provided for in-depth actuarial reviews to be carried out every five years, with interim reviews in the intervening years, but in the event matters took a different course. With continuing inflation, it was found necessary to introduce new legislation almost every year to increase rates of benefit and contribution to keep pace with

inflation, and each new Bill presented to Parliament was accompanied by
a report from the Government Actuary giving revised estimates of income
and expenditure in future years. This situation persisted until the 1970s,
when provision was made for rates of benefit and contribution to be
changed annually by Regulation, without the need for new legislation.
Reports by the Government Actuary on those changes provided only
short-term estimates for budgetary purposes. Preparation of long-term
financial estimates was reserved for quinquennial reviews or when major
changes in the National Insurance Scheme were under consideration.
Long-term estimates allowing for future inflation at an assumed rate
would inevitably have shown such a large increase in income and expenditure that the figures would have been difficult to comprehend, so it became
the practice to present the long-term estimates in terms of constant
earnings. This manner of presentation gave a better insight into the
country's ability to meet the cost of benefits from earnings-related contributions. Also, in view of continuing uncertainty concerning future rates
of unemployment and fertility, and in the increase in longevity of pensioners, it also became the practice to give figures showing the sensitivity
of the estimates to the assumptions made on those factors.

The National Insurance Scheme introduced in 1948 lasted for only ten
years before a major change was under consideration. The government of
the day concluded that 'the developing needs of the old in a community
enjoying rising standards of life cannot be adequately met by contributions which have to be fixed at a level that all can afford to pay'. The result
was a complete departure from the concept of the 'actuarial contribution'
in favour of a 'pay as you go' system, in which the flat-rate contributions
could be held down to a level that the lower-paid could afford, while those
with higher earnings would pay an additional contribution related to their
earnings. This seemed unobjectionable, but those paying the extra
earnings-related contributions would be awarded additional graduated
pensions when they retired commensurate with the extra contributions
which they had paid. Under the 'pay as you go' system, this would mean
that future generations of contributors would have to pay even higher
contributions once the extra pensions came into payment.

Simultaneously, the Parliamentary opposition was planning to introduce even more generous earnings-related pensions, which would
place an even greater financial burden on later generations than the
scheme that the government had in mind. In a pamphlet entitled *An
Appeal to Statesmanship*, the actuarial profession expressed misgivings
about our 'promising ourselves, now, that our children will pay us larger
pensions in the future than we are willing to pay now to our parents', and
warned that future generations might decide that they were unwilling to

accept the financial burden that they were being asked to shoulder if they thought it excessive. The government went ahead with its relatively modest scheme of graduated pensions. Although men still paid a higher flat-rate contribution than women, both paid the same earnings-related contribution. However, women received a smaller graduated pension than men with the same earnings, because women retired earlier and lived longer than men.

The need for a second pension in addition to the basic State pension

In 1968, almost one-third of pensioners were receiving supplementary State benefits, because the basic State retirement pension was insufficient for their needs. There was a growing division between those who had to rely upon the State and those receiving occupational pensions in addition to the State pension. Both of the main political parties drew up plans for improving the lot of pensioners. The Conservative party saw the best way forward as setting up a money-purchase State Reserve Scheme, to which employees who were not members of adequate occupational pension schemes, and their employers, would be obliged to contribute a percentage of earnings. It would be a funded pension scheme, entirely separate from the National Insurance Scheme, with real assets, and the individual's pension would reflect, on an actuarial basis, the amount contributed and the return on the assets. Investment of the assets would be independent of government control.

However, it was the Labour party's scheme that eventually found its way into the statute book. It identified a band of earnings ranging from approximately one-quarter of National Average Earnings (NAE) to $1\frac{1}{4}$ times NAE. Contributions became wholly earnings-related (except for the self-employed and non-employed) and were levied on all earnings up to $1\frac{1}{4}$ times NAE. The basic pension was equal to one-quarter of NAE, and there would be an additional earnings-related pension amounting to one-quarter of average earnings between the limits for those who contributed for 20 years to the new scheme, with proportionately less for fewer than 20 years' contributions. For those who contributed for more than 20 years, only the best 20 years would count. Both pensions would be related to the level of NAE at the time of retirement. Thus, the combined State pensions for those retiring in 20 years' time would range from 100 per cent of earnings for those who had earned no more than the minimum to 36 per cent of earnings for those with $1\frac{3}{4}$ times NAE.

Benefits on this scale overlapped to a significant extent with occupational pensions, so arrangements were made for schemes that met a specified standard to contract out of the State earnings-related pension scheme (SERPS). Members of contracted-out schemes, and their employers, paid reduced rates of National Insurance contribution and, in return, the schemes were required to guarantee the payment of benefits corresponding closely to SERPS. The contribution rebates were thus in the nature of insurance premiums payable by the National Insurance fund to contracted-out schemes, and were calculated to be sufficient to enable a typical funded scheme to provide the guaranteed benefits. However, there was no advance funding for the remainder of State pensions, so National Insurance contributions were expected to increase considerably in the longer term as expenditure on SERPS grew. The government required contracted-out schemes to provide regular actuarial certificates to the effect that, if the scheme were to wind up, the level of funding would be sufficient for it to be able to secure the guaranteed benefits by purchasing insurance policies or paying premiums to the National Insurance fund to reinstate the contracted-out benefits. The amounts of the contribution rebates for members of contracted-out schemes, and the premiums payable to reinstate individual members in the State scheme, were to be calculated by the Government Actuary, with accompanying explanations of the methods and assumptions used. All of these financial arrangements placed a heavy responsibility on the actuarial profession.

Alarm concerning the growing cost of unfunded State pensions

In 1979, the incoming government was alarmed at the growing cost of State pensions and consequently made a number of changes in the National Insurance Scheme. The most significant of these was to provide for the basic pension, and also the lower and upper earnings limits, to be revalued only in line with the index of retail prices in future. For some years after 1980, NAE increased at a faster rate than the prices index to which the basic pension (and other benefit rates) were now linked, so earnings-related contribution income increased faster than the expenditure on benefits. If no changes had been made, the excess of income over expenditure would have continued to grow year by year for as long as the earnings index continued to outstrip the prices index. In the event, an excess was avoided by running down the regular Treasury Supplement from 18 per cent of contributions in 1980/81 to zero in 1989/90, giving a substantial reduction in government expenditure.

Two major changes were made to SERPS in 1986. One was the

introduction of Personal Pensions, aimed at persuading individual employees who were not members of occupational pension schemes to contract out of SERPS. The government offered as an alternative to pay premiums amounting to about 8 per cent of earnings between the lower and upper limits to an insurance company or some other savings organization to secure a Personal Pension. This naturally did not appeal to elderly workers, whose SERPS pensions were worth more than 8 per cent, but it was a bargain for employees in their twenties and thirties, whose SERPS benefits were worth a great deal less than 8 per cent. In the event, about five million young employees accepted the government's generous offer. This would have meant an increase in the earnings-related contribution rates in order that the National Insurance fund would still be able to meet current expenditure on benefits as well as paying the extra premiums, but this proved to be unnecessary because of the continuously growing headroom created by holding down the annual increase in benefit rates by reference to the index of retail prices. The other change made to SERPS was to reduce the target pension from one-quarter to one-fifth of the relevant earnings, and to base the pension on average lifetime earnings instead of the best 20 years. This had little effect in the short term, but made a significant reduction in the anticipated expenditure in the longer term.

Taken together, the result of these two changes has been that, in 1997, more than half of SERPS is being funded in advance, by the payment of premiums for investment in occupational pension schemes, insurance companies, and so on during working life. This proportion could have been as much as three-quarters were it not for the fact that very many of those contracted out and paying reduced National·Insurance contributions are members of unfunded public-sector occupational pension schemes.

If this system remains unaltered, the basic pension payable will fall steadily in comparison with NAE, and SERPS too will ultimately fall in a similar fashion, because the upper earnings limit for its calculation is tied to the amount of the basic pension. This trend will meet the political desire for a reduction in expenditure on National Insurance benefits financed by the 'pay as you go' system but, as each year passes, the National Insurance Scheme itself will become less and less satisfactory as a mechanism for providing financial support for those whose earnings are interrupted by unemployment or illness, or whose earnings cease permanently on invalidity or in old age. The basic pension has already fallen from about 25 per cent of NAE to 17 per cent, and it is only a matter of time before it will become negligible in relation to NAE.

For many years, actuaries from the UK have played an active role in the

Table 7.2 The estimated future UK population (in millions).

Ages	1996	2021	2046
0–15	12.1	10.8	9.5
16–64	37.4	38.6	33.9
65 and over	9.2	11.7	14.5
All ages	58.8	61.1	57.9
65–74	5.0	6.6	6.3
75–84	3.1	3.8	5.7
85 and over	1.1	1.4	2.4

Source: *1994-Based Population Projections by the Government Actuary's Department, OPCS Series PP2, no. 20, HMSO.*

International Social Security Association, particularly in its technical committees. A matter of particular concern at present is the 'ageing' of the populations of the developed countries. The proportions of the populations in those countries at the older ages is increasing and the proportions at the working ages declining. For many years, the official population projections for the UK (see table 7.2) have warned of this development, but the ageing has been more rapid than was anticipated, because the reduction in mortality rates achieved in recent years has exceeded expectations, whereas fertility rates have remained below the level required to maintain the numbers at the working ages; that is, those whose efforts must pay for the pensions of the elderly. The UK is likely to be better placed than most developed countries to meet the growing cost of pensions because, taking State and occupational pensions together, a large and increasing proportion of the liability is being funded in advance following actuarial principles. However, the problem does not end with the provision of pensions for those over retirement age. The proportion at very advanced ages is set to increase dramatically and the number in need of full-time residential care is already on the increase, at very heavy cost to the government-financed National Health Service. Consideration is being given, by actuaries as well as others, to devising methods by which the individual might provide in advance for meeting this cost and avoid having to pay for it out of savings. Possibilities are the payment of insurance premiums to cover the risk of full-time residential care becoming necessary, or accepting a smaller occupational pension to begin with in return for a larger pension later on.

Past progress and future prospects

The twentieth century began with a growing determination to get away from the inhumanity of the old Poor Laws by introducing schemes of national insurance. For many years, the contributions paid by insured persons and their employers to those schemes followed actuarial principles that were already well established in the financing of life assurance and friendly societies; namely, the payment into a fund during the working lifetime of amounts estimated to be sufficient to finance the payment of the promised benefits later on. As time passed, benefits were awarded from these schemes that were greater than the contributions paid in the past would have justified, or for which no contributions at all had been paid, so that a State subsidy became necessary. The position now reached is that National Insurance is unfunded, there is no longer any State subsidy, and the cost of benefits is met from the current contributions of insured persons and employers, assessed by reference to the cash needs of the scheme. Under this 'pay as you go' system of financing, it is of crucial importance for reports by the Government Actuary to display long-term estimates of expenditure on benefits allowing, *inter alia*, for estimated changes in the population structure. These estimates have given forewarning of the financial impact of the ageing of the population and of the sensitivity of the estimates to the main assumptions made, as a result of which steps are now being taken with a view to cutting back the National Insurance commitments entered into by the State on behalf of contributors in later years.

In addition to the growing cost of pensions and of providing residential care for the very elderly, further strains are currently being placed on National Insurance and the welfare system by the changing role of women. Fifty years ago, over 90 per cent of men and women married, and remained married, so that over 90 per cent of children lived with both of their parents, generally being cared for by the mother while the father went out to work. So far as married women and their children were concerned, the social security scheme could generally be directed towards providing support if the husband died or became sick, disabled or unemployed. However, about two-fifths of marriages now end in divorce. Many children are dependent upon a single parent, usually a young unmarried or divorced woman who wishes to go out to work sooner or later, and to have the economic independence which that brings. As it has not been possible to expand the economy and provide sufficient work opportunities to meet the increased demand, there has been an increase in part-time employment, in self-employment, in unemployment and in early retirement. As the century comes to an end, government expenditure on welfare benefits for single parents is mounting, in the form of income support for those on low incomes, or with no income, and housing benefit paid by local councils to those who need help to pay their rent. It is not clear exactly how the State will modify the National Insurance and welfare systems to provide for the changing role of women but, just as it has for the past 100 years, the actuarial profession will continue make available to the government the benefit of its technical skills and advice on this as on all financial matters.

Further reading

Anon. 1911, 1912: Actuarial reports on the provisions in the National Insurance Bill 1911. *Journal of the Institute of Actuaries*, 45, 406; 46, 64.

Beveridge, Sir W. 1942: *Report on Social Insurance and Allied Services*. Cmd. 6404. London: HMSO.

Blackley, M. J. J. 1906: *Thrift and National Insurance as a Security against Pauperism. Memoir of the late Rev. Canon W. L. Blackley and a Reprint of his Essays*. London.

Clarke, C. E. 1950: *Social Insurance in Britain*. Cambridge.

Cox, P. R. 1950: *Demography*. Cambridge.

Government Actuary 1925: *Report on the Financial Provisions of the Widows', Orphans' and Old Age Contributory Pensions Bill 1925*. Cmd. 2406. London: HMSO.

Government Actuary 1975: *Report on the Financial Provisions of the Social Security Pensions Bill 1975*. Cmnd. 5928. London: HMSO.

Government Actuary 1982: *First Quinquennial Review of the National Insurance Fund under Section 137 of the Social Security Act 1975*. HC 451. London: HMSO. See also *Second Quinquennial Review* (HC 582, 1990) and *Third Quinquennial Review* (HC 160, 1995).

Harvey, P. N. 1923: The scheme of National Health Insurance considered in relation to the valuation of approved societies as at 31 December 1918. *Journal of the Institute of Actuaries*, 54, 150.

House of Commons 1969: *National Superannuation and Social Insurance. Proposals for Earnings-Related Social Security*. Cmnd. 3883. London: HMSO.

House of Commons 1974: *Better Pensions. Proposals for a New Pensions Scheme*. Cmnd. 5713. London: HMSO.

House of Commons 1974: *Strategy for Pensions. The Future Development of State and Occupational Provision*. Cmnd. 4755. London: HMSO.

Institute and Faculty of Actuaries 1959: National pensions. An appeal to statesmanship. *Journal of the Institute of Actuaries*, 85, 293 and *Transactions of the Faculty of Actuaries*, 26, 309.

Maddex, Sir G. H. 1954: The Government Actuary's Department. *Transactions of the Faculty of Actuaries*, 22, 146.

Paulin, D. 1901: Old age pensions and pauperism. A present day problem. *Transactions of the Actuarial Society of Edinburgh*, 4, 3.

Royal Commission on Population 1950: *Reports and Selected Papers of the Statistics Committee*. London: HMSO.

Woods, E. 1903: Old age and workmen's pensions in Great Britain and Ireland. *Transactions of the Fourth International Congress of Actuaries, New York*, 1, 690.

Young, T. E. 1891: The German law of insurance against invalidity and old age: a history, analysis and criticism. *Journal of the Institute of Actuaries*, 29, 269.

The actuary and general insurance   8

Graham Lockwood

Fire and marine insurance in the UK was at first conducted in an unscientific manner. In the nineteenth century, an orderly company market was achieved through a tariff structure. At the same time, mathematicians were developing statistical models to represent the experience of an insurance portfolio, in terms of numbers and amounts of claim, although the practical application of such models was limited by the lack of appropriate data. In the 1960s, the UK general insurance market became less orderly and results were more volatile; this attracted greater attention from regulators. Actuaries became involved in the practical management of insurance portfolios, contributing effectively to data collection and analysis, especially in reserving for claims and pricing. In more recent years, this contribution has extended to other aspects of the management of a dynamic portfolio, including the relationship between assets and liabilities, the adequacy of capital and the risk management of the portfolio.

Early marine and fire insurance markets

There is no record to show that any of the buildings devastated by the Great Fire of London in 1666 were insured. However, there is evidence that the disaster was a spur for the introduction into Britain of insurance against fire and other hazards to property and goods on land. Marine insurance, providing financial indemnity in the event of a loss at sea of a ship or its cargo, had been available for a long time. The entrepreneurs who began to issue fire insurance policies were not the marine underwriters. Furthermore, they may not have been mathematicians, but they did have a growing fund of experience from which to learn. This was to be the foundation upon which they made day-to-day underwriting decisions.

As the marine insurance underwriting practices had been long established when others decided to take advantage of the potential demand for fire insurance after 1666, a consequence was that the marine and fire insurance markets developed their own individual structures and approaches to transacting their business. One clear distinction to emerge was that between the limited liability insurance company market and the unlimited liability associated with Names at Lloyd's. Market participants in each sector did their best to ensure that, when excesses of competition did occur, steps were taken to restore an orderly market for their economic benefit. Although the distinctions between the two marketplaces were to become blurred over time, it was a long while before such orderliness was to come under real challenge.

Edward Lloyd opened a coffee house in the City in the late 1680s. It attracted a clientele of all those interested in maritime trade, including those wealthy merchants who were prepared to accept a portion of marine insurance risks by putting their name down for a percentage of the risk described on each policy slip. This process became known as underwriting, and the financial backers as Names. Because of the quality of its clientele and the information that Lloyd himself ensured was made available there, the coffee shop became the recognized centre of marine intelligence and shipping experience. This knowledge has served marine underwriters in Lloyd's to this day, in the series of specially designed buildings that have succeeded the coffee house.

Meanwhile, outside Lloyd's, fire insurance was becoming established. Unlike the marine underwriters within Lloyd's who accepted risks on behalf of named individuals, fire underwriters were employed by companies set up specifically for the purpose – the insurers. For a long period the fire market was fragmented, as the insurers concentrated on a specific region or specialized in the fire risks of one of the many new industries emerging from Britain's economic revolution. In keeping with the commercial freedom of the times, it was easy to start an insurance office, and as competition grew there were inevitable failures. To protect their own position and to restore an orderly market, a small number of fire insurers began to share experience and expertise in respect of new and large risks such as textile mills and other specialist factories and machinery. They also spread the exposure to heavy losses from especially large risks through the mechanism of coinsurance, thereby adopting an established practice among Lloyd's marine underwriters This enabled a single large risk to be shared by a number of underwriters in agreed proportions, and ensured that the whole of the business was retained within the group.

Tariffs

From this beginning, a pricing structure for fire insurance premiums was developed by the participating companies. In 1868 this led to the formation of the Fire Offices Committee, which set minimum premiums based upon the pooled claims experience of like risks, and which established common rates of commission and other terms and conditions. The companies participating in these arrangements became known as the tariff market and those that remained independent of it were known as the non-tariff companies. The term 'tariff' thus became widely used to refer to a collaborative system of rate-fixing rather than to the premium rates themselves. Such rates were subject to periodic revision in the light of experience. Later, the fields of accident insurance (such as personal accident cover from the early days of the rapidly expanding railway networks), motor insurance and compulsory workmen's compensation insurance all became part of another tariff structure, the participants in which were members of the Accident Offices Association, which was formed in 1906.

These market associations helped to sustain relative stability in the financial results of the insurers. Profits from underwriting were augmented by the investment return on funds that the cash flow from premiums generated and from which claims were paid. These funds were invested by each company with freedom from regulation and without the regard for the nature of the liabilities. Concern with that relationship was to come much later. The financial rewards to shareholders inevitably fluctuated from year to year but, overall, were at such a level that there seemed to be no need to call for a more scientific approach. But such stability was not to last. Participation in the tariff structure was not compulsory and the time was to come when Lloyd's underwriters would expand their activity to include non-marine classes, new non-tariff companies would compete with the tariff rates in chosen sectors of the market and, later still, tariffs would become politically unacceptable in a free-market economy.

Searching for a theory

An underlying principle of insurance had always been mutuality of interest in the pooling of risks of a broadly similar nature. Furthermore, for a risk to be insurable, the underwriter needed to be satisfied that there was no exposure to 'moral hazard'; namely, the risk that the insured member would seek to profit from the contract by withholding relevant information or by submitting a fraudulent claim. Members of an insurance scheme were expected to contribute sufficient and fair amounts into a common fund to ensure that the fund was able to meet demands from members seeking to be indemnified for financial loss arising from insured events that happened during the period of cover. In some schemes, fund sufficiency could be ensured by having a levy on members at the end of the period to cover any deficiency. In others, an initial premium payable in advance was intended to be sufficient, and this had to be calculated by recognizing the existence of chance, being the probability that a financially disabling event would occur, and the existence of cost, being that of the financial indemnity which would be paid out by the fund should such an event happen.

Early premium rates for household risks were simply structured: given the paucity of data, this is not surprising. For example, in the first premium rates tabled in the proposals for the fire offices set up immediately after 1666, recognition was given to the lower claims expected from a portfolio of brick-built houses in comparison with a portfolio of houses constructed in wood. Similar simplicity of pricing prevailed in the premium structures right up to recent times – one flat-rate percentage for the fire insurance of a brick house wherever located in Britain and another flat-rate for contents.

This simple approach could continue for as long as no companies were able to gain from additional information that would enable variations in risk to be identified and premium rates to be differentiated so as to attract the more profitable business away from their competitors. In practice, the tariff companies kept the general level of their premium rates under review, adjusting it up or down depending upon overall financial results, which were calculated without any precision. Non-tariff companies had little choice but to adhere closely to the premium structures of tariff companies, usually charging slightly less. As long as these conditions prevailed, the practitioners of the business did not perceive a need for a more analytical approach.

Academic interest in general insurance had existed since the eighteenth century, but the author of a paper on premium rating of fire insurance, published in 1878, expressed some surprise that rates were still being deduced on a non-scientific basis despite the progress that had been made in building an actuarial approach to life assurance. In practice, the prospect of developing such a scientific approach to the rating of fire insurance was hampered by the absence of relevant and reliable data linking the occurrence and cost of claims to appropriate measures of exposure to risk. With the forms of record-keeping and methods of calculating that were available at that time, setting up arrangements for the collection and analysis of such data would have been a formidable undertaking and would have required a high degree of collaboration among the companies. In the absence of a general perception of the potential value of this information, and in a climate in which many underwriters were anxious to preserve the confidentiality of their own office's experience, it is not surprising that no progress was made.

At the beginning of the twentieth century, a mathematical analysis of the structure of insurance business, notably in Scandinavia, led to the formulation of risk theory, and in particular to what became known as the collective theory of risk. This theoretical work, much of which was directed towards the measurement of variability of the experience of an insurance portfolio and hence the vulnerability to insolvency, was developed by actuaries in several countries and resulted in papers of formidable mathematical complexity. It had, however, very little influence over the practical conduct of insurance, partly because the practitioners did not understand the theory but also because they believed that, despite its complexity, it failed to take account of some important characteristics of the business and its environment.

In particular, the insurance industry responded to the rapid growth of an industrial economy in Europe and the USA by offering new types of insurance protection. The early models did not reflect this dynamic nature of an insurance account, with its constantly changing portfolio of risks insured, and with uncertainties both in the potential cost of claims already incurred but not yet settled and in the cost of claims that might yet arise from the current portfolio of insured risks. However, although the gap between theory and practice might have been seen to be widening at that time, there were examples, within a few years, of the potential value of a partnership between the practitioners and those able to develop a theoretical approach to the business.

The partnership begins

Among the new types of insurance that evolved to cater for the risks associated with the industrial and commercial expansion in the nineteenth century was that of covering the liability of employers to provide financial compensation for factory employees who sustained injuries and diseases while at work. Each employer insured for Workmen's Compensation clearly had a distinct claims experience reflecting the nature and conduct of the employer's business as it affected his employees. The problem was to find the premium most appropriate for such experience.

In 1911, some actuaries in the USA, with a special interest in this and

other problems in general insurance, had become associated professionally as casualty actuaries. Their approach to the problem of pricing this
class of insurance, known now in the USA as Workers' Compensation,
was to develop a premium rate that would give proper weight to the
experience of the insured employer relative to that of the pooled experience of all employers engaged in similar business activity and with similar
working conditions and practices. For example, when quoting a premium
to an employer for the first time, the insurer might be faced with a dearth
of information in respect of the actual experience of that employer in
relation to the events to be covered by the insurance policy. At that stage,
the underwriter might have to rely solely on the collective experience of
other employers. Subsequently, as the actual experience of that employer
built up, this record was used to modify the premium by the process
known as experience rating. The premium became a weighted sum of two
elements, one based on the collective experience and the other on the
experience of the individual employer: the greater the volume of data
about the latter, the more credibility could be attached to it and the greater
the weighting given to it in the formula. The mathematical foundation for
this procedure became known as 'credibility theory', and this was developed and extended by actuaries elsewhere, especially in continental Europe.

Examples of experience rating are to be found in personal motor
insurance and, to a limited extent, in household insurance. In the UK, this
became known initially as a no-claim bonus but is now generally referred
to as a no-claim discount scheme. In other countries, such as in continental Europe, where until recently it was likely to be regulated, it
became known as a *bonus-malus* system. The perception was that policyholders who had made claims in the past were more likely to do so in the
future than those who had not. In the UK, where insurers were free to
make their own rating decisions, the no-claim discount became a competitive weapon in the battle to attract and retain the insurance of the
better risks. An extensive range of no-claim discount scales evolved
through the efforts of various insurers but, without careful statistical
analysis, it was by no means obvious whether any one of these scales was
justified.

The demand for insurance protection against the loss of material goods
and business profits continued to grow as the austerity of the 1940s and
1950s in the UK was replaced by a growing affluence. As in previous
times, the insurance market responded quickly with increased capacity
and new insurance products which, together with longer-standing protection of all types, remained an essential part of the economic structure of
society. However, the attitudes of both suppliers and buyers began to

change when the decade of the 1960s saw much social change, with long-standing values held in society being set aside and new freedoms becoming manifest in many aspects of everyday life. For example, judicial awards, which were relevant to the cost of claims under a range of insurance products, reflected increasing attention to the 'duty of care'; there was the increasing knowledge and discernment of insurance buyers, particularly among the managers of risk and insurance in industrial companies.

In the UK, the growth in the supply of insurance also brought further competitive pressures to bear against the bulwarks of the non-statutory tariff structure. Competition for market share continued to grow from both Lloyd's underwriters, no longer confining themselves to pure marine risks, and from new non- tariff companies. The tariffs in fire insurance and motor insurance, in which the majority of UK insurance companies participated, began to be threatened. Indeed, the motor tariff system collapsed at the end of 1968 as some companies broke away in the belief that, by aggressive pricing independent of the tariff, they could increase their market share. The remaining companies responded in a like manner, with the result that – across the market – premium rates were inadequate for the prevailing claims experience. As the adverse implications for profit from this highly competitive state came to be realized, and with the need for more careful selection of risks, the company underwriters needed to set up better systems for collecting and analysing data to help in the formulation of premium rates and other aspects of the financial control of the business.

Much of the information collected in many offices in the 1960s was still rudimentary and well short of the detail required for such analysis. Fortunately, the introduction of the Motor Risks Statistical Bureau (MRSB) by the British Insurance Association in 1967 began to correct this deficiency. The proposal that there should be a pooling of risk statistics as a basis for decisions on pricing had been made in 1965, in a report commissioned by the British Insurance Association as a response to threats from new sources of competition. It took the input and influence of a small number of actuaries on a subsequent working party to establish the nature of the risk statistics that would serve the desired purpose and be useful to participating companies.

This was an important step forward. The old tariff rating system had been based mainly on target ratios of the revenue account claims to premiums, with allowances for expenses and profit. With the introduction of the MRSB, statistics began to be compiled that enabled claims to be related to a proper measure of the corresponding number of vehicles exposed to risk in each of the related risk categories. Each participating company received from the Bureau the results derived from the combined data of all the participants, together with the corresponding results based on its own data. When the number of participants had grown sufficiently, a model based on the combined data was constructed to represent the expected experience, with which the actual experience in each of the subsequent periods could be compared. This made it possible to relate changes in the pattern of results to identifiable risk factors.

During this time of considerable change in the nature of the insurance markets, and an increase in the number of actuaries applying and developing techniques for general insurance, there was a corresponding enhancement in the way in which members of the profession prepared for working with general insurance practitioners. One important initiative was the inclusion of general insurance as one of the subjects covered by the formal education of the actuary: in the UK, for instance, this began in 1978. Sharing knowledge, research and experience was another way forward and actuaries in several countries were doing this: in Australia, for instance, actuaries had displayed little interest in general insurance up to the late 1960s, but within a few years they were contributing academic papers to international conferences and providing professional contributions to the local insurance market.

In Britain in the mid-1970s, actuaries had begun to meet in seminars and working parties to advance the use of actuarial and statistical methods. Early studies related to the assessment of liabilities in respect of outstanding claims, including claims which had occurred in the past but which had yet to be reported. Subjects of study also included assessing the likely variation in these liabilities and in the value of the assets held to meet them. Methods for managing such variation through the use of reinsurance and constraints on premium growth were also explored. Another study group that flourished in the 1980s concentrated on the distinct practices and risk characteristics of the London insurance and reinsurance market, in which Lloyd's and other insurance companies also participated.

The range of topics expanded in response to, or in anticipation of, market changes. Thus among the topics studied by these groups was the development of models intended to achieve some measure of the sensitivity of the financial state of a general insurer under various combinations of conditions in each of the insurance and the investment markets. Such models are inevitably complex, and considerable mathematical skills and computing capacity are required to embrace the full array of possible outcomes. The problem for actuaries was to turn mathematical concepts into practical use, but to avoid the danger that simplification of the model in the interest of practical application would result in a lack of market realism. One solution developed was a model that could be used to simulate a range of possible scenarios of different cash flows of investment and insurance income and outgoings arising over time from both changing conditions and strategies that were characteristic of the real marketplace. From such simulations, it was possible to gain some insights into the financial sensitivity of the business to variable conditions and strategies.

Solvency and claims

The 1960s also saw increasing communication between the supervisory authorities of the UK and those of continental Europe. From its earliest days, the UK general insurance market had been virtually free of government regulation. The regulatory and financial barriers to the entry of new insurance companies to the market were still not onerous, even with the provisions of the Companies Act 1967, which introduced an authorization procedure for new insurance companies. These included a requirement for a modest paid-up share capital and adequate reinsurance arrangements. All general insurers had to maintain a solvency margin of an amount equivalent to one-tenth of premium income for the large companies and a higher percentage for the smaller ones. As the amount available as the solvency margin is calculated as the difference between two much larger numbers – the amount set aside for the technical liabilities of the business and the value placed on the assets of the company – the usefulness of the solvency margin as a measure of the financial strength of a company depends on there being a generally accepted basis for arriving at these two quantities.

By comparison with the UK insurance regulations, those in some continental markets were more detailed and were exercised, until the 1990s, principally through control of premium rates and policy conditions. In 1967, the Organisation for Economic Co-operation and Development began to study the possibility of harmonizing insurance supervision in member countries. Working parties were set up to study technical aspects such as solvency and the adequacy of what are variously referred to as technical reserves or technical provisions. British interests in the working party were represented by an actuary from the Government Actuary's Department (which was also working with the UK supervisory body – the Insurance Division of the Board of Trade) and by an experienced actuary from the industry. In 1973, the European Economic Community, which the UK had joined at the outset of that year, adopted the First Non-Life Directive, the provisions of which included the introduction of a minimum solvency margin equal to the higher of two quantities, one based on premiums and the other on claims, each incorporating an allowance for outward reinsurance. The new formula typically produced a result somewhat in excess of 16 per cent of the net premium income, compared with the 10 per cent that had previously been required in the UK.

Meanwhile, regulations brought into operation after 1970 in the UK extended the annual returns that companies transacting general insurance had to submit to the supervisory authority. Statements of the earned premiums for the year and, in the case of motor insurance risk groups, the number of vehicles exposed to risk during the year, were required for each of a defined set of risk groups. The year-by-year run-off of the claim payments subdivided by year of accident also had to be provided. This information was intended to enable the supervisory authority to test the adequacy of the provisions made by the companies for their outstanding claims, and was regarded as being no more than the information that any competent manager of such businesses would wish to see for their own purposes. The introduction and subsequent development of these requirements encouraged an increased use of actuaries by the companies, to organize the systems needed to prepare the returns and to advise on the amounts of the provisions to be made for outstanding claims.

Another specific application arose from the Lloyd's accounting system that was employed during this period. The members, or Names, whose personal resources provided the financial backing for the insurance underwriting at Lloyd's, were organized in syndicates for the acceptance of business in each underwriting year. The composition of each syndicate was likely to change from one year to the next, as some Names left and others joined. Thus it was necessary for the underwriting to be treated as an annual venture, so as to offer a reasonable prospect of maintaining equity between the Names who participated in one underwriting year and those who participated in subsequent years.

The normal practice was to keep open the account for business written in each underwriting year until the completion of three years from its beginning. The assumption was that, after that time had elapsed, it would be possible to make a reasonable assessment of the eventual outcome of that year of account. That assessment would form the basis for transferring the residual portfolio of outstanding liabilities, together with a matching premium, to the Names participating in the underwriting year just commencing. This transfer of liabilities, known as 'reinsurance to close', could only be made if certain conditions were met, since it was important to be able to demonstrate to the incoming Names that the reinsurance premium being transferred, together with investment income and reinsurance protection, was likely to be adequate to meet the ultimate cost of the liabilities being accepted. From the late 1970s, a number of

Lloyd's syndicates began to obtain independent actuarial verification of such premiums and, since then, actuaries have extended their involvement with Lloyd's for commercial and regulatory purposes.

The problems of the long tail

General insurance is frequently characterized as 'short term', because the period of insurance protection is usually for one year at a time and claims, when they occur, are often reported promptly and the settlement cost quickly identified. Prudence therefore requires that the balance of those premiums, after deducting expenses, should be invested in readily realizable assets of the sort that might not be expected to vary very much in value. For other types of insurance, the financial consequences of each underwriting year may take many years to become final. Such business is said to have a 'long tail', and it is a characteristic of liability classes of insurance.

In employer's liability, for example, disease arising directly from long-term exposure to an unfavourable working environment can take years to become apparent, and it can take more years still to determine the degree of damage that the worker has sustained. Improvements in medical diagnostic skills have increased the likelihood that a disease identified late in life can be attributed to a period of exposure to an unfavourable

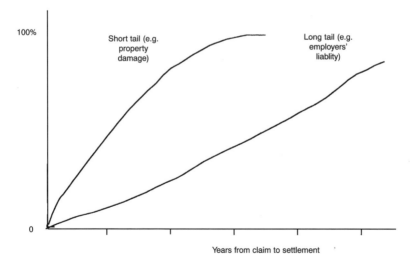

Figure 8.1   Proportion of ultimate claims cost patterns.

working environment many years earlier. Legal awards have tended to be larger, in real terms, the greater the perception has been that there has been a failure to observe a 'duty of care' towards the injured party.

These awards become the claims of insured defendants against their relevant liability insurance policy. Such claims costs were likely to be considerably in excess of those assumed when premium rates were calculated, possibly years earlier. This created increasing uncertainty for insurers, especially in the 1970s and 1980s. It was necessary to make substantial additional provision to allow for the possibility that claims already reported would ultimately cost more than originally anticipated, and that the number of those yet to be reported would also increase. For some insurers, the total amount of such increased provisions became very large in relation to the premium income and the capital base of the company. The financial condition of the insurer therefore became sensitive to such adverse variations in the amount of the provisions. This awareness was spread to investors in insurance companies as investment analysts, including some actuaries who had become employed in that capacity, began to comment on the effectiveness of insurance management in mastering this problem and the adequacy of capital. Familiarity with statistical methods for estimating the economic cost of such long-term liabilities presented actuaries with an opportunity to put forward practical solutions to this problem.

So much time could pass before the actual ultimate cost of claims arising from a cohort of similar policies underwritten in recent years would become apparent from reported and settled claims that, at an early stage in the development of each underwriting year, it became important to make a reliable estimate of that ultimate cost, so that the insurer could ensure that sufficient provisions were made in the underwriting accounts. To do this, actuaries made statistical models to represent the pattern of claims settlement which might be expected to emerge from such business, and which could be applied to the recent years, with adjustments for the volume and any significant changes in the characteristics of recent business. Such patterns could be built up from the actual data from the underwriting years which had been running off for several years, and where reliable and appropriate data had been collected. Where this was not the case, data from an alternative source might be available to provide a suitable benchmark for the account under review. The purpose of the exercise was, naturally, to have a better informed view of the outlook for the ultimate cost of the claims incurred in each of the recent years. By following this process for all incomplete years of account and totalling the amounts, one estimate of the reserves needed for outstanding claims was provided.

This method was applicable to several classes of business, but for really long-term liability it was apparent that some of the claims reserve might not be needed for many years. Furthermore, as the ultimate cost of many claims might be expected to increase with cost or wage inflation, as well as from increases in the amounts that were awarded in the Courts, there was a case for investing the assets held to meet such liabilities to match the requirements of cash flow and to provide some hedge against claims inflation. Investing in ordinary shares offered one such possibility.

Some insurers reasoned that allowance could be made for the time value of money by discounting the claims liability to an amount which, when increased by some or all of the expected return on the supporting investments, would be sufficient to meet the ultimate cost of claims on final settlement. The effect was to reduce the amount of claims reserves recorded in an insurer's balance sheet. This increased the solvency margin in the short term but the reduction was, in effect, achieved by borrowing against those future investment returns needed to top up the current reserves from year to year. Actuarial methodology was useful for this purpose. Within the accounts, care was needed to ensure that, year to year, the investment return was appropriately split between that required for building up the claims reserve and that which might be available for distribution or other balance sheet purposes. Such accounting concerns are now covered by European Community Accounting Directives and UK legislation.

Equitas

When the Lloyd's market experienced a series of major losses, beginning in the late 1980s, actuaries were provided with an opportunity to contribute their skills towards the arrangements that were adopted as the best solution to an important market problem. Since being active in the non-marine market in the 1880s, Lloyd's underwriters had shown a receptive attitude to risks located in the USA, and had been especially innovative in the growing market of reinsurance, including excess of loss business. The latter enables insurers to protect themselves against losses arising from catastrophic events which accumulate to amounts beyond which they are able or willing to bear.

A sequence of such disasters began in 1988, and these coincided with losses of even larger proportions that accumulated more slowly from the litigation environment in the USA, where Courts were making awards of a scale and nature that penalized product manufacturers (and hence their liability insurers) for circumstances not conceived of when the insurance was priced and underwritten. These losses, compounded by poor under-writing and weaknesses in monitoring aggregations of exposure arising from exposure to the retrocession market (where reinsurance is itself reinsured), produced potential losses to Lloyd's of a magnitude that threatened its future as a distinct insurance market. As a result, many underwriting years were not able to be closed after the normal three-year period. Many Names were left with very large potential losses, and they were reluctant to pay for their share in the face of what they perceived to be ineptness and deception within Lloyd's.

In an effort to restore the financial standing of the Lloyd's market after the huge losses incurred in the underwriting years 1989–92, and to deal with the uncertain losses of earlier underwriting years, the ruling body of Lloyd's recommended to members a radical new approach. This required the establishment of a new, authorized insurance company, the sole purpose of which was to take in, by way of reinsurance from every syndicate underwriting non- life business, their liabilities relating to all their open years of account before 1993. In recognition of this transfer, each syndicate was required to pay a reinsurance premium calculated as being the amount sufficient to cover the emerging cost of transferred liabilities.

The new company was to be known as Equitas – a name prompted by the need to maintain equity between different generations of Names. Although the company would not be accepting new business, it was, of course, necessary for it to satisfy the statutory solvency requirements. Estimates therefore had to be made of the size of the liabilities that the company would be taking on, and of the extent of the uncertainty attached to those liabilities. These estimates would enable an assessment to be made of the assets that could be regarded as sufficient to exceed those liabilities by an adequate margin. The assets were to be provided partly by a contribution from the central fund of Lloyd's and partly by way of reinsurance premiums from the individual syndicates. The members of each syndicate had to be assured that the proposed reinsurance premium would be fair, having regard to the nature and scale of the liabilities being transferred. Many actuaries, on both sides of the Atlantic, were engaged in this project, which led to the authorization of Equitas in 1996. This was a vital step in restoring the international reputation of Lloyds and in increasing the security behind insurance and reinsurance placed in that market.

The 1990s

The actuarial involvement in Equitas was directed essentially towards the financial management of a general reinsurance company that will be running off a closed book of past business. For those underwriters continuing in business and for most insurance companies, the objectives for the 1990s were to continue to accept business on terms that would meet business objectives, such as that of achieving an adequate rate of return on the capital employed. As this history shows, the confidence of general insurance underwriters to price and to accept insured risks has been based upon a steadily increasing fund of experience and a sensitivity, not always wisely applied, to market conditions. Furthermore, the changes following the breakdown of tariff markets, the accumulation of relevant data by individual offices, the increased use of computers for analysing and making projections, and better informed supervision have all facilitated a more responsive and analytical approach to the financial management of a general insurance business in the UK. In many other countries too, regulators have become more demanding of authorized insurers in the financial measures to be taken to ensure the prudent management of portfolios of insured risks. In Canada, regulation has been introduced requiring a general insurance business to have an Appointed Actuary with responsibilities similar to those of an Appointed Actuary in life assurance.

Another example of regulatory involvement concerns a measure of the relationship between insurance liabilities and the corresponding assets as an indicator of financial security of an insurance operation. This measure is intended to indicate whether, for a given insurance account, a prudent level of risk-based capital is being maintained, having regard to the level of risk implicit in the type of insurance underwritten and the nature of the investments of the insurance fund. In the USA, after considerable simplification of a potentially complex analysis, the regulators set minimum ratios of capital to premiums that depend upon both the perceived risk of the insurance liabilities, including the use of reinsurance, and the risks associated with different categories of the underlying investments. When ratios fall below specific levels, action is required by the company, or in worse situations by the regulator. At Lloyd's, where investment freedom is limited, the minimum acceptable ratio of capital to premium volume is governed principally by the nature of the insurance underwritten, higher ratios of capital to premiums being required for classes judged by the regulatory body to be riskier.

There have also been important changes in rate making. For example, the simple application of nation-wide premium scales for personal lines business, such as the insurance of property and contents, which had been a feature of the tariff system for so long, has been replaced by a much more detailed rating structure, which reflects the appropriate risk characteristics. Rating according to the address postcode can reflect the nature of the terrain of the insured house, which might be exposed to a greater than normal chance of flooding or subsidence, and can also reflect characteristics of the risks in motor insurance. More generally, the price of an insurance product at any particular time might, depending upon the state of competition in the market, contain an element of payback for past losses or, perhaps, a conscious underpricing to obtain or retain business upon which a better price might be achievable on a future renewal. In essence, the effect is the proper funding of variable experience over time within the insurance fund.

This is possible because the volatility of outcomes from portfolios of insured risks is usually measurable and manageable. A portfolio of motor or household damage insurance policies might be large in terms of the numbers of policies and experience a high frequency of claim, but the range of the cost of individual claims is not large relative to the size of the business. For most of the time, the cost of claims can be met from the insurance fund, but the insurer must be aware of the exposures to events which can, in a very short period of time, bring to such portfolios an exceptionally large number of claims and a potential financial loss of such magnitude that there is no prospect of managing out the problem over time in this way. The occurrence of an earthquake or hurricane in areas in which the insurer has many insured risks is an obvious example. The purchase of reinsurance which performs in such circumstances is the traditional risk management mechanism used by an insurer to protect the insurance fund.

The importance of managing exposure to occasional large losses is increased when the insurer also underwrites commercial risks where there is a low probability of a claim arising but, when it does, the amount claimed can be very large. This latter group could include the insurance of a large chemical plant, oil rigs, fleets of aircraft, or the acceptance of inward catastrophe reinsurance. In both personal lines and commercial accounts, awareness of the exposure to, and the potential frequency of, all such events, and an understanding of the means of financing them through reinsurance programmes or other forms of transfer of financial risk to other parties, are all essential to the risk management process that an insurer must adopt and for which the methodologies of the actuary are increasingly appropriate.

Methodologies do not provide the complete solution, since much also depends on the quality of the assumptions used in their application. These assumptions must reflect changing conditions, increased knowledge and alterations in risk characteristics. Technological advances can act to the advantage of insurers. The knowledge gained from an industrial disaster can lead to important changes in loss prevention methods for the future, with a consequence for future loss probabilities. Aircraft crashes, for example, are invariably followed by investigations into their cause, and often lead to changes that are aimed at preventing a recurrence. More difficult for insurers are changes in social attitudes that might alter moral hazard or influence Court awards for environmental, industrial disease and personal injury claims. The consequences are evident in the claims experience of classes such as liability insurance in the UK and Workers Compensation in the USA, where there have been threats to the supply of insurance capacity in recent years. All of these changes place additional demands on the managers of portfolios of insured risks, and from time to time there are bruising examples of the failure to take account of them.

During the 1990s, patterns of involvement by actuaries in general insurance have widened considerably and the actuary can be found in a number of roles. One such role is that of a guardian of the prudential interests of the different generations of insurance policyholders, and as an advisor on matters of equity between parties when commercial or judicial decisions must be made. Sometimes, the actuary can be the watchdog of the regulator, perhaps with statutory powers to ensure that insurers act in a manner which maintains solvency, and to ensure the availability of funds to meet the obligations to policyholders. The actuary can also be the verifier of values for a book of liabilities, and perhaps of assets as well, with such verification required by regulation, or for commercial transactions involving the sale, purchase or transfer of a general insurance business. Among other roles is that of the actuary as one of the advisers on financial risk management or the commercial strategy of an on-going insurance business.

Further reading

Abbott, W. M. 1986: Actuaries and general insurance. *Journal of the Institute of Actuaries*, 113, 299.

Abbott, W. M., Clarke, T. G. and Treen, W. R. 1981: Some financial aspects of a general insurance company. *Journal of the Institute of Actuaries*, 108, 119.

Beard, R. E. 1963: Some statistical problems arising from the transaction of motor insurance business. *Journal of the Institute of Actuaries Students' Society*, 17, 279.

Craighead, D. H. 1979: Some aspects of the London reinsurance market in world wide short term business. *Journal of the Institute of Actuaries*, 106, 227.

Daykin, C. D. 1984: The development of concepts of adequacy and solvency in non-life insurance in the E.E.C. *Transactions of the 22nd International Congress of Actuaries*, T3, 299.

Daykin, C. D. and Hey, G. B. 1990: Managing uncertainty in a general insurance business. *Journal of the Institute of Actuaries*, 117, 173.

Daykin, C. D., Pentikainen, T. and Pesonen, M. 1994: *Practical Risk Theory*. London.

Hooker, N. D., Bulmer, J. R., Cooper, S. M., Green, P. A. G. and Hinton, P. H. 1995: Risk-based capital in general insurance. *British Actuarial Journal*, 2, 265.

Miller, T. 1880: Fire insurance: a theory of statistics. *Journal of the Institute of Actuaries*, 22, 108.

Morris, C. 1747: Essay on the science of insurance. Reprinted 1995 in S. Haberman and T.A. Sibbett (eds), *History of Actuarial Science*. London.

Raynes, H. E. 1964: *A History of British Insurance*, second edition. London.

Walford, C. 1878: On the scientific application of data to the purpose of deducing rates of premium for fire insurance. *Journal of the Institute of Actuaries*, 21, 1.

Whitney, A. 1918: The theory of experience rating. *Proceedings of The Casualty Actuarial and Statistical Society of America*, 4, 274.

Desmond Le Grys

Having established the principle of insurance by pooling risks, the pool needs to be protected from abnormally high risks, large claims and adverse selection. In the early days of life assurance, this was achieved by only allowing entry to those who conformed to exacting criteria, by limiting the amount of cover and by charging heavy premium rates. The concept of reassurance was not then established.

Before 1850, a proposer usually had to appear before a committee of the directors of the life office to establish that he was healthy and of good character. No medical examination was conducted and, generally, a medical doctor was not present. The underwriting decision was made by the directors on the basis of the proposer's general appearance.

The need for more expert knowledge led to invitations to medical doctors to attend and advise the directors. The medical officer and the company's actuary started to take an increasing responsibility for the underwriting process, and the requirement to have a medical examination by a physician appointed by the life office was established. This was a universal practice by 1900, and the examinations became more scientific, with the introduction of urine testing and blood pressure readings. In 1893, the Assurance Medical Society was formed by a group of senior medical officers who met regularly to discuss problems of underwriting in the light of their clinical experience.

The aim of underwriting was the exclusion of any life that was not considered first class and, also, to ensure that adverse selection was eliminated. A proposer who failed the test was generally not offered cover at an extra premium or other underwriting terms, but was declined outright. Offices also limited the size of risk that they accepted.

The beginning of reassurance

In the early 1800s, a person wanting a large insurance would have to effect a series of independent insurance policies with several offices. Relative to the size of the insurance funds and the surplus arising from the funds, the amount of risk retained by a life office then would appear dangerously high today. Actuaries in the Scottish life offices were the first to draw up an agreement, in 1850, that one office could accept the whole amount of cover and then pass a part of the risk to one or more of the other offices. This led to the 1900 Reinsurance Agreements, to which most British life offices subscribed. There were no professional reinsurers established in the UK, although reassurance of life business by professional reinsurers was already established in continental Europe. Reassurance even between life offices was considered with a great deal of unease, and an office would take great care in choosing the partners with whom they would exchange reassurance cases.

All reassurances were effected on a 'facultative' basis. This means that the principal office would choose the reassurer, who would decide whether to follow or reject the underwriting and premium rates of the principal office. The Reassurance Agreement defined the terms and the documentation on which the reassurance was finalized. Generally, the reassurance was completed on the premium rates, terms and conditions of the principal policy. On with-profit policies, the reassurer followed the bonuses paid by the principal office. Other variations that could be used were also defined in the Agreements. Commission was normally paid at the same rate as the agent's commission on the principal policy.

Offices considered reciprocity as highly important, with each office obtaining a reasonable amount of inwards reassurance to balance the amount passed out. Offices would informally develop a circle of other like-minded offices and pass reassurance around the group.

Reassurance on the 1900 Agreement and on the original terms basis lasted for many years, and still influences facultative reassurance today.

Non-medical assurance

As the volume of new business grew, the use of a full medical examination became cumbersome for handling the majority of apparently fit proposers. One office developed non-medical assurance for certain categories of proposers, and this had become the established market practice by the 1920s. Originally, the sums assured and age limits were severely restricted, but with the gradual realization that the non-medical mortality experience was only marginally higher than for medically underwritten business, the limits were extended. Actuaries at the time argued that the reduction in expenses balanced the slight increase in mortality.

The non-medical proposal forms in those days were long, and asked for many details of the proposer's medical history and of his family history. A report from the proposer's medical attendant was often required, and the office retained the right to call for a full medical examination in case of doubt. A medical examination was invariably required if underwriting terms were likely to be imposed or the proposal declined.

Actuaries emphasized the need for protection of the insurance pool and the exclusion of all but first-class lives. However, they came to realize that the pool of insured lives covered a range of people, some of whom were super-fit and others of whom were slightly unhealthy. The concept evolved of the 'standard life', the health of which fitted within this range of lives. Non-standard lives could be offered assurance, but they would be charged more penal terms.

Although evidence was available of the mortality of standard lives, very little evidence was available in the UK on the mortality of non-standard lives, and consequently on how to derive appropriate extra premiums. There was no standard approach for rating the various medical impairments; within each office, the actuary and the medical officer derived a standard peculiar to that office. Little inter-office comparison took place except on reassurance cases. The medical officer's responsibility was to advise the actuary on the severity of the impairment, and the actuary set the underwriting terms on this advice.

It was customary to ask the doctor who examined the proposer what addition to age he considered necessary so that the impaired life would have equivalent mortality to an average life at an increased age. The doctor would be given a table of life expectations to help him make the recommendation. This recommendation was then re-examined by the chief medical officer, and the actuary then used an age uprating table to fix the terms. An exception was made to this age uprating system if the proposer was considered to have a predisposition to an infectious disease, such as tuberculosis, that imposed an immediate or short-term risk. The need for more information on the mortality of impaired lives was being voiced at that time, but would not be answered for many years.

The variations in population mortality according to socio-economic groups were well known, and all offices had scales for occupation groups, military personnel, residence in India and other Empire countries, and climatic extras.

There was little conformity on extra premiums for female proposers. Although the 'Eagle and United Empire' office had been charging lower premiums for females since 1827, most offices charged female lives higher premiums, especially if the proposer was young and recently married. Evidence of the relative decline of female mortality became progressively available and the practice was modified. Reduced premium rates for females became almost universal for life assurance.

The profession's Joint Mortality Investigation Committee developed tables for assured lives mortality accepted at standard terms. Subsequent tables showed consistent improvements in mortality, which in turn led to a progressive reduction in premium rates. The pattern of causes of death was changing – better hygiene, housing and lifestyles were reducing the incidence of infectious diseases.

Measurement of blood pressure readings was becoming increasingly required at medical examinations during the 1920s and it was believed (but not fully established at that stage) that high blood pressure readings were associated with increased mortality rates.

Two developments in the USA were to have an impact on the way in which British actuaries assessed impaired lives and measured the amount of extra mortality. The first was the large-scale medico-actuarial studies in North America, which confirmed conclusively the relationship between high blood pressure and mortality. Secondly, the 'numerical rating' system was developed and, although this was not immediately accepted in the UK, it would influence underwriting practice in the second half of the twentieth century.

Reassurance

The Mercantile and General (M & G) was the first reinsurance office established in the UK and it transacted some life business from the 1920s. It mainly transacted facultative business and its early treaty business was from overseas. Under the treaty method, the life office agrees to reassure all cases of a certain type of business with the reinsurer who automatically accepts the business. The treaty sets out the terms of the agreement, including the premium rates, retention levels and any limits on the size of the reassurance or the degree of extra mortality. Within defined parameters, the reinsurer follows the underwriting decision of the life office. Cases which were not covered by the treaty would be handled facultatively – often with the same reinsurer.

After 1945, the M & G grew strongly and progressively established treaty business as the main method of handling reassurance. Later, other reinsurers with European and North American backing also became established in the UK and created a wider market.

In the 1950s, the bulk of reassurance transactions were still on the 'original terms' method, but increasingly 'risk premium' reassurance came to be the most common form for risk transference. Original terms reinsurance was still retained for term assurance contracts, since it was more convenient to administer.

Under 'risk premium' reassurance, the life office effects a decreasing term assurance with the reinsurer and pays a relatively small risk premium. The life office retains the bulk of the office premium, pays out the commission and expenses for that policy, and has the responsibility to build up reserves, invest the assets and eventually to pay out the claim value. The reinsurer only has the responsibility to pay out the sum reassured on the decreasing term policy if the policyholder dies. In the original form, the level of the decreasing sum assured was fixed at the outset and the sum at risk each year was also fixed according to the office reserve basis at the outset. The reassurance premium was then the multiple of the sum at risk and a risk premium rate for the policyholder's then age, on a scale of premiums agreed at inception. This method was popular with some life offices because the bulk of the premiums, and profit potential, was retained by the life office and only a small premium (and some of the mortality profit) was paid to the reinsurer. Some of the mortality profit would be passed back to the life office, as treaties generally included a profit-sharing arrangement.

In general insurance, many offices protect their pools by effecting 'non-proportional' cover. The reinsurer takes the excess of losses if a catastrophe happens or if a run of losses occur independently. These covers are agreed on a yearly basis. Because life assurance is long-term, these covers have rarely figured in risk management arrangements of life offices. However, some offices do buy catastrophe cover. There is a catastrophe risk pool operated by the Association of British Insurers.

Life underwriting

Mortality in the UK has declined progressively over the past century. The introduction of antibiotic drugs after 1945 had a large impact on mortality, and deaths from infectious diseases declined dramatically. So, with more comprehensive statistics, a more liberal view was taken on the definition of a standard life for an office's insurance pool. Some offices traditionally had wide limits for defining a standard life and consequently charged relatively high premiums. Other offices, which were more specialized, had stricter entry conditions and charged lower premiums. With improving mortality, most life offices started to charge fewer occupational groups with extra premiums and they also relaxed the medical standards.

The aims of underwriting were also changing. Initially, the prime purpose had been to prevent early death claims and to avoid adverse selection. Although these were still of consequence, other considerations were becoming important. The actuary's responsibility in underwriting was seen as ensuring that the office's actual mortality experience – both in the short term and the long term – was in line with the assumptions in the premium and the valuation. There was no consensus on how underwriting terms should be calculated and, also, there were no UK statistics on which to base assessments. A. J. Steeds published a definitive paper on under-writing, and so in the 1960s actuaries were able to be more objective in making decisions and could abandon making decisions largely based on personal impressions or whim.

Rating methods

The numerical rating system was developed in the USA soon after 1900. It was based on the assumption that the majority of impairments can be measured by a percentage addition to standard mortality, and that this percentage addition could be assumed to apply for the rest of the person's lifetime. The Americans considered that the concept should not be a theoretical exercise, but a practical method of assessing and rating risks.

Under this system, a proposer is given a number of debits or credits for poor or good features according to his medical history, state of health and lifestyle. The debits and credits are based on percentages of standard mortality. An average proposer would rate at 100. If the summation of the debits results in a total score below 125 per cent, then the proposer would be considered a standard life. For higher scores, additional underwriting terms would be charged. No reduction in premiums was given for scores below 100.

Although actuaries in the UK admitted that they had few statistics on which to base underwriting terms, they were in general more concerned with the incidence of the risk – whether the additional mortality was increasing, decreasing or constant relative to standard mortality. They therefore considered that the numerical rating system (which in its origi-nal form ignored the incidence of the risk) was defective.

The issue was resolved because more and more data was becoming available from North America. The studies showed that measuring the degree of impairment as an extra percentage of standard mortality was approximately correct for most impairments, and that decreasing risks could be accommodated by charging additional terms (normally a flat extra premium for a short period of years).

However, there was little data for impaired lives directly from the UK. Perks showed in 1952 that the ratings for all types of impairments charged by his office were greater than the actual experience, and that they were correctly slanted according to severity of the impairment. Another important contribution was from Clarke in 1965, revealing data from the impairment study of another large life office. He demonstrated that the ratings of that office for major medical impairment groups were generally adequate and correctly shaped.

A standard method of assessing extra mortality was introduced when the first UK underwriting rating manual was published. Underwriting manuals were published by North America and European reinsurers both for their own use and for their client offices. The ratings were largely influenced by statistics from North American and European countries, and from a wide range of independent medical and epidemiological studies.

The old informal arrangement for passing reassurances around offices began to lose popularity, since the professional reinsurers were able to give automatic cover and good underwriting limits, and could advise on difficult cases. The old method of swapping reassurances led to administrative problems and was expensive to operate. Offices tended to move out of London, and that the close circle of underwriting actuaries was being loosened.

A significant development was the formation by Mercantile and General of the three specialized pools for cases of diabetes, hypertension and coronary artery disease. The pools were organized so that life offices could offer terms on cases that they might otherwise have declined. Each pool worked on the principle that risk premiums were credited to the pool and the cost of claims debited to it. At the end of a year, the participating offices shared proportionately in the profits or losses. The reinsurer underwrote all cases accepted for the pool so that a consistent standard was obtained – strict criteria were laid down for acceptance of suitable cases. The other principal purpose of the pools was to obtain knowledge of the amount and incidence of these impairments. As life offices gained more confidence in underwriting these types of impairments, they started to retain the risks in their own accounts rather than use the pools.

By the 1970s, the underwriting philosophy of most offices was similar, and the day-to-day underwriting of cases was passed on from the offices' actuaries to a new generation of life underwriters, who were skilled in interpreting medical data and translating it into underwriting terms with the help of the medical officers.

Each office developed its own set of underwriting rules on what level of medical evidence was required: many offices set limits so that around 60 per cent of new business was accepted on the information on the proposal form alone. Medical evidence was only requested automatically for the larger sums assured and elderly people. Although the office would have its own concept of extra terms for impaired lives, the life office underwriter relied heavily on the reinsurer's underwriting manuals. Generally, it was the reinsurers who undertook the detailed investigations to determine the appropriate ratings for the medical impairments.

Practice among offices varied, but over 90 per cent of proposers would have been accepted at standard terms, with only a small percentage declined for life assurance.

Underwriting in practice

The method of charging underwriting terms would allow for the level of extra mortality, incidence of risk and type of policy. The main methods of imposing underwriting terms are shown in table 9.1.

Variations in this underwriting approach are possible. Some offices which were principally selling endowment assurances used the decreasing debt approach almost exclusively. With those policies, the policyholder was principally interested in savings and investment and so a reduction in cover, rather than an extra premium, was appropriate. Since the sum at risk on an endowment assurance runs down quickly (unlike a whole-life policy), this approach could be used for any incidence of risk. Debts were only used for whole-life policies if the amount of extra risk was small and of a decreasing nature.

Table 9.1   The main methods of imposing underwriting terms.

Type of policy	Decreasing incidence of extra risk	Constant percentage of basic mortality	Increasing incidence of extra risks
Whole-life	Flat premium for a limited period	Extra premium	Extra premium (sometimes a reduction in length of cover)
Endowment	Flat premium for a limited period or decreasing debt	Extra premium or decreasing debt	Extra premium (sometimes a reduction in length of cover) or decreasing debt
Level term	High flat premium for a limited period	Extra premium	Extra premium and limitation to length of cover
Decreasing term assurance	High flat premium for a limited period	Extra premium	Extra premium

Some offices did not want to retain the risk on lives who were severely impaired or who suffered from a combination of impairments. The reinsurers would underwrite these difficult cases and accept the mortality risk on the whole sum assured. It was possible for lives with estimated mortality of five times standard mortality to be offered life assurance cover. It was unusual for terms to be offered for higher amounts of extra mortality.

Much of the life assurance industry in the 1970s and 1980s concentrated on selling investment plans and single-premium bonds. The actuary now just fixed the mortality basis for standard cases; fixing the level of mortality for substandard lives and determining the underwriting criteria was generally delegated to the life underwriters.

Mortgage-linked contracts

In the late 1970s, some offices began to write endowment assurances issued as part of a mortgage repayment package. In many cases, there was no requirement for medical evidence at all: the argument was that house purchase was a selective process because very few people in ill-health would commit to it. The scheme rules were carefully limited to first-time housebuyers, young people and small sums assured. Any additional mortality costs were considered to be balanced by the saving in underwriting expenses. The experiment was largely unproven. In 1983, the way in which mortgage interest was relieved against income tax was changed and all existing mortgages had to be reviewed. Actuaries were pressed to use the 'no underwriting' approach to all existing mortgage holders, including those with a traditional mortgage repayment system who wished to switch to the endowment method, the latter being more favourable under the new tax conditions. Large numbers of policies had to be written in a limited time, the 'no underwriting' approach was extended to people with existing mortgages and the limits were widened and, in some cases, were virtually dropped altogether. The result was large-scale adverse selection and a rapidly deteriorating mortality experience. By April 1984, the scheme was withdrawn and insurers introduced short non-medical proposal forms, which eliminated the adverse selection. Mortality losses were made, and increased mortality experience is likely to persist into the long term for these policies.

Unit-linked contracts

In the early 1980s, the flexible whole-life contract was introduced into the UK. This was a unit-linked policy under which premiums were invested in units, some of which were then surrendered to cover mortality and expense charges. Within limits, the policyholder could select a maximum cover plan (akin to a ten year term assurance) or a standard plan (equivalent to a whole-life policy on very favourable terms) or a minimum plan (equivalent to a ten-year endowment). The premium terms were not guaranteed. The plan was reviewed periodically, and the level of premium and the amount of cover adjusted in the light of actual experience. It was customary to build in automatic increases of cover in line with the retail price index. Guarantees to increase cover substantially on marriage, house move or birth of a child were also included, as were extra increases at regular intervals. This led to some controversy on the cost of these options, how they should be charged and the implications for under-writing. There were two schools of thought. The first argued that the cost of options was low and would be balanced by improvements in mortality over time, and no special underwriting considerations applied. The second school (who may have had experience of US renewable-term policies) argued that the mortality experience would progressively deteriorate, that the options were expensive and that, when fixing underwriting terms on substandard lives, all options should be removed, since the sum at risk on maximum and standard plans could increase steadily for 30 or 40 years, thereby exposing the office to the possibility of substantial loss. The debate was resolved when the industry became aware of the potential cost of AIDS, and most options to increase cover were withdrawn. It is now academic to consider which school of thought was more likely to be correct, but this does demonstrate that life offices had moved into an era in which underwriting was considered far less important than marketing advantage and new business flow.

Smokers

An increasing number of offices have introduced separate premium scales for smokers and non-smokers, because of the growing evidence that smoking is associated with a significantly higher incidence of cancer, respiratory and cardiovascular disease. Offices initially gave relatively small discounts/additions for non-smokers/smokers. Recent evidence tends to show that the difference in mortality experience of the two groups is wide, and several offices now quote larger differentials. A present-day view is that non-smokers should be considered as the standard life for the underwriting pool, and that smokers should be considered as abnormal risks that require underwriting terms based on twice standard mortality. Actuaries have the problem of establishing the new standard mortality basis, bearing in mind that there is considerable mis-statement of the smoking habit and definite adverse selection.

AIDS

AIDS was first recognized in 1979 in the city centres of the USA. The new infectious disease had no cure and it was growing very rapidly. The number of people with the virus (HIV – Human Immunodeficiency Virus) and the number with the full syndrome (AIDS – Acquired Immune Deficiency Syndrome) were both doubling every eight months or so in the early 1980s in the USA. Once a person suffered the full AIDS syndrome, death appeared to be imminent. This was the first new disease that life underwriters and actuaries had to face in living memory. Actuaries were confronted with the problem of how to measure the possible incidence of the disease and how to adjust underwriting terms.

Attempts by the actuarial profession to forecast the growth of AIDS in the UK were tentative, as there was very little information on the per-ceived high-risk group in the UK (male homosexuals), or whether the transmission rates recorded in North America would apply in Europe. It was suggested by the Institute of Actuaries AIDS Working Party that basic premium rates for young males would need to be increased significantly, that good underwriting practice alone would not protect insurance pools, and that blood testing should be an automatic part of underwriting. Life offices followed the advice on premium levels, introduced lifestyle ques-tionnaires, extended proposal forms to ask questions on previous blood testing, but only required blood testing for large sums assured.

The actual incidence of AIDS was much lower than the first forecasts, and it now appears that the increase in mortality in young males, both for the population and for insured lives, has peaked much earlier and much lower than originally forecast. Premium rates were reduced gradually by most life offices. The right of life offices to ask some of the questions that were originally included in proposal forms was disputed by some pressure groups, who argued that asking questions on previous blood tests could deter people who might be at risk from taking a test and then receiving counselling. Whether this is the case is not proven, but the contentious questions were modified.

Business expansion

During the 1980s, there was a rapid expansion of life assurance business and a number of offices (particularly the newly established ones) had difficulty in financing the growth. The reinsurers were able to assist by reassuring the extra growth and, in return, paid high commission, or some other consideration, to the life office to defray the selling and marketing costs. The reinsurer was then responsible for creating reserves and for absorbing the valuation strain, in addition to taking the mortality risk.

Many complex reassurance arrangements were designed to solve the special needs of each office. In their simplest forms, the treaties were 'original terms' treaties, under which a quota share of business (an agreed percentage of each policy of the defined class of business) was reassured. Much recent business has been written on a unit-linked basis, and the reinsurer has been unable or unwilling to match the asset performance of the life office. In some cases, the reinsurer deposited cash equal to the reserves with the life office, for it to invest. Alternatively, a reassurance system was used that gave the desired financing effect to the life office, but the reinsurer was not involved in reserves and investment.

Most reassurance treaties effected by life offices had been placed with UK-based reinsurance offices, or continental offices with branches in the UK that were regulated by the Department of Trade. Due to the different tax regime applied to foreign reinsurers, it was possible to use reassurance treaties to arbitrage between tax systems and to design very attractive policies for UK policyholders. The tax regulations were changed in 1995 and these reassurances are no longer arranged.

Current issues

The view that the life assurance industry is still moving towards the provision of savings, investment and pensions may not prevail in the future. The public's expectations on the care, comfort, income and services that they require when old, infirm, disabled or hospitalized is growing at a time at which the State is facing difficulty in covering the basic costs.

In 1997, actuaries are discussing the following:

- Have the underwriting limits for the 'standard life' (ordinary rate classification) been extended too far? There is scope for giving cheaper rates and terms to low-risk groups and for charging different rates for the relatively high-risk groups.

- With critical illness insurance, a sum insured is paid on diagnosis of certain diseases. The underwriters have followed traditional life assurance underwriting, but perhaps a fundamental reappraisal of the underwriting process is necessary – especially as the concept may well be extended to other types of cover.
- The advent of sophisticated and comprehensive expert systems will change the way in which life offices operate, and could substantially change the underwriter's process. Telemarketing methods are also likely to require new underwriting approaches.
- That additional services are required for the elderly/infirm is not in doubt. Not only does this raise opportunities for life offices for long-term care insurance, but it may lead to new partnerships between the State and life offices on a whole range of care and health insurance services.
- The science of genetic testing is under development, and it will be possible to make predictions on a person's future health patterns with increasing certainty. The whole philosophy of underwriting and risk selection is likely to change, and much more emphasis will have to be placed on the forecasts of the health profile.

Further reading

Brackenridge, R. D. C. 1992: *Medical Selection of Life Risks*, third edition. London.

Clarke, R. D. 1960: An investigation into the mortality of impaired lives. *Journal of the Institute of Actuaries*, 87, 196.

Clarke, R. D. 1979: Mortality of impaired lives. *Journal of the Institute of Actuaries*, 106, 15.

Institute of Actuaries Working Party on AIDS 1989: *Bulletin 4*.

Leigh, T. S. 1990: Underwriting: a dying art. *Journal of the Institute of Actuaries*, 117, 443.

Perks, W. 1951: The treatment of sub-standard lives in practice. *Journal of the Institute of Actuaries*, 78, 205.

Steeds, A. J. 1964: Some considerations affecting the selection of risks. *Journal of the Institute of Actuaries*, 91, 231.

Bill Abbott

Investment management is a matter of balancing acceptable risk against higher returns. The traditional view of investment markets is that they are ruled by fear and greed. The actuarial approach to investments has been to seek to resolve these tensions in a coherent way, to quantify the acceptable risks and the corresponding return. The natural emphasis on sound and prudent management has to be viewed in the context of satisfying customer needs. Typically, the customer may be purchasing the products of a financial institution or the services of an investment manager.

Actuaries have been involved at two levels of investment management: at the corporate level, which is now normally described as asset/liability management; and in the management of the investments within set objectives. As computing power and databases have expanded and as the mathematical modelling facilities have increased, new financial instruments and consumer financial products based on derivatives have emerged and new investment techniques have developed.

There are now a fair number of actuaries who describe themselves as 'investment actuaries'. Nevertheless, investment and asset/liability management is a core actuarial discipline, being part and parcel of the activities of all actuaries involved in the prudential management of a financial institution and in product pricing.

The evolution of the investment actuary

Sound and prudent management of a financial institution has always involved the assessment and management of both its liabilities and its assets. The origin of the actuarial profession stems from one type of financial institution, the life insurance company. Product design and pricing, and the establishment of appropriate provisions, have required assumptions to be made on the investment returns available in future and consideration of what would happen if those assumptions were not achieved.

Life insurance companies are major corporate investors and, together with friendly societies, were for many years the dominant corporate investor. It was natural that some company actuaries, with their mathematical and financial skills, became investment managers for those funds and were at the forefront of institutional investment. Pension funds created from defined benefit schemes emerged later, with actuaries also being appointed as investment managers for those funds.

The skills of these investment-focused actuaries were transportable to the market-making and intermediary institutions; for example, to stockbroking, where they found roles in the marketing and analysis of both fixed interest investments and equities. As these other institutions developed their own fund management activities, including the management of collective investment vehicles such as investment trusts and unit trusts, a wider market for fund management services emerged. Some of the fund managers of these vehicles were actuaries.

Two other developments established actuaries in the investment world. First, pioneering work in the production of investment indices led to a role in monitoring the performance of the investments, and even of the managers of those investments. Secondly, for many years the Institute and the Faculty of Actuaries provided the only professional examinations in investment expertise.

The past 30 years has seen the evolution, initially by American academics but including actuaries, of theories of financial and investment economics. These have had a profound effect on investment markets. There have been major developments in derivative instruments and trading systems, and markets are now supported by the use of mathematical models and theory. The practice of investment management reflects these developments.

The provision of financial advice to individuals has been subject to increasing regulation in recent years, with particular emphasis on training and competence. A small but increasing number of actuaries are now emerging as independent financial advisers to individual clients.

Genesis

The primary issue for the profession in the financial management of insurance companies was to identify the principles of managing the money of those companies. Investment fashions come and go, but certain principles should remain. For example, there was a lively debate in 1918 when the insurance companies reviewed their portfolios following the massive increase in gilt holdings as a result of the demands of government to invest in War Loan. There was concern over the volatility of these security prices related to international events, and at that time actuaries revisited the principles by looking back over the previous century.

At the start of the nineteenth century, few insurance companies had funds that were sufficient to make investment policy a top priority. The exception was the Equitable, where by 1810 the funds were £3 million and increasing by £300 000 each year.

The management of an institution's money depends on four factors: what the management is empowered to do by its corporate constitution; what the institution's contract with the customer is and the expectations that arise as a result of this contract; what constraints are imposed by law; and what objectives in practice are given to the investment managers. Thus the Equitable had powers of investment in its deed of settlement which referred to 'Government and other good and sufficient securities'. The initial practice was to restrict investments to gilt-edged fixed interest stocks. The policyholder expectations were covered in the company prospectus issued in 1778, which reminded the members of the wider powers given to the executive. More definite powers were given later, starting in 1858 with powers to make policy loans.

The earliest accounts in 1767 showed funds growing very slowly, because more than half the business was for one year or less. Liquidity requirements were quickly discovered when the Society borrowed £650 from its vice-president to pay a claim without selling stocks! By 1778, it was making switches from one investment to another. (This was viewed with some interest in 1918, when the wisdom of an active policy that precipitated the realization of capital gains and losses was part of the debate.)

The first mortgage borrowings appeared in the portfolio in 1779, and by 1799 these accounted for one-third of the portfolio. Then, for ten years or so, no new money was invested in mortgages. This was consistent with the adoption of an investment policy based on a broad outlook over a number of years, because when yields fell back towards their pre-1800 levels, profits were taken and switched into mortgages. The realization of these profits led to the decision to restrict the flow of new business, so that profits arising from a temporary advantage, which might not recur, should not be spread over a large number of new policyholders.

This provides an early example of asset/liability management by the actuaries concerned with new business management. In the 1918 debate, it was used to illustrate the dangers of regarding market values as permanent and the ramifications of considering surplus in terms of inflated values. The appropriate valuation of assets has remained a key issue for actuaries considering distributions or funding requirements.

The tension between investing for security of capital, risk and return naturally led to actuarial debate on the principles on which life assurance funds should be invested. This led to Bailey's 1862 paper, which set out five canons, namely:

- security of capital is paramount
- subordinate to that, the highest practicable investment return should be obtained
- a normally small liquidity requirement should be maintained to cover claims
- the remainder should be invested in securities that are not readily convertible, as these are unsuitable for private individuals and so command a higher rate
- capital should be employed to aid the life fund

By 1871, over half of the assets of the top ten life companies were invested in mortgages on UK property, but the proportion started to drift down so that by 1905 it had fallen to one-tenth, a level that was maintained until relatively recently. Gilts in 1871 accounted for 7 per cent of total assets, falling to near zero in 1914 when railway and similar stocks accounted for about one-third of the total. The forced investment policy of the war years resulted, ten years later, in nearly 40 per cent in gilts. Policy loans were in the 5–10 per cent range until after the Second World War, and life reversions – an actuarial niche – accounted for less than 5 per cent.

Investment in equities was for many years negligible. (The analyses available refer to 'Railway and Other Preferred Ordinary and Ordinary stocks and shares'). Never more than 8 per cent of the portfolio until 1930, they accounted for 16 per cent in 1935, before reverting to 10 per cent in the 1940s. Raynes spearheaded the actuarial debate in the inter-war years into the virtues of equity investment and the comparison between ordinary shares and fixed interest yields, at a time when equity investments were more generally becoming popular. Part of the debate related to the extent to which the reduction in yields as a result of this increased demand for equities had resulted in non-repeatable appreciation.

As late as 1951, insurance companies were being castigated by some economists for an over-cautious attitude to equity shares, with a resultant lack of investment in the creation of wealth for the nation. Aided by the lack of surrender value guarantees in their products, the investment profile of insurance companies moved significantly with substantial equity investments in the 1950s. By 1962, over 20 per cent of the investment portfolio of the UK life companies was in equities. Investment in property also became popular over the same period, growing to 10 per cent.

The 1862 canons remained perceived wisdom for many years. Criticism built up against these principles, and Binns in 1965 said that there were now two generally accepted basic principles of investment for a long-term fund:

- to earn as high a yield as possible, over a long period broadly commensurate with the future development of liabilities
- to spread the investments to secure the advantages of favourable (and minimize the disadvantages of unfavourable) political and economic trends, varied in accordance with views of possible future trends

The investment mix of life assurance funds further developed towards equities over the next 30 years. By 1995, the balance sheet of UK life companies, which included linked funds, had in aggregate over 60 per cent in equities, of which one-fifth were overseas equities. The property proportion had dropped to 7 per cent. The basic investment principles are now honed, from asset/liability studies, into fund-specific objectives and guidelines.

Exodus

Into fund management

Throughout the nineteenth and most of the twentieth centuries, life insurance companies were the major institutional investor as they developed products both for individuals and for groups. Various tax advantages on life and pension products encouraged savings to be directed through these companies, which grew their own fund management expertise.

There were some other institutional investors in the nineteenth century, most of whom were concerned with 'segregated' portfolios of individuals. There were trust companies, and at least one Victorian actuary was the manager of such a company. Other collective investment vehicles were to emerge later.

Until the Big Bang of 1986, which radically altered the way in which the investment markets worked, securities on a UK stock exchange could not be sold directly by one investor to another. Listed securities had to be sold (or bought) through the agency of a stockbroker to a market-maker – the jobber. The broker in turn gave advice on the merits of individual stocks. They would also act as fund managers for individual clients, taking the actual investment decision for them.

The trust funds of pension schemes emerged as major institutional investors after 1945. The management of these fund investments was initially contracted out, either by insuring the benefits or by appointing an external fund manager, such as a stockbroker. With funds above a certain size, an in-house manager was regarded as more efficient. Aided by their knowledge of pension fund liabilities and asset/liability requirements, a number of actuaries assumed responsibility for the investment management of pension funds.

One such pension fund manager was Ross Goobey of the Imperial Tobacco Pension Fund. He realized that equities were a suitable investment for a pension fund with continuing substantial cash inflows and acted upon this belief. This stance was adopted by other fund managers, including insurance companies. Aided by inflation, the consequence was sufficient money going into equities in the 1950s to reverse the yield gap that had previously existed whereby the dividend yield on equities exceeded the yield on fixed-interest securities.

The major development that arose in the 1960s was that of the linked life contract, which established unitised funds within an insurance company's portfolio. Typically, in 1960 an insurance company would have just two funds to manage, the long-term fund and the general business fund. This is in stark contrast to the situation in 1997, with a plethora of niche funds.

Although fund management is not the sole preserve of actuaries, many actuaries have proved to be good fund managers. Techniques of fund management have developed in which quantitative investment methods are used, and actuaries have a particular aptitude for understanding the use and misuse of such methods.

Into stockbroking and investment banking

Stockbrokers acted not just as execution agents; they also provided advisory services to their clients. These included investment recommendations to clients, investment analysis relating to particular stocks, and economic analysis on their expectations of shorter-term movements in interest rates and stock markets.

The compound interest knowledge relating to fixed-interest investments led, from the early days, to actuaries working not only for the institutions that bought bonds but also those that marketed them. Thus teams of fixed-interest specialists were built up by the brokers: a major part of their work was to analyse the gilt market, studying and developing the concept of yield curves, and combining actuarial and economic skills. Given that the objective of the broker was to create selling opportunities, models were developed not only as an aid for traders but also to give the salesmen a benchmark for discussing cheapness/dearness pricing indicators. Pepper's 1963 paper on the selection and maintenance of a gilt-edged portfolio was a watershed. Traditional gilt-edged valuation techniques were becoming obsolete as computing power emerged that could handle increasing volumes of statistical data. The 'cult of the equity' had been in progress for many years, with gilt-edged securities regarded as old-fashioned, and the paper reconsidered the role of gilt-edged stocks in a modern portfolio.

The contribution of actuaries to a systematic assessment of default or counterparty risk has been spearheaded in the USA, where equity investment plays a lesser role for insurance companies, and competitive advantage is hopefully gained through the higher yield obtained on low-quality corporate bonds. Rating agencies have provided a benchmark – albeit not an infallible one – for the default risk, based on a fundamental view of the credit standing of the issuer. Not all bonds have ratings, and statistical analysis can provide some perspective on the risks.

As a consequence of Big Bang, the separate roles of brokers and jobbers disappeared, but the fund management activities of the brokers had to be clearly separated from market-making to avoid conflicts of interest. The industry further consolidated into investment banking groups, with global coverage, and with departments specializing in innovative financial products and servicing particular industries. Actuaries have moved with these changes; perhaps from being gilt-edged specialist salesmen with a broker to giving specialist advice to a market-maker and then to becoming the market-maker. The work of the actuary on the equity side includes specialist investment analysis on the insurance industry and on investment trusts, and now extends to financial conglomerates.

Into performance measurement

The development of indices by the equity specialists in order to understand the markets better led to indices being used to track performance. The first performance measurers were the fund managers themselves. The need for objectivity led to the creation of a separate industry with the independence naturally provided by firms of consulting actuaries, given their responsibilities for advising pension clients, or by firms spun off from fund managers.

The performance measurers may track the performance of a fund against an index, or of the managers against other managers. This may not be sufficient to form a view, as the performance will depend on the objectives that have been set for the manager, and such objectives may have more regard to a liability profile or tax situation. Nevertheless, an analysis of the performance that explains it in terms of risks accepted, asset allocation and stock selection should provide a valuable insight.

Into academia

The development of actuarial science in the UK mainly emerged from the work of actuaries in commercial practice; UK chairs of actuarial science only began to be created after 1970. The investment aspects of actuarial science have to be set in the context of financial economics, the use of which in actuarial work continues to be controversial. Financial economics is the application of economic theory to financial markets. Its study is a postwar phenomenon and has produced several specific models which have come into widespread use in the financial community. Nevertheless, it is this work that has led to wholesale changes in the nature of the products traded on the market and the ability to manage funds in an apparently more structured fashion. The initial work was on the pricing of commodity futures, and from these pricing studies it has been possible to develop a large number of derivative products related to various securities; futures, options, swaps, and so on. These products range from those traded on a market to 'over the counter' hybrid products specifically designed by an investment bank to meet the needs of a client.

A whole generation of investment bankers and fund managers have grown up with these products. Business schools teach the underlying theory as the heart of a course on capital markets. A more limited number of graduates with a mathematical (or nuclear physics) background, sometimes called the 'rocket scientists', are market participants and provide the intellectual support for the 'quants'. The 'quants' apply quantitative investment methods to portfolio management.

There have been many examples of substantial losses being incurred through improper assessment of the risk being run. Any actuary with a detailed understanding of the markets and the underlying models can provide advice on the riskiness of any business using the products and methods that are now available. More generally, shared corporate objectives can be achieved by getting added value from the collective corporate advice of fund managers, traders, 'quants' and actuaries.

The contribution that actuaries can make in the development of a prudential approach to the financial management of investing institutions was recognized in the establishment, by the International Actuarial Association, of a specialist investment section (AFIR).

Into corporate finance

The management of the asset/liability position embraces not just the management of the assets covering the liabilities and the capital regarded as essential to support those liabilities, but also the management of any excess assets to those requirements. An insurance company, and similar corporates, will have operational plans for organic and acquired growth, and financial projections will indicate the extent to which the corporate has to access fresh capital. The raising and management of corporate capital has many common features with the investment of monies into such capital. Actuaries are naturally involved with corporate finance activities for insurance companies and may also be involved on the investment banking side.

There are some specific forms of corporate finance for the insurance industry, such as financial reinsurance, where actuaries are heavily involved. There are non-reinsurance products which produce similar added value. These may include the reduction of the strain of writing new business, giving value to assets which may be disallowed for statutory purposes (or even for financial reporting to shareholders), or financial synergies. The capital raised may be debt or equity and will be tailored to the needs of the insurance company or its holding company.

The skills of the actuary in the management of risk/return relationships have led into a wider field of opportunity, in which advice is now being given on investment into capital projects.

Indices

Other than for shares in railway and telegraph companies, few ordinary shares were held by insurance companies until the 1920s. Douglas in 1929 showed how the yield averages and price indices of government stocks, debentures, and preference and ordinary shares could be related to the economic cycle. From this work emerged a committee that started the Actuaries' Investment Index – just in time to take in the effects of the 1929 boom and the subsequent Wall Street inspired crash.

The purpose of this index was to assess markets against the economic cycle and to aid research into investments. This contrasts with its current usage of measuring investment performance and providing a base for passive fund management.

The compilers of the original index chose to calculate it as an unweighted geometric average of the price relatives, which is only satisfactory if markets do not change too rapidly. The volatility of currencies and defaulting interest payments caused the discontinuance of a foreign bond index in 1935. The production of the equity index, by hand, continued until 1953, using a wider selection of shares arranged in more numerous industrial groups. A revised second series in 1957 reflected the increasing necessity to compensate for the geometric basis.

By the 1960s, it was recognized that a stock market index needed to be available and widely disseminated daily, and on a market-value-weighted arithmetic mean basis. The theoretical actuarial work of Haycocks and Plymen, the willingness of the *Financial Times* to publish the full range of industrial group and total market indices, and the increasing availability of computing power to do the calculations enabled the introduction of the *Financial Times* – Actuaries All Share Index in 1962. In 1997 this index, now renamed the FTSE All-Share, was published in real time, not merely once a day.

From being pure research tools, indices now face the commercial reality of performance measurement and index tracking, and can affect the remuneration and retention of investment managers. The *Financial Times* and the Stock Exchange had commercial motives for promoting generally accepted indices, and there is now a grouping of interests identified with them that produces a wide range of interlocking indices.

Actuaries continue to play a role in the production of the various indices and their associated legacy, the industrial classification system. One of the great strengths of the FTSE–Actuaries All-Share Index series is the comprehensive classification of the companies into, as far as possible, homogeneous industrial groupings. In particular, the actuaries provide a rigorous intellectual basis, dependent on the objective of an index, and an audit function to establish respectability for an index.

The knowledge of index construction also provides a role for actuaries in three related fields; performance measurement, passive fund management and determining investment strategy. For example, the Pension Act 1995 codifies the functions and responsibilities of pension scheme trustees, including full responsibility for the investment of the assets. Trustees now have to have a working knowledge of the operation of these indices and not simply accept that the indices exist.

Performance measurement

Although the achievement of a superior investment return has always been a competitive advantage, the demand to 'benchmark' the performance of the funds under management, and by implication the performance of the fund managers, has been a recent development. In particular, the growth of pension funds with large equity portfolios has put obligations on trustees to have a defensible rationale for the choice of investments and managers. The growth of equity vehicles such as unit trusts and unit-linked funds was a parallel development, in which the individual consumer could make choices. Investment performance thus became a major marketing tool.

Performance measurement is essentially a statistical task. It has been relatively easy to measure the historical performance of a fund either against an index of some description or against a set of competitors, although even here there are a vast number of technical complexities that obscure comparisons. It has been less easy to relate that performance to the specific objectives that may have been set for a fund, particularly with regard to the risks that the fund may be prepared to accept, or to the constraints that may attach, such as those relating to specific tax situations or ethical investment.

The measurement of past performance has developed into a significant industry with a major actuarial input. Data from the various funds has to be collected on a regular and timely basis, and has to be collated on a like-with-like basis to obtain an independent view of the performance of any single fund relative to others. The comparisons for pension funds were initially limited to the funds to which the performance measurer, quite often a firm of consulting actuaries, had access. More recently, there has been a trend to consolidation of the databases. Nevertheless, there can be substantial differences between the databases available to different measurers which, in turn, have to be fully understood by the investment manager – whose livelihood may depend on their measurement.

The availability of fund performance measurement services itself opens a debate as to whether it encourages short-term management of a fund to its long-term disadvantage. This is leading to measurement against specific objectives, rather than emphasizing short-term achievements. Investment actuarial consultants may advise on the choice of investment managers. Their advice depends not only on a knowledge of the past performance of these managers, but on their style. For example, one manager may feel that stocks with growth rates that are above average earnings offer the best prospective returns; another that smaller companies offer more scope for outperformance. A consultant needs to determine from the manager, whether traditional or quantitative, what the manager's style is.

Financial economics

The initial academic research on the quantitative analysis of shares was in 1952, when Markowitz drew attention to portfolio diversification and how an investor could reduce the standard deviation of portfolio returns by choosing stocks that do not move exactly together. He described some basic principles of portfolio construction, which were based on a relationship between risk and return.

The definition of risk chosen was the standard deviation of returns, or a similar statistical measure such as variance. Risk can be changed in a portfolio for a given expected return by combining securities in different proportions until a position is reached beyond which return cannot be increased for a given risk – an efficient portfolio. The theory ties in with the efficient markets hypothesis, which requires all investors on average to be rational and driven by the profit motive.

Twelve years later, the Capital Asset Pricing Model (CAPM) emerged, providing the first quantitative framework for investment management. This linked expected returns on an asset to the risk of the asset by a single factor (*beta*). The theory was that risk-averse investors do not accept a given risk without a commensurate level of reward. They demand a higher return from an investment in a portfolio made up in exactly the same proportion as the stock market (the indexed portfolio) than from a risk-free investment such as a gilt-edged stock, the excess return being the market risk premium. *Beta* measures the market risk of a single investment, effectively the sensitivity of the investment to market movements. The *beta* of the market is one and *beta* of a 'risk free' asset is zero. The expected *beta* of a portfolio is simply the weighted average of the *beta*s of the underlying stocks, and the expected return on a portfolio is the risk-free return plus the product of the portfolio *beta* and the expected market risk premium.

Arbitrage Pricing Theory (APT) emerged in the 1970s as an alternative expected return model to CAPM, to compensate for the perceived deficiencies of CAPM. In APT it is assumed that there is a relationship between a number of factors and expected return, these factors being flexibly chosen. APT maintains that the expected excess return on any one stock is determined by the stock factor exposures and the factor forecasts associated with those factors. Option pricing models, based on the work of Black and Scholes, now underlie the market in financial derivatives.

Quantitative investment management

This has been defined as investment management based upon formal research in which objective factual information is examined, implemented within a structured, explicitly defined decision-making environment. Whilst traditional fund managers continued in their belief that they could add value, 'quants' accepted the notion of 'efficient markets' and developed passive techniques. The acceptance by clients of passive management was itself a function of the development of indices that enabled performance measurers to demonstrate whether a fund manager was able to add value over the years compared with a passive policy. It also enabled a passive policy to be adopted on the basis of an appropriate index.

The growth of the index-tracking funds required new techniques as well as indices. The techniques vary from full replication to sampling methods such as stratified sampling and optimization, with the twin objectives of minimizing tracking error and keeping dealing costs low. Portfolios have to be continually rebalanced, but over-frequent rebalancing increases dealing costs. Successful index-tracking depends to some extent on having an index that represents stock availability in the market. If, say, half of a heavyweight stock is held by an inert shareholder, be it the government, family or parent company, then an index with a weighting that allows for 100 per cent of the stock will be considered by the trackers as a distorted index. A similar argument can apply to shares with restrictions on holdings by overseas investors. Moreover, if the actions of index-trackers can be anticipated in advance, then use of this knowledge can in itself produce inefficiencies in the market. The more money that is indexed, the more opportunities there should be for skilful active managers to exploit.

The availability of index-tracking funds has led to core/satellite strategies, in which it is assumed that risk can be better controlled by splitting a portfolio into two, the index core plus an active higher risk portfolio as the satellite, taking advantage of the differing expertise of managers.

The work of the 'quants' involves devising rigorous tests on passive techniques. These tests in fact cast doubts on the efficiency of markets and have led to 'active quant management'. Both traditional and quantitative management fall into a bracket between chartists (who do not believe in even the weak form of market efficiency) and the semi-strong form (where only insider information is of any value).

The success of index-tracking of indices may be measured by their tracking error. The error is the percentage variation each year of the actual portfolio performance from that generated by the index. There are expectations on what would be a reasonable tracking error, based on a probability equivalent to one standard deviation. Thus 1 or 2 per cent per annum is a reasonable tracking error for an efficient equity market (such as the USA), as is 1 per cent for a less efficient market (such as smaller UK companies). The tracking error provides a measure of risk and the incremental returns on active funds can be measured by reference to index fund tracking errors. This measure of risk can then be used as a risk control device. Tracking errors can be influenced by the difficulties faced by all fund managers, whether active or passive, in acquiring sufficient shares of newly listed companies.

The globalization of investment markets means that most investment portfolios have a significant overseas element. Quantitative investment techniques exist alongside other techniques to control the additional currency risks. 'Currency overlay' is the separate management of such overseas currency exposure and usually denotes a hedging activity designed to reduce foreign currency risks. In contrast, 'currency allocation' is the treatment of currencies as a separate asset class from which an extra return may be generated. If the risk of a currency loss may be associated with the volatility of a currency, then a risk-control led currency overlay may be used. Forward currency markets or currency options can be employed for this purpose. Currency allocation models are very reliant on technical analysis factors, such as charts and momentum measures, for determining views on future movements. Fundamental economic forecasts may be used in currency overlays.

The efficiency of currency markets is not proven, with central banks, as one market participant not driven by a profit motive, being more concerned with reducing the volatility of their currency. Quantitative techniques can then be used in a way which is designed to detect inefficiencies in the market and simple rules for highlighting market opportunities.

A major active quantitative technique is the use of multi-factor models in an attempt to outperform a benchmark, where expected returns on a stock demonstrably correlate with certain key explanatory variables, such as the stock's price : earnings ratio or its price movement in the previous month. A typical model would use multi-factor regression techniques on the chosen explanatory variables. The modelling depends on the choice of factors and on maintaining stability from one economic scenario to the next. Any volatility of relationships between factors is a clear weakness of this approach.

Quantitative techniques can be used to aid the management of a portfolio where a manager believes that he or she can make money by identifying stocks which are moderately undervalued. Such 'market neutral' strategies depend on buying undervalued shares and short-selling overvalued shares. The manager is taking a view on the stock-specific incremental returns, independent of overall market movement. The risk attaching to the portfolio has to be carefully controlled, and quantitative techniques are used, for example, to achieve required levels of intra-sector offset in order that successful stock selection is not dissipated by the wrong sectoral mix.

Tactical Asset Allocation models allocate portfolio monies between different asset classes in a quantitative manner. They operate in a similar manner to the currency overlay model, and vary exposures on an existing portfolio through derivative usage. Compared with a traditional management process, which may refer such decisions to an asset allocation committee (or manager), the 'quant' version may automatically follow an objective measure of prospective returns.

A further overlay to a portfolio may be achieved by an equity-style management system, based on the manager's style as discussed previously. Models have been developed to tilt portfolios towards the most favoured factors. Style analysis begs the question as to whether one style that has been effective will continue to be effective in the future. This is one area in which traditional and modern quantitative techniques are converging.

The search for better techniques is a continuing process. The research area now embraces neural networks, based on a set of mathematical functions that have an ability to learn, and represent a more powerful statistical tool to analyse data in a non-linear way, which makes them more realistic. Genetic algorithms are a tool for machine learning and discovery based on Darwinian evolution; for example, a population of stock trading rules could be modelled and allowed to evolve. In chaos theory it is assumed that a variable's value depends on one or more variables in the past according to a non-linear equation, on the basis of the concept of infinite regression.

'Quant' techniques can be blended back into the old-fashioned driver of 'human insight'. Knowledge-based quantitative forecasting systems build in this extra factor to address the fact that models are 'back tested' on past performance data, and that the models often do not work as well in practice. The full range of artificial intelligence techniques is available, including fuzzy logic and case-based reasoning. Knowledge-based systems are being used to run bond portfolios. They do not have the problems of 'quant' techniques which mine a lot of data, some of which is bound to exhibit an apparent profitable relationship. They do share an 'in-sample' bias with other 'quant' techniques, in which 'back-tested' results are based on information that could not have been known at the time.

Asset/liability management

Asset/liability management was perceived by many to have been created in 1979 and to have been associated with the US banking industry. In reality, it has always been a standard part of the actuary's process of sound and prudent control of the financial institution with which he or she has been connected.

The US banking and thrift industry had relied heavily on the structural benefits of the yield curve, borrowing heavily on short-term rates and lending to long-term borrowers at high fixed rates of interest. This comfort proved illusory during the fallout from the collapse of the junk bond market, when lenders' interest costs shot up to 19 per cent while their earned return remained at 8 per cent. The shock triggered financial crises, insolvencies and runs on the bank. It also generated the need for a stronger, more disciplined and analytical approach to risk management. This led to the creation of the concept of an Asset/Liability Committee to monitor structural risk across an institution's entire balance sheet, and to establish policies and procedures for managing that risk.

Asset/liability management applies to any institution that has primarily financial assets and liabilities. The fervour with which it has been taken up within banks, where the activity may be monitored on a week-to-week basis by full Board committees, is not necessarily replicated elsewhere in other financial institutions, where the process may be managed in a different way. For an institution such as an insurance company, a specific manager of the liabilities, such as the actuary, may exist. For example, the liabilities of a life insurer may be assessed on a less frequent basis, possibly once a year for a full review. The process is that a review of the asset/liability position should generate a set of portfolio objectives and guidelines for the investment fund manager and the fund manager.

If the fund manager operates within too narrow guidelines, then the major gains or losses from the investment of the institutions funds will arise from the setting and review of the objectives, rather than the fund management itself. For a major institution, rapid transition may not be feasible, not only because of dealing costs and the impact of planned programme trades on the market itself, but also because of the tax consequences of changing a portfolio.

The asset/liability management process has to establish the nature of the assets and liabilities being managed and their valuation. One normal starting point is a cash flow projection of the liabilities. This will depend on a number of actuarial and economic assumptions. For a pension fund, it will additionally depend on future salary progressions and exits. General insurance cash flow projections have been overwhelmed by catastrophic risk exposures, by the full extent of retrospective legal liability awards and by reinsurance company insolvency. Nevertheless, for any institution a cash flow projection is the start of the asset/liability management process, in which the determinable effect of various movements in asset values and investment returns on those cash flows are considered.

These tests cast further light on the required excess of assets over liabilities to cover with safety margins in the potential cash flows. Additionally, the cash flows are discounted to provide a balance sheet snapshot of the institution's capital. Sometimes discounting replicates a market value basis, typically for assets. At other times the discount rate is zero – for instance, undiscounted general insurance liabilities – or is at a rate which is common to both the asset income and the liability outgo. Asset/liability management will consider the conflicting requirements of the different perspectives, which may well include the resultant volatility of reported earnings.

The cash flow asset/liability models that have been developed are based on a projection of investment cash flows, a projection that may be deterministic or the result of a stochastic investment model. They facilitate a number of studies which can lead to crucial decisions for the management of the institution, such as:

- what financial resources are necessary to support the various 'futures' indicated by the cash flows
- what investment strategy is suitable for a given level of resource and liability
- what guarantees can be given on the liability side for a given level of resource and investment strategy
- the computation of economic value of ownership of the flows

The time period of these models is crucial. Bank models look to the exposure to a sudden market movement in the near future. The longer-term models for life insurers and pension funds should incorporate not just cash flows to third parties, but also cash flows that are locked in – for instance, for solvency purposes – and are not then available to the provider of the capital.

A deterministic model will require a choice of investment assumptions or a set of scenarios that may happen and are considered suitable for stress testing of the financial solidity of the institution. A stochastic approach is increasingly accepted as adding value to the risk analysis of financial institutions.

Stochastic models will depend on a choice of fundamental economic variables to be modelled and a set of relationships between these variables. The value at time t of each variable, say $A(t)$, will depend on consistency with past history, economic intuition, efficiency, and the ability of the modeller and manager to understand the model. The value of $A(t)$ may depend on previous values of itself, or on other economic variables. Such processes do not look forward and are therefore termed 'non-anticipating'. The introduction of dependencies on previous values makes the model autoregressive. The family of stochastic models is known as the Wilkie model, and has the feature of being mean reverting. Thus, if in one year the return on some asset category is less than expected, this increases the likelihood that it will be greater than expected in the following year.

Wilkie's work stemmed from a 1980 review by a professional working party on reserving for maturity guarantees for periods of up to 40 years on unit-linked insurance contracts. This report effectively stopped the granting of such guarantees. More recently, guarantees for shorter periods have re-emerged, but on the basis of costing techniques that have blossomed with the emergence of the derivatives market. The Wilkie model with subsequent modification has become, by default, a benchmark model for stochastic investment modelling, although its limitations are well understood.

Actuaries and others are continuing to develop models that are more tailored to usage in asset/liability management. A static strategy is one that rebalances a portfolio from time to time back to a static benchmark weighting: such rebalancing prevents a portfolio drifting away from the original benchmark. In contrast, a dynamic strategy will be one that varies over time by more than market drift correction. An example of a dynamic strategy is one which maintains a high equity weighting when solvency capital (or minimum funding requirement for a pension fund) is well covered, but with progressive reductions as the cover falls. Such strategies may be achievable through derivatives.

A major feature of market returns is that their distribution is not normal but is skewed. The current generation of models is being developed to take this into account, with asset/liability modellers having to decide on the outliers to incorporate in their models.

The management of money has come a long way over the past 100 years. The categories of investment available, and the potential different approaches to investment, have increased hugely, with new ways of making and losing money. Indeed, some investments can now lose far more than the amount originally invested. Many new techniques of identifying and controlling the risks have been developed, but managing the money successfully still depends on a mix of intuition and rigour.

Further reading

Anon. 1980: Report of the Maturity Guarantees Working Party. *Journal of the Institute of Actuaries*, 107, 101.

Bailey, A. H. 1862: On the principles on which the funds of life assurance societies should be invested. *Journal of the Institute of Actuaries*, 10, 142.

Binns, J. D. 1965: *Institutional Investment*. Institute of Actuaries and Faculty of Actuaries.

Black, F. and Scholes, M. J. 1973: The pricing of options and corporate liabilities. *Journal of Political Economy*, 81, 637.

Clarkson, R. S. 1996: Financial economics – an investment actuary's viewpoint. *British Actuarial Journal*, 2, 809.

Douglas, C. M. 1929: The statistical groundwork of investment policy. *Transactions of the Faculty of Actuaries*, 12, 173.

Elderton, W. P. 1918: Investments a hundred years ago. *Journal of the Institute of Actuaries*, 51, 32.

Haycocks, H. W. and Plymen, J. 1964: The design, application and future development of the *Financial Times* – Actuaries Index. *Journal of the Institute of Actuaries*, 90, 267.

Imam-Sadeque, F. 1996: *Quantitative Investment Techniques*. Staple Inn Actuarial Society.

Kemp, M. H. D. 1997: Actuaries and derivatives. *British Actuarial Journal*, 3, 51.

Markowitz, H. M. 1952: Portfolio selection. *Journal of Finance*, 7, 77.

Pain, R. 1996: The Actuaries' Investment Index. *The Actuary*, April 1996, 21.

Pepper, G. T. 1964: Selection and maintenance of a gilt-edged portfolio. *Journal of the Institute of Actuaries*, 90, 63.

Raynes, H. E. 1935: *Insurance Companies Investments*. London.

Smith, A. D. 1996: How actuaries can use financial economics. *British Actuarial Journal*, 2, 1057.

Symposium on Institutional Investment, 1971: *Transactions of the Faculty of Actuaries*, 32, 363.

Wilkie, A. D. 1995: More on a stochastic investment model for actuarial use. *British Actuarial Journal*, 1, 777.

The future of the actuary

Chris Daykin

Although the actuarial profession is 150 years old, it continues to be forward-looking rather than backward-looking. In recent years, there have been global trends for actuaries to be given more direct professional responsibility in matters affecting the continuing financial health and strength of financial institutions. Many actuaries have moved into the wider field beyond the traditional one of life insurance and pensions. Therefore, the actuarial profession is looking forward to an exciting and challenging future.

Actuaries are accustomed to developing models for projecting the financial consequences of future events, but they do so on the basis of statistical analysis of past experience and in the expectation of some stability of that experience into the future. Such techniques provide limited scope for projecting the future development of the actuarial profession, since the major influences in the future can be expected to be very different from those experienced in the past. This is particularly true if one takes an international perspective, since there are many areas of the world in which there have been significant discontinuities over the past few years in the role of the actuary and in the part played by actuarial associations.

Some important trends can be observed in many countries: a new emphasis on deregulation of financial markets, with a loosening of rigid regulatory controls; and increasing competition and the development of multi-faceted financial supermarkets. It would be wrong to see deregulation as a move away from protecting the consumer: rather, it should be viewed as a re-evaluation of the balance between the benefits of consumer choice and paternalistic protection. 'Consumerism' is probably stronger than ever, and is of great concern to politicians and to regulators. What is different is that centralized controls are no longer seen as giving the best deal to consumers or as being the only way of creating a secure financial environment. A more flexible solution is to place greater reliance on the role of professionals (including the auditor and the actuary) who are close to the business of the financial institution. Greater disclosure of information is also seen as important, and the actuary can play an active part in making disclosure more meaningful.

The Appointed Actuary

In life insurance, the trend is towards widespread adoption of supervisory systems based on the Appointed Actuary concept, first established in the UK through the Insurance Companies Act 1973. Although there are almost as many variations on the basic idea as there are jurisdictions, common features are likely to include some devolution to the actuary of decisions on product pricing and liability reserving, an emphasis on the adequacy of assets to meet liabilities, and professional responsibilities to advise the company on a wide range of financial management issues, including capital adequacy, profitability and risk management. The role of Appointed Actuary involves continuous monitoring of the current financial condition, an obligation under certain circumstances to 'blow the whistle' to the supervisor, and looking ahead and reporting on potential financial strength (or weakness) under possible future scenarios.

Analogous developments can be expected in the sphere of complementary pension schemes, (that is, schemes, generally funded, which are established to complement social security schemes, including both occupational and personal pensions), as has already happened in the UK with the enactment of the 'scheme actuary' concept in the Pensions Act 1995. The actuary in such a role is, in part at least, carrying out the functions of the regulator, in helping to ensure continuing satisfactory financial condition, appropriate funding levels, prudent investment strategy and protection of the interests of the pension scheme members.

General insurance

There seems little doubt that there will be a rapid growth in the involvement of actuaries in general insurance. The Task Force on the Future of the Profession (in the UK), which reported in September 1995, identified the general insurance practice area as that likely to offer the most rapidly growing employment opportunities for actuaries over the next decade.

A tougher operating environment, fierce competition, catastrophic losses, and the emergence of long-tailed liabilities that are difficult to control (for example, in relation to asbestos, pollution and health hazards), has forced general insurance companies to adopt tighter financial controls, and to seek assistance from actuaries in developing a more scientific basis for the business than was hitherto usually the case. This has become a necessity for assessing a proper level of provisions for outstanding claims, including estimates of claims incurred but not reported.

Better reserving also has implications for setting appropriate levels of premium and for understanding the likely profitability of underwriting strategies. Actuarial approaches to asset/liability management and dynamic financial analysis (described in chapter 10) also have potential for adding value in the management of the business and will probably play an increasingly important role in the future.

It seems likely that trends in regulation and supervision will lead to a demand by supervisory authorities for a much more active actuarial involvement in the overall financial management of the business, expressed in terms of an Appointed Actuary (or similar) role and requirements for future financial condition reporting. While some people have argued that actuaries do not have a monopoly on the skills that are necessary for the calculation of reserves required in general insurance, there is increasing recognition of actuaries' ability to undertake a broad financial management role, particularly as a fundamental requirement of supervisory authorities is likely to be that the work is carried out to acceptable and enforceable standards within a well-defined professional framework. It may only be a matter of time before general insurance companies in most countries are required to have an Appointed Actuary.

The life insurance industry

Most observers expect some reduction in the number of companies operating in the UK life insurance market. This could have adverse consequences on the number of actuaries employed in life insurance, or at least act as a brake on further growth. Nevertheless, in addition to the formal Appointed Actuary role, actuaries may find other roles thrust upon them in relation to adequacy of premium rates and consumer-oriented measures such as marketing disclosure. North America is already seeing the advent of the 'illustration actuary', with specific professional responsibilities for what is disclosed to customers. Increased disclosure to potential and existing policyholders seems to be an inevitable trend, in which actuaries will need to participate actively.

Actuaries will no doubt continue to be closely involved in the design of new products, to meet the needs of the market (both domestic and international). Although the process may continue to be a slow one, the European Union will develop into a genuine single market. There will be gradual convergence of world-wide markets, with growing prosperity in many countries in which insurance penetration is currently low, and rapid advances in global communication. The regulation of insurance will become increasingly international, with many common elements in supervisory practice across borders, and an expectation that accountants and actuaries will be operating to internationally agreed professional standards.

The life insurance industry offers prospects for very rapid growth and development in southern, central and eastern Europe, the Far East, the Caribbean, South and Central America and the Indian subcontinent. The demand for actuaries in many of these areas is likely to outstrip supply for many years to come; so there will be a demand for consultancy services from the more mature markets such as the UK, North America, South Africa, Australia and the Netherlands.

With the increasing sophistication of techniques, actuaries will need to specialize to a greater extent within the life insurance market. Even quite sizeable companies may find it cost-effective to 'outsource' specific tasks, rather than developing or maintaining all the necessary capabilities in-house.

Investment

Investment management will continue to be of fundamental importance to both life and general insurance companies as well as to pension funds, with an increasing emphasis on asset/liability management. This is a rich vein for actuaries to mine, as it corresponds well to the skill mix which is derived from an actuarial training, even though there will be many others from different backgrounds who have expertise in investments. The investment area is now so broad – and continuing to broaden – that it is unrealistic to expect actuaries to be the dominant profession in all areas, particularly as the breadth of the actuarial training (and its length) may be seen as an unnecessary distraction by many investment specialists. If the actuarial professional is to continue to be a major supplier of training to investment personnel, it will be necessary to tailor an investment specialization that has more weight in investment and finance, and less in life insurance, general insurance and pensions, than the current general qualification.

This having been said, the likelihood is that most actuaries will need in future to know more about investment and to have a better understanding of the characteristics and pricing considerations of modern financial instruments, such as derivatives. The development of the actuarial role to cover assets as well as liabilities will offer particular challenges in other parts of the world, where actuarial training has hitherto concentrated on the liabilities.

Pensions

Demographic pressures on traditional social security schemes, combined with arguments about economic efficiency, are leading to complementary pension schemes acquiring a growing importance all over the world. The defined benefit occupational pension schemes which have played such a key role in the UK are tending to give ground to defined contribution (money-purchase) schemes, which are seen as simpler, less of a long-term commitment (from the point of view of employers), and not requiring so much complex regulation. It seems likely that there will continue to be a major role for actuaries to play in the UK in relation to defined benefit schemes, particularly with regard to the provisions of the Pensions Act 1995 for 'scheme actuaries' and the introduction of a minimum funding requirement. These responsibilities will reinforce the role of the actuary as protector of the interests of members, but may sometimes threaten to undermine the relationship as adviser to the sponsoring employer. Overall, rather more actuaries may be needed, as there will sometimes be a need for a second actuary to advise the employer, and the role of the 'scheme actuary' is likely to be more intense than the previous 'valuation actuary' role.

In so far as there is a trend towards defined contribution schemes, rather than defined benefit schemes, there may be less demand for pension actuaries. However, there will continue to be a role for actuaries with this type of product. Annuity business will increase, even if providers other than insurance companies play a part in handling the investment build-up. Many employers and trustees will continue to use actuaries to assist in the design and control of such schemes, including improving the targeting of the resulting benefits so as to bear a sensible relationship to final salary, and managing the impact of expense structures and guarantees.

The development of new legislative frameworks for complementary pension schemes can be seen as a major programme for the next decade (or two) in many countries around the world, particularly where complementary schemes have not up to now played a significant role. Undoubtedly, this will lead to increased opportunities for actuaries in these countries, even though the potential may not be as great if the new pension schemes are defined contribution schemes. Although many such countries may be inclined to set in place defined contribution systems at first, there may well be subsequent moves towards defined benefit schemes. In any case, it will be essential to develop strong systems of actuarial pricing and control for the annuity markets that will be needed.

Social security

Alongside the development of complementary pension schemes, there will be widespread re-evaluation of the scope and nature of social security schemes. Indeed, the new emphasis on complementary schemes will in large measure be in response to such reviews. Many countries have already recognized the importance of actuarial involvement in the design of social security schemes and in reviewing their financial viability on a regular basis. Such reviews demand a very long term perspective, close integration with thinking on future demographic and economic developments, and interaction between the actuary and those responsible for policy development, including politicians.

It will no longer be good enough for politicians to make social security promises without testing the long-term cost implications and hence their financial viability. Actuarial reports required at intervals under social security legislation should be used as an essential policy-making tool, and not treated as a formality. There is an urgent need for actuaries with an appropriate training for this work to be accessible to social security institutions all over the world.

Wider fields

Although the actuarial profession in the UK has historically been active predominantly in life insurance, pensions and investment, and, in more recent years, in general insurance, there is considerable scope for the application of similar mathematical, statistical and financial models in many other areas. Since most such areas have managed without actuaries up to now, it will certainly be necessary for actuaries to show that they can add value, in order to compete with economists, operations research experts and others, in quantifying the problems and providing practical solutions.

Health and long-term care

Although most private medical insurers use actuaries, they control only about one-tenth of the UK health market. Greater penetration by actuaries into the health sector will mean working for the National Health Service (NHS), for purchasing authorities, for general practitioner fundholders and for NHS trusts. Actuaries will be able to make a useful contribution in this area, applying a combination of modelling skills, financial awareness and business acumen. They will need to become familiar with the operating methods and technology of the sector, and to work alongside a variety of other professionals and experts.

World-wide, the health sector will be a major area of developing actuarial involvement. Some health-care systems will require significant input from actuaries as a matter of necessity. Others will offer natural opportunities for the application of actuarial skills, particularly when major changes take place in countries in which other relevant professions do not have a track record of involvement.

Actuarial skills will be particularly applicable in finding solutions to the problems of financing long-term care, whether it be through insurance products or through structures such as health maintenance organizations and retirement communities. The long-term planning perspective needed, with a mixture of indemnity payments and longevity protection, makes an actuary ideally equipped for work in this area, which is likely to be high on the political agenda in many countries.

Pre-paid funeral plans may grow in popularity and will need to be subject to appropriate financial controls, with the mandatory involvement of an actuary to ensure pricing and reserving adequacy, as well as security for the assets held to back future liabilities.

Capital projects

One of the most promising future fields of activity is the appraisal of proposed capital projects, to help decision-makers to decide whether or not they should proceed. Such projects include buildings, transport infrastructure, power generation schemes, oil and gas exploration, hospitals, and the development of new products. Typically, they involve the investment of a capital sum at the outset, on the basis that the investors will be remunerated out of the net income generated by the project during its lifetime, or through savings compared to other alternatives.

Such appraisals involve a deep consideration of risk and finance over long future periods – exactly the skills that the actuary has developed so painstakingly in connection with life assurance and pension funds. There is plenty of evidence to show that these skills are more widely needed. Numerous projects that have not drawn on actuarial expertise have gone badly wrong, resulting in delay, overspending, insufficient income or lack of use. A survey conducted in 1994 by the Confederation of British Industry revealed that only one-quarter of British manufacturing companies use any form of quantified risk assessment when appraising their projects.

An example of how the profession can help occurred in 1996, when it responded to a request from the team in charge of the UK government's

Private Finance Initiative to develop a methodology for evaluating private-sector bids. The aim was to demonstrate whether, after allowing for the transfer of risk, such bids offered better value for the taxpayer than the alternative of carrying out the project wholly within the public sector.

The technical problems in carrying out a proper assessment of project risk are significant. The first step is to identify all of the relevant risks and to estimate the likelihood of their occurrence. The next step is to evaluate the impact that each risk event would have, if it occurred, on the financial outcome of the project. By using simulation techniques, a series of possible financial outcomes can be generated and an assessment made of the range within which the end result will probably lie.

In addition to the appraisal itself, actuaries have much to contribute in the management of a project's risk. Good risk management at the outset is one of the keys to a project's success and to the achievement of the anticipated rate of return by investors. Moreover, a 'portfolio' approach to overall risk can be developed in some situations in which a number of independent projects are taking place.

A few actuaries are already working full-time in this field, and many others have helped their employer or a client to appraise an occasional project at some time during their career. It is likely that this involvement will grow significantly as we move into the next century. This is partly because there will be a need for substantial capital investment, to enable society to provide the infrastructure to cope adequately with changing demographic factors. More importantly, on a world-wide basis, there will be a need for detailed analysis of proposed projects, to assess the positive and negative impacts that they will have on the increasingly complex infrastructure that will already exist. There is a growing recognition of the need for adequate risk analysis and risk management, to improve the chance of the project's success, and it is likely that this trend will continue.

Personal financial planning

Most actuarial advice is geared towards institutions and hence is on a relatively large scale. However, the actuary's understanding of financial products and investment possibilities may make personal financial planning a natural activity for some. Inevitably, an actuary moving into this field would have to acquire the necessary detailed knowledge of products and providers, including the full range of tax-efficient non-insurance products, the complications of the personal tax regime and the relevant regulatory requirements.

Figure 11.1   The Millennium Dome – a capital project appraisal.
Source: photograph courtesy of the PA News Photo Library.

Some actuaries may be attracted by the possibility of offering a personal service to individuals, probably at a local level (the 'high street actuary'). This could be either as part of a multidisciplinary independent financial adviser (IFA) firm, as a sole practitioner or with other actuaries in partnership.

Court awards

It is likely that actuaries will increasingly assist the Courts to address problems of value, whenever uncertain future contingencies are involved. Divorce settlements are one such area, where legislation has been moving in the direction of dividing up the assessed value of accrued pension rights – unequivocally an actuarial task.

Actuarial evidence is now admissible in the UK Courts (through the Criminal Evidence Act 1995) in cases involving the assessment of damages arising from personal injury. Industrial Tribunals are already accustomed to making use of actuarial considerations to determine compensation in unfair dismissal cases. These specific instances are likely to lead to an increased understanding by the judiciary and the legal profession of the role that can be played by actuaries and hence to increasing reliance upon them.

Actuaries giving expert witness in Court will need to become familiar with the relevant procedures, and to develop the ability to provide robust, defensible explanations that will hold up under the fiercest cross-examination.

Other financial institutions

It is perhaps surprising that actuarial skills have not been more in demand in banks and building societies, as they have moved into more complex financial products than their traditional cash and cheque handling and deposit-taking. In many cases, being unaware of what an actuarial training might have to offer, some similar skills and techniques have had to be developed within the banking sector. Both the banking sector and the insurance industry stand to gain from greater interchange of ideas and personnel, as may be seen with the development of the involvement of banks and building societies in insurance. We may come to see an increasing number of actuaries working for banks.

Unit trusts present many problems which are closely akin to those in unit-linked life insurance, but have grown up with quite different traditions. Actuaries can offer new insights into pricing, financing and the assessment of provisions.

Actuarial skills

Consideration of the potential for actuaries to develop new roles inevitably focuses attention on the core skills that actuaries possess by virtue of their training. These certainly include a strong mathematical and statistical background, the ability to analyse and interpret statistical information, mathematical modelling, using both analytical and computer-based tools, effective treatment of uncertainty, analysis and management of risk, understanding of investment possibilities and hence the ability to evaluate the financial consequences of future contingencies and financially based ways of addressing them and preparing for them.

The actuarial skill-set will need to develop and adapt over time to meet the challenges and opportunities, both in traditional areas of activity and in new ones. There seems little doubt that investment knowledge will need to be increased. This will be true even in the UK, but it will be a critical area of development in many parts of the world, as the combination of asset skills and liability expertise will become one of the hallmarks of actuaries.

It is likely that traditional present-value techniques will continue to give ground to techniques based on cash flow modelling, such as dynamic financial analysis. This allows the exploration of a wide variety of potential scenarios, and an explicit analysis of the effects of uncertainty and the value of adopting alternative strategies, in terms of potential return and the associated level of risk.

The recipients of actuarial advice will expect to be more involved in the process of setting assumptions and in the development of recommendations, with the result that actuaries may need to improve their communication skills, while still maintaining professional standards and knowing where to draw the line. Particular emphasis will be placed on the quality of professional judgement, rather than simply on technical ability, although the latter will still be an essential component and may involve a wider range of skills than hitherto. Actuaries everywhere will need to present themselves as skilled problem-solvers, with a strong understanding of the relevant business environment as well as good business acumen.

The internationalization of business, and of the profession, is likely to bring pressure for actuarial qualifications to be more strongly coordinated world-wide, so that mutual recognition can become more a reality and the quality of qualified actuaries can be ensured. It may not be too difficult to achieve a reasonably uniform technical education, but harmonization at the level of understanding of principles and practical applications in the different practice areas may be more of a challenge, as will ensuring similar standards of testing, particularly when it comes to higher-order skills of analysis, synthesis and judgement, and understanding of issues related to professionalism. The debate will continue as to whether or not greater specialization is a good thing. Specific knowledge of local law and practice may become increasingly compartmentalized into modules that are separate from the internationally recognized qualifications, with perhaps an increasing emphasis on continuing professional education and development (of which some might be examinable) and on the use of practising certificates issued by actuarial associations.

A public-interest role for the profession?

It is easy to approach the opportunities and challenges of the future from the perspective of what might be attractive to members of the actuarial profession. However, much of what the profession has to offer is for the benefit of customers. We can expect to see this in the increasing importance of quasi-regulatory roles (such as that of the Appointed Actuary), but a broader objective for the profession, and a defence against accusations of being an actuaries' trade union, will be the concern that the professional bodies, in the UK and elsewhere, demonstrate for public-interest issues.

When individual actuaries are working for their employer, or advising a client, their perspective will inevitably be narrower. It could be argued that it is the responsibility of the actuary's employer or client, not the actuary, to take the public interest into account. This does not absolve the actuary from drawing attention to any public-interest issue that he or she is particularly well-placed to identify.

Around the world, we can expect to see emphasis being placed on actuaries as members of a profession, rather than purely as technical experts. The role of actuarial associations can be expected to be strengthened in this direction by the development of relevant activities within the International Actuarial Association (IAA), as seen in the establishment of the International Forum of Actuarial Associations (IFAA). Since the challenges that now face the actuarial profession, and are likely to face it in the future, have many similarities across national boundaries, the profession will increasingly need to think and act globally. There will be particular opportunities for the profession to develop rapidly in some of the countries in which there have until recently been few or no actuaries. The more established actuarial societies have a responsibility to lend a helping hand to ensure that these opportunities are grasped.

The IAA will help to support actuarial associations as they develop into professional bodies. It will also provide the framework within which a more uniform qualification process can be designed for actuaries worldwide, leading to greater clarity in defining the core skills of actuaries and increased scope for mutual recognition and transferability of qualifications.

It is likely that the IAA will increasingly be called upon to speak on behalf of the global actuarial profession and to provide an interface between actuarial associations and international bodies such as the Organisation for Economic Co-operation and Development, the World Trade Organisation, the International Accounting Standards Committee, the International Association of Insurance Supervisors and the International Social Security Association.

The role of the IAA will evolve over time to create the most effective structure for handling these key issues of professionalism, education, mutual recognition and representation at the international level. It seems inevitable that the profession will become increasingly international in its orientation.

An exciting future

As actuaries look to the past only to be able to bring greater certainty to managing the future, the most exciting conclusion from this analysis is that there is a bright future for the profession, and an increasingly global one. Even if some practice areas may be less buoyant than hitherto in countries in which the profession is well-established, new areas of practice are opening up, and in some countries the growth rate will be extremely rapid, as developments that evolved over many decades in the UK and North America look set to take place very rapidly in these new situations.

Actuaries have had a rather staid image. The reputation is unfair, but has been due to a tendency to shun publicity, and to revel in clever mathematics and in the technicalities of the insurance business. The actuary has always been a problem-solver, but has sometimes failed to communicate fully with customers, and has therefore been seen as remote from practical business problems. If this were ever the case, even only for some actuaries, it is likely to be less and less so in the future.

The role of the actuary will lose much of its potency if he or she neglects the fundamentals of mathematics and statistics on which the science is based. However, the actuary of the future is likely to need to be much more in the public eye, and to be seen as a problem-solver with a strong appreciation for the business context, a manager and indeed a decision-maker with exceptional awareness of financial and risk management issues. After all, the financial security of millions depends on the work of the actuary.

Further reading

Daykin, C. D. 1996: The future of the profession. *British Actuarial Journal*, 2, 325–427.

Daykin, C. D. 1997a: A crisis of longer life – problems facing social security systems worldwide and options for reform. Paper presented to a seminar organized by the House of Commons Select Committee on Social Security.

Daykin, C. D. 1997b: The internationalisation of the actuarial profession. Paper presented to the Third Argentinean Congress of Actuaries, and posted on the World Wide Web site of the International Forum of Actuarial Associations (http://www.actuaries.org).

Johnston, E. A. 1989: The Appointed Actuary. *Journal of the Institute of Actuaries*, 116, 27–100.

Lewin, C. G., Carne, S. A., de Rivaz, N. S. C., Hall, R. E., McKelvey, K. J. and Wilkie, A. D. 1995: Capital projects. *British Actuarial Journal*, 1, 155–250.

Orros, G. C. 1996: The role of the actuary in the National Health Services. *British Actuarial Journal*, 2, 19–128.

Index

tracking errors, 190–1
transfer of engagements, 59
Trenchant, J., 16
trustees, 115, 118
Trustee Investment Act, 57

underwriting, 12, 147, 165–77
underwriting aims, 169–70
underwriting terms, 172–3
unemployment insurance, 129
unequal treatment of sexes, 133, 167
unisex tables, 37, 119
unistatus tables, 119
unit-linked life insurance, 77–80
unit-linked insurance guarantees, 195
unit trusts, 206
unitised with-profit insurances,
  79–82, 102, 174
unlimited liability, 148

usury, 27

valuations, 50, 61–80
value of company to policyholders, 98

Wallace, R., 25
Watson, A. W., 51–2, 130–1
wider fields for actuaries, 202–6
widows' and orphans' pensions,
  130–2
Wilkie model, 195
William of Tottenham, 15
Witt, R., 17; *see also* de Witt, J.
Workers'(Workmens') Compensation,
  135, 151–2

yield curve, 183, 193

Zillmer, A., 65, 84